Our Messianic Age

May God bless

JB

Our Messianic Age

The Story of a Spiritual Legacy

Jerry Lynn Ray

Our Messianic Age
The Story of a Spiritual Legacy

© Jerry Lynn Ray 2012

Published by
Lighthouse Christian Publishing
SAN 257-4330
5531 Dufferin Drive
Savage, Minnesota, 55378
United States of America

www.lighthousechristianpublishing.com

For Collin, Katherine, Madison, and Jonathan—May this story encourage you every day—Dad

CONTENTS

Prologue
"Memory Rock"

If there is a golden age in every spiritual life, the time around 1970 was that epochal era for me. True, these were the days of my youth, and there is an undeniable nostalgia that surrounds this season of one's life, especially when looking back upon it from the grizzled perspective of later years. Yet in my case—and of numerous others with whom I shared the experiences of this formative period—there is a magical, or more accurately, a supernatural aura that pervades it.

I like to call it "our messianic age." It was an extraordinary time when I and many among my peers entered into relationship with the Christian Messiah, Jesus of Nazareth. Our spiritual eyes were opened to the understanding of God, the eternal salvation He offers, His general plan for our lives, and the biblical truths about our existence. It was then that I acknowledged Jesus Christ as Savior and Lord, started to grow in my walk with Him, and came to know His calling upon my life. The messianic age dawned as a religious reality for me personally.

It was far more inclusive than one person, however. It was a spiritual venture I gladly shared with others among my little company of friends, whose perpetually teenage faces are forever etched into my psyche. Like me, they attached themselves to Jesus, and for a while, at least, our relationship with Him was our highest priority. We came to be known as "the Seekers" because we were seeking the Lord and His will, and nothing else in life mattered so much.

I tend to compare our religious movement—with considerable audacity to be sure—to those few short years the first disciples spent with Jesus prior to His death. As with Peter, James, John, and the rest, we heard the Lord's call to follow Him. We left the nets of our desires and future goals to travel the well-worn path of the Galilean Carpenter. We, too, witnessed miracles of God's presence and power, and saw sin and evil exorcised and conquered. We observed many of our contemporaries enter God's kingdom and begin a life of Christ-like service.

Like the Twelve of old, during our messianic age there were less than stellar moments of ignorance and selfishness, argument and doubt. Denial and betrayal sometimes intruded. Yet trumping our immaturity and pettiness was a genuine hunger for God, an all-consuming desire to journey with Jesus that is still palpable these many years later. It was a divine mountaintop to which I long to return, and do so in my mind's eye time and time again. It is my Memory Rock.

I first came across that scintillating phrase in a lecture series I attended as a college student. The guest speaker's name has long been forgotten, but his message—about returning to one's spiritual moorings—has stayed with me all of my life. He entitled his address simply, "Memory Rock."

The biblical texts the orator chose were from the book of Genesis, which relates how the patriarch Jacob journeyed to a location he eventually called Bethel. There he experienced God in an unexpected way as he fell asleep and dreamed about a ladder reaching from earth to heaven—Jacob's ladder!—with angels ascending and descending. God spoke to him in the dream, and when Jacob awoke he declared, "Surely the Lord is in this place—and I did not know it."

Afterward he took a stone, the one he had earlier used for a pillow, fashioned it into an altar, and dedicated himself to God. Jacob never forgot his extraordinary experience with the divine, later revisiting the sacred spot. Remarkably, the theophany was repeated, and once again he took a stone and used it for an altar of praise. Bethel forever became Jacob's Memory Rock.

Just so, each of us who knows the Lord has in our spiritual past a Bethel beckoning us to return, the lecturer proposed. There is someplace, somewhere, sometime that God has met with us in a wondrous way, enabling His presence to be an unmistakable reality in our lives. Perhaps it's where we met Christ in salvation—a church, school, house, or field that now is hallowed ground. It could be a revival, crusade, camp, or conference in which we came to know with certainty the claim of God upon our lives. As with Jacob, it may have been a critical moment when we were in need of guidance and felt God's assurance promising to lead. We, too, every so often need to go back to Bethel—if only in our dreams.

Memory Rock for me centers upon a particular time and place, along with many of the people and events that intersect them. The time encompasses the tumultuous years of the late 1960's and early 70's. The place is anchored by a small Deep South community and its leading church. The people include a faithful pastor and his wife, along with several young men and women under their enormous influence. The events that occurred then and there and with them comprise the substance of

3

the following pages, my own little altar of praise to the Lord. It is full of fond memories that constitute the essence of my spiritual being and the story of our messianic age.

It's a story that should be chronicled, and not only because it deserves its own historical narrative. It ought to be shared especially because it will glorify God in the highest for the "great things He hath done." My prayer is that it will also bring challenge and inspiration to current and future generations of "Seekers" everywhere.

Chapter 1
"Beauregard"

Back to Bethel for me is back to Beauregard. My Memory Rock lies there in a small, east central Alabama community of mostly country folks. Located in Lee County, Beauregard sits seven miles due south of Opelika, about the same distance southeast of Auburn, and approximately twenty miles west of the Chattahoochee River that serves as the Alabama / Georgia border. It's a speck of a place that falls under the large shadows of bustling cities like Montgomery and Columbus, with the metropolis of Atlanta lurking a hundred miles away.

You probably won't find Beauregard on a Rand McNally road map. No traffic signals govern our comings and goings, though two or three caution lights attempt to slow us down a bit. We've never had our own system of government, nor post office or newspaper. Until recent times, just a few mom and pop stores, a number of churches, and a couple of schools comprised the architectural landscape. Ranch houses and modest farms, back roads and untidy creeks mark Beauregard's largely flat terrain. Pine trees, row crops, and pasture land still dominate its acreage, with commercial and residential development steadily encroaching.

"Rustic charm" is a polite way to describe our little community, although it would never be the subject of a Thomas Kinkade painting. Overall there may be as much Beauregard blight as Beauregard beauty. It has its share of weed-filled yards, run-down shacks, and butchered parcels of land that stand out with a brazenness that will not go away. But for many of us who grew up there, a timeless grandeur surrounds this place, a spiritual air that designates it as holy ground—if of non-biblical proportions.

The community name is a telltale sign of its character, and correct pronunciation is important. The first syllable is the key to accuracy. We call it "Bō'-ri-guard." Alabama's Beauregard begins with the same four letters as South Carolina's Beaufort (Bū'-firt), but that may be all it shares in common with the decidedly more sophisticated low country destination. There are no captivating bed and breakfasts in our Beau. No chic shops, art galleries, or espresso cafés, either. Four or five convenience stores and a barbeque shack are more our style.

The name is distinctly Southern, although with French flavor. Confederate General Pierre Gustave Toutant de Beauregard of New Orleans is our proud namesake. History says General Beauregard is the Southern officer who ordered the first shot to be fired in the conflict known around these parts as the War Between the States. We like that about him. It shows decisiveness, courage, spunk—all marks of ideal Southern character. Of course, most among us no longer agree with all that he was defending and are secretly glad the other side won, but we still like our man Beauregard and are pleased to have his name adorn our community.

I doubt there are any villages of the same name located north of the Mason-Dixon Line. Like mixing peanut butter and ketchup, they would not go well together. Beauregard belongs to the South, as much a part of our culture as the renowned figure of Robert E. Lee. To hold birthright in the community of Beauregard and in the county of Lee binds one forever to the Southern heritage. We may humbly admit that our wisdom in going to war a century and a half ago was questionable, but past and present loyalty to the men who fought on our behalf is indubitable. Territorial names are living testimony to steadfast devotion.

The Beauregard accent is as Southern fried as its name, with country drawl and penchant for running words together and omitting parts of syllables. Our brogue, in fact, is a source of great regional pride, serving as a badge of identity, a way of preserving long-held tradition and paying tribute to Deep South roots. It's our own little dialect, one of the few things Sherman didn't take when he burned Atlanta to the ground and marched a path of destruction through our land.

We're well aware that our language often befuddles those from other climates. We love words like "yawl" and "yonduh," "heepa" and "reckon." "Hyyu" and "awraht" punctuate the start of many conversations. While some find it charming, others think it churlish. To us it's folksy and friendly, denoting that we are an informal, laid back, loosely strung breed of people.

Using proper conversational English doesn't feel quite right to a purebred Beauregardian—like eating oatmeal instead of grits for breakfast, or putting snow tires on the car in winter. Any native who attempts to use "hifalutin" language sounds awfully suspicious to our ears. It's not so much that we are unacquainted with how to pronounce words correctly or lack the capacity to learn. It's simply not natural for us, as absurd as asking a cat to bark or a chicken to quack.

My Beauregard twang and slang initially caused considerable concern when I left for college and majored

in—of all things—English. Thankfully, Miss Frances
Garner was head of the English department at Mobile
College (now the University of Mobile). She was a native
Alabamian with impressive degrees from Vanderbilt,
Duke, and the University of Tennessee. Relatively tall
and slim, with a taut, unwrinkled face housing beady little
eyes and thin pursed lips, her head topped by graying
light brown hair, Professor Garner oozed the dignity and
deportment of a genteel Southern lady. She never
married, her beloved fiancé tragically killed before their
wedding day.

Dr. Garner devoted her life to academia and to her
students, spending the better part of three decades
teaching language and literature at Mobile. She instilled
in us the correct way to construct sentences with good
grammar and syntax. She lauded the literary classics,
insisting we read, analyze, and write on the likes of
Hawthorne, Joyce, Hemingway, and James.

It was obvious, however, that she reserved a
special fondness for Southern authors: Poe, Twain,
Faulkner, O'Connor, and Welty among them. She
reveled in Southern culture, teaching her students to
appreciate it as a unique part of the wider expanse of
literature and life. To my great satisfaction, Dr. Garner
was not averse to dropping an occasional "yawl" or
"reckon" into her classroom lectures, paying homage to
her geographical heritage and finding no apparent
contradiction between educational theory and social
practice.

Perhaps this is why I still relish the
"Beauregardese" I hear whenever I'm home. A family
member says she's "fixin' to go to town, be back
directly." A friend laughs about how his grandson "let go

of the hose pipe and it went ever-which-away!"
Someone else mentions "it's comin' up a cloud." Still
another licks his lips and declares he's "eatin' high on the
hog with peas and cornbread and the gospel bird." The
talk is as delicious to my ears as the food is to my belly.

****

Although Beauregard is home, I didn't always
reside there as a child. Born in Opelika in April of 1954, I
grew up in various houses in and around the city,
including at least two stops in Beauregard. I actually
attended elementary school in another little Lee County
community named Beulah, before moving back to
Beauregard for good when I was twelve. Beulah and
Beauregard are not very different—an "a" in the first
syllable and about fifteen miles is mostly what separates
them.

Beauregard is my mother Shirley's native soil,
Beulah the stomping ground of my father Ernest—better
known as "Junior." In 1958 we relocated to my dad's
side of town, moving into a brand new Jim Walter home
situated at the end of a quarter mile dirt track off Ridge
Road. The Jim Walter Company built the shell of the
house and my parents finished the interior when not at
work or caring for me and my two younger siblings, Vicki
and Tim. It seemed palatial to my young eyes, though
there were only seven hundred square feet of living space,
the four rooms and a bath little bigger than many master
bedroom suites of today.

*"Junior," my father, in the
Air Force around 1950.*

The well we used for household water was located
on the right side of the house looking out, only a few
steps from the front door. Referred to disgustedly as "the
well from hell" due to the frequent aggravation it
provided, the well was not very deep and periodically ran
dry, often necessitating trips to borrow water from
neighbors. When water returned to the well, my dad was
given the laborious task of priming the pump so water
could reach the pipes under the house. In winter those
pipes sometimes froze, provoking a few choice words
from my frustrated father, and inevitable trips by mama
for water to flush the potty.

The opening at the top of the well was at ground
level, measuring three or four feet in diameter, and was
built in such a way that it was difficult to cover securely.
Wild animals occasionally fell in. Skunks were the worst,
polluting our water supply and stinking up the yard until
we somehow fished them out with a bucket. A recurring
childhood nightmare was that I, too, might suddenly

plunge into the deep dark watery hole and struggle to get out alive.

*My mother Shirley and sister Vicki
pose in their Sunday best. The
"well from hell" is behind them.*

I'm surprised that one of my all-time favorite pets never wandered into the well—there were certainly ample opportunities. The much-loved creature was a pig that I affectionately called Arnold, named after the celebrated porker on the old Green Acres television show. The TV Arnold was perpetually small, and smarter and more talented than any man or woman living in the fictional rural community of Hooterville. Arnold's owner, Mr. Ziffel, treated his pig like a wunderkind, often taking him to visit misplaced city slickers Oliver and Lisa Douglas, where comedic chaos invariably ensued.

My Arnold was actually a 4-H Club project. Each club member was required to engage in an agricultural venture, and the specific task I chose involved raising a piglet to maturity. Arnold started out little in stature, but within eight months grew into a 250 pound behemoth by faithfully emptying his trough of daily rations. He loved all the pig feed, kitchen leftovers, and mishmash of slop I could provide.

Black in color, with a patch of white upon his forehead, Arnold and I bonded early on. I treated him like my dog, walking him on a leash up and down the dirt road, into the nearby woods, and around neighbors' houses. I built a small pen out of concrete blocks, locating it in the trees and brush across the dusty lane from our house. The pen worked fine for a few months, but as he grew larger Arnold learned to knock over the blocks and periodically escape his makeshift prison. Fortunately, Arnold always hung around the yard for his next meal, and when discovered, wore the appearance of a rascally grin beneath his snout. More than once I told him to go jump in the well.

The object of raising a 4-H pig was to put some bacon, sausage, and pork chops in the freezer. When the time came to slaughter poor Arnold, I was heartsick at the prospect. Unlike Charlotte and her web, my pig story did not end happily. Never thrilled to have a hog around the house, mom and dad insisted I fulfill my club obligation. Arnold was dutifully taken to a nearby butcher, and afterward we packed our freezer with pork. He had grown so hefty, however, that it was riddled with fat and barely edible. That was fine by me—I'd already taken a dramatic oath never to partake of my erstwhile friend, and I never did.

Something else seared into my memory at the Jim Walter house is the front porch seat I occupied in witnessing one of our country's engineering marvels. The Eisenhower Interstate System was under construction, and I-85 came right through our front yard. Watching them build such a mammoth roadway was great spectator sport for a kid. All the noise, big machinery, strange smells, and different people coming and going kept each day interesting as I observed the highway unfolding in the distance.

The Jim Walter house of my childhood. From its porch I watched the construction of I-85.

Our house was built on property owned by my widowed grandmother, Willie Belle Ray, and for a short while her home was only a hop, skip, and jump down the dirt road from our own. But when the government exercised power of eminent domain to purchase part of her land for the superhighway, her property was permanently divided into two disconnected portions. The unpaved road was split apart, putting my immediate family on one side of the new highway and my grandmother on the other.

The simple five minute walk to her house became a convoluted ten minute ride by car. Getting there by bike was no longer an option, though traveling by foot was an adventure I savored as a kid. It entailed climbing two chain link fences erected on either side of the great highway, each topped with barbed wire, then negotiating cars and trucks traveling at a high rate of speed while making sure not to fall into the drainage ditch in the median. Once, I lost my balance, slipped into the ditch, and ended up with a bloody gash that is still marked today by a four inch scar on the inside of my left knee.

Granny Ray's home was where my dad grew up, a white, wood-frame, five-room dwelling with a tin roof and two long porches protruding from its front and back sides. I loved to be there when it rained to hear the steady pitter-patter of precipitation banging off the old house's metal top. Its soothing rhythm enabled me to appreciate one of nature's many wonders while remaining dry and safe inside.

Granny knew her way around the kitchen and was quite adept at using her culinary prowess to persuade visitation from the grandchildren. I especially came running when she prepared a favorite dish like mashed potatoes or blackberry cobbler, which she cooked like no other. The secret to their palatal goodness was the gobs of mayo she put into the former and hunks of butter scooped into both. Granny's kitchen, no doubt, is the origin of many cholesterol and hypertension battles waged later in life.

Willie Belle, my Granny Ray, in her kitchen.

Her covered back porch was one of my regular hangouts. It extended approximately forty feet alongside the kitchen and bath, and rose about four feet off the ground, though it looked twenty feet high to my little boy eyes. Made of wooden boards painted a grayish blue color, the porch contained no rail and served nicely as a launching pad for younger kids to exhibit their courage. High-jumping off Granny's back porch became a favorite playtime sport. I was told I'd better be careful, however, because my Granddaddy Ray had taken a fatal fall off that porch—a dire warning not to horse around too much.

My paternal grandfather, also named Ernest, of whom I have no memory, has always remained an elusive figure. I'm told that he "doctored cows" for a living, among other things. Although not a veterinarian by degree, he didn't charge their fees either, and he knew enough about nursing sick animals back to health to make money at it during an era when many folks depended upon their livestock for the everyday staples of milk and butter. Selling honey from his beehives and milk from his own cattle were other sources of income for the family.

From all accounts he was a decent, hard-working man I would have been proud to know.

For many years the porch explanation of my grandfather's demise sufficed, with his name rarely called and photographs absent from our home. The distinct impression I received was that his death in 1956 was a terrible tragedy, and a subject to be left unmentioned. I often wondered if he had committed suicide.

Later I learned that shortly before my birth, Granddaddy Ray was involved in a serious car accident that left him with severe and lingering pain. In a time when physicians and their patients didn't know or heed the dangers of prescription pain medicines, he became addicted and could not find release. At times he grew delusional, and eventually entered Bryce Hospital, a state psychiatric facility in Tuscaloosa, to deal with the problem.

After residing at Bryce for several months, he returned home, attempting to manage the pain and conquer the addiction on his own. He was not successful. In a terribly unstable moment of chemical-induced agony and rage, he fell off the back porch and sustained a fatal head injury. An ambulance rushed him to the local hospital, but there was nothing they could do. He was forty-nine years old.

Not long after my grandfather's death, I began the process of preparing for formal education. With no publicly funded pre-school or kindergarten programs in Alabama at the time, my sister Vicki and I were sent to Helen Johnson's Opelika Nursery School, a white, clapboard, non-descript house located on First Avenue near Fourteenth Street. The house served as both business and residence for Mrs. Johnson, a bespectacled, overweight woman in her fifties.

Along with twenty or so other preschoolers, we did the usual things of learning letters and numbers, eating snacks and playing on the small playground out back. Mrs. Johnson also created a kindergarten band to perform during music time. Appropriately enough, I was given the least important instrument to play, the triangle—and loved it! The highlight of each day was incessantly banging the three-sided gadget while standing next to the kid relentlessly clanging the cymbals. Hearing aids may well be in our future.

The only thing I abhorred about Mrs. Johnson's was her method of "potty time." Periodically throughout the day she herded us into the house's large living room where several conspicuous portable potties were placed. On cue we promptly lowered our garments and sat together on the pots in unisex style until each did his or her business. The modest and shy among us have been irreversibly scarred.

Graduation day for me at the
Opelika Nursery School.

Before receiving my diploma from the Opelika Nursery School on September 2, 1960 and entering first grade, there were also other caregivers utilized by my parents. Aunt Lola, Granny Ray's sister, was a rotund, big-boned woman of little education but enormous heart. Lola was unable to have children, so she loved and disciplined us as if her very own. She often kept us through the day and cooked a big supper before departing, taking leftovers home to her husband Homer. Mama thought it was a wonderful arrangement.

Liz was another provider who kept us for awhile. A thin black woman in her thirties, we "younguns" became quite attached to her. She was more entertaining than Mrs. Johnson and Aunt Lola, having the energy to amuse us they often lacked. Liz's home life was difficult, and it ultimately led to her termination. On two occasions her husband made an appearance at our house while inebriated. Liz was properly warned the first time, and then necessarily, although reluctantly, dismissed following a second occurrence.

As we took Liz home on her final day of employment, she turned to me in the back seat of the car, pointed, and gave my mother a prediction. "That boy's gonna be a preacher," she declared in no uncertain terms. Her words must have registered strongly; they were remembered years later when the Lord was indeed calling me to preach. I like to think Providence was at work as our two lives intersected in time.

It was during the Beulah years that I was introduced to spiritual things. Liberty Baptist was the church of my grandmother, located only a mile or so up U.S. 29 from her home. Typical of the time, Liberty was a small, white, wood-frame building with a porch in front that invited small talk from attendees before and after church. My earliest memories of Sunday worship are at Liberty—sitting in the pew in my Sunday best of dress pants, white shirt, and bow tie, with a flattop hair style popular at the time; the preacher, Howard Land, raising his voice about something that excited him in the Good Book; the congregation of perhaps fifty singing "Amazing Grace" and "Victory in Jesus" from songbooks held in their hands; an uncle praying lengthy prayers that tested my patience but made me feel all good inside.

Liberty's worship style wasn't unlike something you'd see on the old Andy Griffith Show, first broadcast on Monday nights at about that time. In one memorable episode entitled "What's Your Hurry?" there's a scene at the Mayberry church where town citizens are gathered for Sunday worship. As the preacher waxes eloquent about slowing down the pace of life, various members of the congregation unwittingly put his sermon into practice. Barney nods off, prompting Andy to poke him in the ribs. Opie attempts to catch a fly buzzing around his head, causing dad to remind him to focus on the sermon. Gomer falls asleep and snores so loudly that it embarrasses one and all. There is humor in such a scene, but also an idyllic innocence that I tend to attach to my early worship experiences at Liberty.

Not all country churches in the years around 1960 were blessed with life's modern conveniences. On one of my first Sundays at Liberty, I made the mistake of needing to go to the little boy's room, and immediately was ushered out the back door and toward the ancient equivalent of our twenty-first century port-o-potty. It looked quite primitive—unpainted weathered wood, swinging door decorated with a cutout crescent moon, wooden seat containing a large potty hole. Its conventional outhouse features were accompanied by a smell that made you want to lop off your nose.

I don't recall visiting Liberty's outdoor latrine twice. I thought it worse than sitting half-naked on the potty at Mrs. Johnson's nursery school, and vowed to simply hold it and hurt all the way through the final "Amen" of the benediction. Mercifully, my childhood prayers for indoor plumbing were soon answered.

It was at Liberty that I first met one of my oldest and dearest friends, a soul-mate by the name of Gary Dennis. Only two weeks apart in age, we sat together through many Sunday School classes and Vacation Bible School sessions. Neither of us knew the Lord at this early stage of our lives, but spiritual seeds were being sown in our hearts and minds that would later germinate, grow, and bear fruit in Beauregard.

****

During my seventh grade year, we moved back to Beauregard. My folks purchased two acres of land and built a red brick house that was more than twice the size of our former residence. It was an attractive home site, carved from the edge of pasture and adjoining forest along Marvyn Highway, the major route through the community. I particularly enjoyed exploring the thick woods in back and frequenting a secluded pond about a hundred yards therein. Our home was located less than

two miles from the epicenter and namesake of the area—
Beauregard High School.

First organized in 1890 as a one-room
instructional facility, the Beauregard school has enjoyed a
long history of educating children living in the southern
tier of Lee County. Students residing beyond the city
limits of Opelika and Auburn, as well as between the
outlying communities of Smiths Station and Loachapoka,
attended Beauregard. It was originally known as Whatley
School, named for a local benefactor who donated land
for the institution. In 1928, following consolidation with
eleven other small schools on the same side of the county,
it was renamed for the Confederate general. A member of
the faculty, Dolf Parker, proposed the new name, reason
unknown. Gradually the entire community took on the
moniker.

It's kind of neat that I was educated at the same
school as my mother. She attended Beauregard when it
was a white, wood-frame, U-shaped structure during the
years inclusive of World War II and the Korean Conflict.
I followed in her steps during the Viet Nam era, although
by that time it had given way to a sleek brick complex of
buildings. Mama and I even shared the same principal
and at least one beloved teacher.

Lore has it that J. W. Harris had been principal at
Beauregard since the days of Teddy Roosevelt and the
Spanish-American War. He, indeed, seemed ancient to
fresh-faced teenagers who passed him in the halls each
day.

Mr. Harris was an old school, drill sergeant kind
of headmaster, a leader who ruled with an iron fist, and
whose piercing gaze scared the living daylights out of
you. Tall and lean, distinguished by charcoal hair

streaked with gray, and wearing thick, black-rimmed glasses, he liked to stand in the halls before and after classes like a military commander, positioning himself in a conspicuous corner spot to see and be seen.

Dapperly dressed in dark suit, white shirt, and striped tie, Mr. Harris possessed the disconcerting habit of twirling a chain full of keys back and forth around his fingers. The sound of distant keys rattling put every student on notice to immediately straighten up, if necessary, or face J. W's wrath.

No student wanted to cross Beauregard
principal J. W. Harris.

When not policing the halls, Mr. Harris retreated to his office—the notorious Beauregard "dungeon." No student wanted to enter the principal's lair, a fearsome place where hellfire and brimstone reigned down upon wrongdoers in the form of painful paddling, stern lecture, short-term suspension, or permanent expulsion. The dungeon was situated near the front of the building, overlooking the student parking lot. From his office window the school boss could survey the campus for punishable offenses like smoking cigarettes on school property or fraternizing too intimately with the opposite gender. Drugs and guns were still a few years away. J. W. rarely missed a student trick while making us toe the line. Beneath his strict, brusque façade, some say, beat a genuinely caring heart, his tough-guy persona masking an earnest concern for those in his charge. Though no doubt true, he seldom revealed his softer side, the stern image an effective deterrent to bad adolescent behavior. On Mr. Harris' watch there were relatively few discipline problems among the four hundred or so students at Beauregard.

The only trouble I personally encountered was not with the principal, but with a coach. Billy Pope was in charge of baseball, my favorite sport. Like a lot of boys my age, I dreamed of playing in the big leagues, and with that hope firmly in mind I went out for the Beauregard varsity as a freshman.

Although I couldn't hit a lick, I played shortstop for the Hornets. My glove tended to offset my bat, the only reason I found my name in the starting lineup. At the plate I was pitifully inept. The entire ninth grade season, in fact, I blasted all of two hits—both of the infield variety.

Coach Pope took a liking to me despite my skinny size and lack of slugging ability, perhaps because I was so fervently in love with the game. I also took a shine to him. He was young, handsome, and single, with an air of cockiness about him. Not too tall but solidly built, he gave the distinct impression that women thought him to die for.

Coach and I did not always get along, however. Once at Chavala High School in neighboring Russell

County, we were playing a doubleheader. In those days the games often started before school concluded for the day, with last period classes allowed to attend. There was a large crowd watching us play on a warm spring afternoon. In the middle innings of the first game, the score was close. Chavala had a runner on first with less than two outs when the batter hit a slow roller to me at short. I gobbled it up, looked toward second, but decided to take the sure out at first.

Beauregard's coach was not pleased.

"You shoulda thrown to second, shortstop," he shouted from the third base bench. "You coulda gotten him. Now he might score! Use your head out there, Ray!" His criticism was accompanied by demonstrative gestures and a look of disgust.

The fact that my teammates heard his rant was not what bothered me; coaches sometimes chew out their players in front of the team. I had already received a tongue-lashing or two that season, particularly with regard to my futility at the plate. And I was certainly not alone in facing my coach's wrath from time to time.

What troubled me was the embarrassment he caused in front of the other team and the large contingent of spectators. Many clearly heard him censure his shortstop, and I didn't like being shown up by my own coach and labeled a dummy in the field. I might not hit my own weight, but I prided myself on defensive skills and general baseball moxie.

Feeling all of this inside, I proceeded to commit the cardinal sin for any high school athlete. From my position on the diamond, I mouthed it right back to Coach Pope.

"He woulda been safe at second, Coach, and then we wouldn't have gotten anybody out!" I yelled back, my voice pitched with emotion, my face full of hurt, and my right hand clinched in a fist.

The one sentence outburst promptly resulted in riding the pine for the rest of the doubleheader. Coach was not happy that I dared talk back, questioning his judgment and authority. He didn't allow me to easily forget it, either. To his credit, he started me against our next opponent, but only after informing the team that it was dependent upon me keeping my mouth shut and running some laps. I did both, but also noticed in future games that he wasn't so rough on his young freshman.

In contrast to the hard edge sometimes displayed by Principal Harris and Coach Pope, leadership's gentler face was presented by Miss Flora Wright, who taught us our algebraic formulae and geometric theorems. Miss Wright was a Beauregard institution, having probably taught half the community at one time or another, including my mom and her siblings. Mama, in fact, once called her "Miss Wrong," and was promptly threatened with banishment to the dungeon. A prototypical schoolmarm and spinster, Miss Wright was also a devout Christian who enthusiastically taught Bible verses to accompany square roots and logarithms.

One of my most vivid educational experiences occurred in Miss Wright's classroom, though far removed from her subject of expertise. She was the sort of teacher who could easily be distracted, and that's how in the midst of geometry class I finally learned how a girl became pregnant. Up until then the only birds and bees I knew anything about were the kind that sang and made honey. The term "pregnant," and what caused this mysterious female condition, had always hovered just beyond my comprehension. It's like I preferred to remain naïve, or believed I could lose a measure of virtue if confronted with the facts of life.

When Miss Wright lost her arithmetical focus, the conversation invariably drifted away from points, lines, and angles. Talk among budding male teenagers frequently centered upon the forbidden wonder of making babies. Put on the spot by hormonal classmates, I had no choice but to admit—shame-faced—that I wasn't exactly sure how the fairer gender got pregnant. Portly Larry Webb, self-appointed class clown and sex education guru, used some choice non-mathematical language to describe the practice in no uncertain terms, scorning my ignorance and scuttling my innocence.

A decade later the word "pregnant" again brought me grief, this time as a ministerial student at the Southern Baptist Theological Seminary in Louisville, Kentucky. I had been called to be the interim pastor of Immanuel Baptist Church near downtown Louisville, serving on the staff with good friends and fellow seminarians Charlie and Darlene Williams, who later became longtime missionaries to Japan.

At one time Immanuel was a leading church in Louisville. Its expansive facilities included a large auditorium, lots of classroom space, and a gymnasium, all built to accommodate a growing membership. When I arrived in 1977, the church was down to less than a hundred in attendance.

A major reason for their decline was the changing demographics of the community, a neighborhood whose most famous native son was Cassius Clay, later renamed Muhammad Ali. White flight slowly occurred for decades, escalating especially in the sixties and seventies. Many of Immanuel's more affluent members relocated to outlying suburbs, changing churches in the process.

Another factor, however, was the supreme difficulty members encountered in getting along. A disgraceful instance was their recent dispute over the placement of a number board. Statistical displays, on which numbers are reported for weekly attendance, offering amount, and other general items of interest, were once a common sight in mainstream churches. Immanuel decided to purchase such a board, but feuded over its exact location. Some wanted it in the sanctuary for all to see. Others wished to house it in a less conspicuous spot, added to a hallway or to the vestibule. Congregational friction grew to the point where some of the numbers found placement elsewhere on the Christian Sabbath.

One Sunday evening during the Christmas season I was preaching from the passage in Luke where it mentions that Mary was "great with child," as the King James Version delicately puts it. In my sermon I was not so delicate. I remembered the word I had learned in Miss Wright's geometry class, using "pregnant" profusely during my message. Little did I know I was also using it profanely.

After the service a church deacon met me on the sidewalk in front of Immanuel's sanctuary. Nobody else was around to hear our conversation, in which he proceeded to dress me down for using a vulgarism in the pulpit.

"Son, what the hell are they teaching you at that damned seminary?" he scolded, eyes bulging and face contorted in anger. "Don't you know any better than to use filthy language in the Lord's house?"—obviously believing it was alright to spout profanity outside the Lord's house.

I was stunned, and initially had no clue as to what he was referencing. "Wh...what are you talking about?" I stammered.

"The word you kept using tonight—'pregnant.' You don't disrespect God's house by talking about that!"

Flabbergasted, I was momentarily at a loss for any kind of words. Had I more of General Beauregard's spunk, I would have gone back inside and shouted "PREGNANT!" at the top of my lungs. Instead I meekly muttered something to the effect that I would surely not commit that offense again. I also remember thinking that this deacon was probably an excellent example of why Immanuel had arrived at its current state of decline.

Later I spoke with friends Charlie and Darlene, and with another deacon, Chuck Cissle, about the incident. They were as dumbfounded as I was and encouraged me to continue as interim pastor, which I did for several more months. I made certain, however, not to utter the word "pregnant" in the pulpit again, a skittish avoidance I have tended to maintain over the years. "Great with child" is a much safer alternative.

****

The new house we occupied in 1966 was surrounded by several notable landmarks, community icons that defined the Beauregard landscape. Our home was located on the main thoroughfare, Alabama state route 37 (since changed to 51), also known as the Marvyn

Highway. A little over a mile up the road, north toward Opelika, was Beauregard High School. Half-way between sat another geographical monument, the Beauregard fire tower, our one and only skyscraper.

Positioned on what some say is the highest peak from that point to the Gulf of Mexico, the fire tower has stood its lonely vigil for as long as most anyone can remember. When younger, mama and her siblings often climbed the 75 or so steps leading to the top to visit with my second cousin, Elizabeth Stringfellow. Elizabeth worked for the forestry service, operating the little glass-enclosed, square-shaped work station at the pinnacle of the tower, utilizing binoculars and telescopes to sight impending incendiary problems. She occupied the observatory from dawn until dusk, receiving time off whenever it rained.

The Beauregard fire tower
still keeps its lonely vigil.

Down the hill from the fire tower, in the shadow of Beauregard High, was Lloyd's Grocery, a small cash-and-carry where you could always get a loaf of bread and half-gallon of milk, along with other items you might need to cook supper. A precursor of contemporary chain convenience stores—minus the pre-pay gas pumps— Lloyd's was owned by longtime Beauregard couple Lloyd and Wylene Bush, who lived across the road from their business. It probably should have been called Wylene's, since she ran it much of the time while Lloyd worked another job.

The greatest thing about Lloyd's was the candy, chips, and Cokes it offered after a hard day's instruction at school or practice on the ball field. Stopping there was a treat, all the more because Lloyd and Wylene were raising two of the prettiest daughters who ever attended Beauregard High. You never knew when Susan and Cathy would be there to help you find that little something you were craving.

I was especially smitten with Cathy, a year or so my younger. In my teenage eyes she was the perfect heartthrob, a petite brunette with a gorgeous face and the softest voice and "girliest" walk I'd ever heard or seen— and smart as a whip to boot. Of course, I never managed to get to first base with Cathy. I called her up a few times and tried to strike up a meaningful conversation at the store or school, but quickly found she was out of my league. Cathy was more the star quarterback's steady companion than that of a lowly shortstop. Nevertheless, many a night she lived in my dreams as the quintessential Beauregard girl.

The teenage crush I exercised upon
Cathy Bush went unrequited.

There were other small stop-and-shops like
Lloyd's in the community—Whatley's, Blue Top,
Dupree's, Parker's, R & D's, Spring Villa. The latter was
located next to Spring Villa Park, Beauregard's star
recreational attraction operated by the city of Opelika.
With swimming pool, picnic tables, barbeque
grills, swings, and slides, Spring Villa was a popular place
for families, especially during the hot summer months.
Water from natural free-flowing limestone springs was
pumped into the swimming pool, making it the coldest
plunge around—a big deal in the sweltering South when
air-conditioned homes and automobiles were few and far
between. Friends and I delighted jumping with abandon
into the ice cold waters of Spring Villa.
Originally Spring Villa was a 455 acre Southern
plantation. A Georgian, William Penn Yonge, purchased
the property in 1850 and built a magnificent antebellum
home upon his return to the South following success in
the California gold rush. The house was restored to its
former glory in 1934, and later served especially to haunt
young visitors during Halloween season. Legend has it

31

that Yonge was murdered with an axe by a disgruntled former slave on the thirteenth step of the home's interior circular staircase. Attempts to display one's courage by sneaking into the creepy house became a favorite pastime for scouts, 4-Hers, and church youth camping at the park.

If Spring Villa was Beauregard's recreational pride and joy, taking another route led to the community's foremost eyesore. Adjacent to the park, on Lime Kiln Road, were the remnants of the old Chewacla Lime Works. Here diggers mined the earth for years, scarring the land, leaving gaping holes, and constantly stirring up dust in their effort to extract the limestone purchased for use by farmers, contractors, and industry.

Chewacla was once the South's largest producer of cooked lime. By the time of my youth, it had been abandoned, a shell of its former glory. The walls of the rock powder house and commissary, along with rubble from the conical shaped rock kiln, were all that remained amid the pock-mocked earth. Ironically, the quarry and kiln were first operated by William Penn Yonge, the same gentleman who established the beautiful Spring Villa estate.

About the only eating establishment in Beauregard was a half-mile to the south of our house. DuBose Dairy Bar was a godsend from a kid's perspective. The Beauregard version of Dairy Queen had no inside seating and a very limited menu apart from the cones, sundaes, and shakes it served. Walking or riding bikes to taste a fifteen cent vanilla cone or thirty-five cent chocolate milkshake was one of youth's delights.

As good as it was, DuBose couldn't hold a candle to Mrs. Story's Dairy Bar in Opelika, still an East Alabama culinary institution. To go there on a Sunday afternoon meant we children had been especially good, or that mama had an ice cream craving. Mrs. Story's malts and banana splits were the absolute best. Her most celebrated concoction, however, was the greasy foot long hot dog, an especially scrumptious treat due to the secret recipe homemade chili sauce she lavished on top.

Although Mrs. Story passed away long ago, her legacy endures among those who continue to run her little road-side stand. It's still known as Mrs. Story's. It remains located a few doors down from the hospital where most of the locals are born. And, as in the past, you either take your food with you or sit in your vehicle to eat it. Often when I'm in town I'll sneak over to Mrs. Story's for a foot long, chips, and chocolate malt. Nothing beats nostalgic junk food satisfaction.

****

Down the road a bit from DuBose Dairy Bar, and on past the R & D Grocery, was found Sanford High, Beauregard's school for blacks. It stood next door to my grandparents' small farm where my mother was raised. Originally a quaint three-room school-house, it had grown through the years to include a multiplex of classrooms, playgrounds, and ball fields built to accommodate the minority citizenry of Beauregard. According to the 1970 U. S. census, 28% of Lee County's population of 61,268 was non-white, almost all of whom were African-Americans.

Of course blacks and whites in 1960's era Alabama were thoroughly segregated, with separate schools, churches, hotels, restaurants, water fountains, and restrooms. Beauregard's blacks, like those throughout the South and nation, suffered inequitable economic, educational, and residential deprivation that especially manifested itself in squalid living conditions.

I was largely sheltered from the African-American world of hardship, even while growing up amid the social disparities of the community. Perhaps my earliest encounter with black poverty involved a woman who did a lot of cooking and cleaning for our family. Izora Darby was in the employ of my maternal grandparents for what seemed like generations, doing everything from picking cotton in the field to washing and ironing in the house. Often she worked only for the food she carried home to her family. Sometimes she ate with us, but not at the same table. Typical of the times, she duly fixed her plate and ate alone in another room.

Izora endured a harsh life marked by repeated woe. Her husband Joe suffered a drinking problem, making it difficult to maintain steady income for the family. Of her twelve children, only two survived to adulthood, sons with the biblical names of Isaac and Jacob. Several children were stillborn, buried at a gravesite across from her home.

She lived in an unpainted shotgun shack adjacent to Sanford school and within eyesight of my grandparents' farm. Going inside the three-room dwelling further illustrated her indigence. The house featured broken windows taped over by cardboard, and floors pocked with patchwork repair. Old newspapers stuffed into the cracks of walls prevented outside air and insects from entering. Its furnishings were sparse, plain, and frayed.

That kind of hardship was all too common among African-Americans in the Alabama of my youth. Later, as a college student, I observed wholesale penury up close while working on the Opelika City Directory for the R. L. Polk Company. The summer job required me to canvas all-black neighborhoods, going door-to-door and asking residents a series of questions. I sought to verify information regarding their name, address, phone number, employment status, number of people living at a residence, and whether the home was owned or rented.

I walked up to one dilapidated structure, carefully negotiated the broken front steps, tiptoed around a sizable hole in the wooden porch, and knocked on a tattered and torn screen door, half expecting it to fall off its hinges and topple onto my head. As I stood there wondering how anyone could live in such abject poverty, an elderly black woman emerged from the darkness within. Short and thin, with gray hair neatly tied in a bun, she wore a cream-colored dress with a plain brown apron fronting it. Seeing that I was white and carried pen and notebook in hand, she looked at me warily.

"Can I hep ya, sir?" she asked, in characteristic black dialect.

I identified myself and started my litany of questions. She patiently answered each one, and finally I came to the last of my rehearsed queries.

"Do you own your own home?" I asked.

She looked me in the eye, and with the slightest smirk on her face, replied matter-of-factly, "Mr., I don't own nothin', 'cept my Jesus."

Her answer momentarily stunned me, and then my eyes began to moisten. As a committed Christian, I wanted to tell her how rich she really was, that she owned what no money could ever buy, that she possessed treasures in heaven far more valuable than anything she lacked on earth. But I hesitated, and she closed the door before I could utter a single syllable. Perhaps it was just as well. My words might have sounded hollow and condescending, coming from someone who had never experienced her kind of privation.

A black man who seems to have known her level of destitution became a legendary figure in Beauregard circles. Known for his mystery and eccentricity, he was simply called "the Rootman." Like everyone else in the community, I saw him numerous times walking up and down the Marvyn Highway between Opelika and his domicile somewhere within the wilds of Beauregard. From all appearances the Rootman was indigent in the extreme—ragged clothes, unkempt appearance, apparent homelessness, without transportation, and living the life of a hermit.

I first met him when I was fifteen years old and working as a bagboy at the Big Apple Supermarket in downtown Opelika. His face was chiseled and grizzled with an unruly, matted dark gray beard that appeared to have been seldom cut or cleaned. Long locks of grayish-brown hair overflowed from beneath a shabby and grimy floppy hat that he wore pushed down close to the scalp. His distinctive attire consisted of a green knee-length military overcoat with tatty pants and badly stained shirt underneath, accompanied by soiled, outdated tennis shoes. Like an inverted version of Santa, he carried a large brown bag flung over his shoulder where his valuables were kept—money purse, chewing tobacco, and purchased goods.

The Rootman stank to high heaven! When knowledgeable Big Apple employees and customers, black or white, saw him entering the store, they scattered to and fro, lest his malodorous scent remain with them the remainder of the day. He never wanted his groceries bagged, which was fine and dandy with me. He always preferred self-service, carefully placing each item in his over-the-shoulder sack. Speaking to him always elicited the same characteristic and unintelligible grunt in reply.

How the Rootman attained his nickname is unclear. His real name was Willie Wilbur, and not much is known about him other than he served in the army during World War II. Scuttlebutt opined that injury, trauma, or abuse during the war harbored the origin of his strange behavior. As a disabled military veteran, he received a small government pension, enough to support his lonely lifestyle.

As with a lot of legends, there are conflicting accounts of the Rootman's demise. One version has it that he was hit by a car while walking the highway, and like a dog yelping in pain, hobbled back into the woods where he died from lack of medical attention. Another story claims that robbers poured jugs of acid over his head while attempting to steal a stash of horded cash. Long after his death, his body was found near the lean-to hut he called home, with no cause of fatality ever determined. Some declare that the Rootman's ghost still walks the highway and lurks about the community, his foul odor detected here or there, and that he can yet be heard late at night screaming in agony deep within the Beauregard woods.

****

Black and white relations in Beauregard experienced a revolutionary event in1970, an epochal time for many communities in the Deep South as full-blown integration came to our schools. A couple of years earlier, nominal desegregation had begun. Alabama's polarizing governor, George C. Wallace, made his infamous schoolhouse door stand of defiance against court-ordered integration in 1963, but only succeeded in delaying the inevitable. At Beauregard High, a young man named Alvin Baldwin was the first black student to enroll at our previously all-white school.

Alvin was our local Jackie Robinson. Jackie, the black baseball star of the old Brooklyn Dodgers, was the first to integrate the major leagues in 1947, receiving universal accolades for the courage, patience, and perseverance he displayed in the midst of exceedingly trying circumstances. Along with Rosa Parks and Martin Luther King, Jr., he was a major reason discrimination laws were overturned in this country. There were, of course, a host of lesser known principals in the battle for civil rights, individuals no less brave or persistent. In Beauregard, the vanguard for racial justice was Alvin.

A gifted athlete, Alvin particularly excelled at basketball. He brought energy and excitement to the court, was fast on the dribble, and possessed lightning-quick reflexes. Almost effortlessly, he brought the ball down from the basket and put it back up again. His signature move was the delayed jump shot, where he leaped into the air and hung suspended for a moment before thrusting the ball toward the goal.

The 1968 Beauregard Hornets varsity basketball team.
Alvin Baldwin was our first African-American player.

Alvin quickly became a celebrity of sorts at
Beauregard, as everybody knew who he was and why he
was there. He was our token black; thanks to him we
were technically not in violation of the court decree. We
were all curious to see how he handled the pressure-filled
role of racial pioneer—the loneliness, taunts, insults, and
ridicule that would surely accompany his presence. To
our pleasant surprise, Alvin managed it all with
impressive aplomb.

The same cannot be said for the society around
him. Racial hatred frequently reared its ugly head,
reaching the boiling point during the early days of
desegregation. A regrettable scene in neighboring Macon
County illustrates the volatility of mixing the races during
this turbulent era. Alvin and his white teammates played
a game in Tuskegee, a city 80% African-American
according to the 1970 census. Tuskegee's high school
was the reverse image of Beauregard—an all-black
student body except for a handful of whites.

The large crowd that entered Tuskegee High's gymnasium on that occasion was split along racial lines, Beauregard's whites versus Tuskegee's blacks. A potentially combustible situation was made worse by the old gym's odd configuration. The stands were positioned entirely on one side of the court, and there was only one door to enter and exit the building. This meant that the two schools' supporters had no choice but to intermingle, sit within a few feet of each other, and use the same concession booths and restrooms.

Tension was thick and comfort thin and it didn't take long for rowdiness to rule the roost. By the end of the first quarter, racial epithets were flying as two sets of different colored fans cursed one another and tossed rolled up drink cups, wrappers, and napkins back and forth. Shouting matches and a few fisticuffs erupted, the boisterous multitude tenuously near abandon. An ample contingent of law enforcement kept order as best it could.

The closeness of the competition on the court added fuel to the incendiary mix. The scoreboard displayed a seesaw affair throughout the night, a tight contest going down to the wire, with Beauregard tallying the winning points in the final seconds. When the ballgame ended, state troopers immediately escorted Beauregard's players, coaches, and cheerleaders to the visitor's locker room until the raucous crowd could be dispersed. An hour later, all were herded to a waiting bus where a number of broken windows were found, with shards of glass littering the seats. Many came away that night convinced that integration of the races would never work in Alabama.

Nevertheless, in the late summer of 1970, at the beginning of my junior year of high school, total desegregation arrived in Beauregard. Minimal black or white representation in our schools was not good enough for the courts; complete integration was mandated. To avoid the expected violence and / or to placate racial prejudices, numerous parents enrolled their children in private institutions outside the community. My siblings and I were sent to a brand new educational enterprise in Opelika, Scott Preparatory School, from which I graduated nearly two years later.

Many Beauregard students attended Scott, while some scattered to other so-called "white flight" establishments like Lee Academy in Auburn, Macon Academy in Tuskegee, and Glenwood School in Phenix City. Most classmates and friends remained at Beauregard to witness firsthand the shotgun marriage to Sanford and the dramatic alteration of their school.

The new age of Southern society ushered in on our watch was a tough situation for the youth of my day. We were suddenly torn asunder, going in a host of different directions, no longer part of a familiar, cohesive group, but strewn into a variety of new educational communities on the local map. As I soon found out, God would use the necessary upheaval of Alabama's apartheid culture for His greater glory in Beauregard.

****

My mother's side of the family is indigenous to Beauregard. Her father, Reedy Long, was born there, while his wife Alma was from nearby Little Texas. She married Reedy at the tender age of fourteen and moved to his community, where they remained for the rest of their lives. The marriage produced thirteen children, among whom my mother Shirley arrived precisely in the middle. Mama still resides on the same property where she and most of her siblings were raised.

My Granny Long was the picture image of a grand Southern matriarch—more round than thin, always adorned in an understated dress, and with a pleasantly inviting face that communicated comfort and ease to those around. She was big-hearted and full of homey wisdom, possessed a sunny disposition, and was not a little mischievous. A dilettante, Granny was kitchen gourmet, expert seamstress, master gardener, and nurse practitioner. She even wrote poetry, once penning the prize winning ode, "Blue Buckle Overalls." I often think of her as Beauregard's version of Betty Crocker, Aunt Bee, and Dear Abby all incarnated into one blue ribbon package.

Granny had no formal education to speak of. Her mind, however, was wired like a hard drive, with an astonishing ability to remember names, dates, and circumstances. You could ask her what happened in Beauregard on Saturday, September 17, 1949 and odds were good she could tell you who got married, who had a baby, whose house caught fire, or who died. Her conversations were replete with Beauregard history because she had lived there so long, was acquainted with everybody, and could remember so much.

She was also our Beauregard weather prognosticator. In the days before Doppler radar and the Weather Channel, if you ever needed to know the forecast, Granny was your best bet. By monitoring the sky, discerning animal behavior, remembering past

weather patterns, and faithfully watching meteorologist—
and legendary chalk flipper—Doug Wallace on WRBL in
Columbus, Granny could pretty well tell you whether to
pack an umbrella or wear a sweater.

She didn't need Punxsutawney Phil to help predict
the more distant future, either. Paying absolutely no
attention to the sun or her shadow, Granny could walk
outside on February 2, closely examine plants and trees,
carefully observe the movements of birds and insects, and
confidently calculate how much longer it was until spring.
She nailed it far more often than the Pennsylvania
groundhog.

About the only peccadillo Granny possessed was
her fondness for taking a pinch of snuff a few times every
day—Honeybee Sweet her favorite brand. She was so
addicted to dipping that she bought it by the case and hid
it, lest it be found and disposed of by her loved ones.
When imbibing, Granny would gather the snuff into her
fingers from the handy little can, stick it in her mouth
between the lower lip and jaw, and commence to sucking
on it.

Of course this produced no end of tobacco juice,
which she promptly deposited every so often into a
portable spittoon fashioned from an empty can of peaches
or diced tomatoes, label missing. Between spits, she
talked as many syllables as possible before politely
saying, "'Scuse me," whereupon she let out another ugly
stream of black liquid. I never remember thinking her
habit was gross or uncultured or impolite, perhaps
because it was so much a part of the daily life of this
grandmother I loved.

Granny was especially happy around
Christmastime, and she got into the holiday spirit as much

as anyone. For the grandchildren—there were thirty-four of us before it was all said and done—this meant her annual visit with Santa on Christmas "Eve-Z," her designation for the day before Christmas Eve. Granny mesmerized us little ones by telling of going into the nearby Beauregard woods to have a cup of coffee with Santa. There they conversed about our past year's behavior and current Christmas wishes. According to Granny, the red-suited visitor from the North always gave his assessment of her grandkids' conduct and announced something he might bring them the following night.

Afterward Granny took us aside and shared about her visit, first exhorting us to be more obedient before revealing the identity of a special toy coming our way. As a youngster I was amazed that the gift would often be under the tree, just as she said. Of course this gave me even more incentive to believe in Santa—and in Granny. It's also the reason I was ten years old before finally admitting that Granny had been pulling some fast ones on Christmas Eve-Z.

Granny married Reedy back in 1924. They moved around Beauregard a few times until 1947 when they settled down on the farm I remember as a boy. It was a 180 acre spread on the southern end of the community, toward Marvyn and Society Hill. "Pawpaw," as his grandchildren called him, dabbled in several related lines of work while providing for his considerable family. Running a saw mill, operating a general store (now R & D Grocery), growing cotton, making syrup, farming marketable fruits and vegetables such as watermelons and corn, raising hogs and cows and chickens—these were the types of income he pursued at one time or another.

He made a living at all of this despite exceedingly poor eyesight that kept him out of World War II, even as four siblings left home to serve. Robust, wearing thick glasses, white haired in his older years and still strong late in life, Pawpaw carried with him a sly grin that made you think he probably hadn't laid all his cards on the table.

Mischievous Alma and sly Reedy,
my Granny and Pawpaw Long.

He was, in fact, an excellent card player, long a Long forte and tradition. Setback was his pastime of choice, an amusement played much like the game of Rook, with a kitty that's bid upon and a goal either to make your bid or "set back" the winning tender. Pawpaw could sit for hours delightfully dealing one deck after another. His grin served him well—you never knew whether you had him or he had you, but more times than not it was the latter. If he held the upper hand, it didn't take long for his dense glasses to magnify the twinkle in his eye, or for his impish little smile to blossom into a full set of teeth. You could also count on a loud cackle reverberating around the room—rubbing it in was at least as much fun to Pawpaw as beating you.

His wily nature may have contributed to once running afoul of the law. When I was seven, Pawpaw was arrested for operating an unlicensed distillery. Like numerous respectable farmers before him, he saw selling moonshine as a way of making a little extra income. The early 1960's version of the ATF caught wind of the clandestine activity, and the "revenuers" came calling.

He and a partner had entered into a business arrangement whereby Pawpaw provided the ingredients and barn for manufacturing and storing the spirits, while his associate supplied the machinery and customers, along with a man to cook the mash and bottle the liquor. It was a bad deal. His cohort was a shady figure tied to the last vestiges of the notorious Phenix City mafia. When federal agents moved in, Pawpaw took the fall.

The illegal operation was housed on Pawpaw's land, so he was taken into custody. Although offered immunity from the charges in exchange for testimony against his partner, he refused to identify the fellow bootlegger. Likely he feared for the safety of himself and his loved ones. Pawpaw was indicted and found guilty, spending three months in Montgomery's Federal Prison Camp on the grounds of Maxwell Air Force Base. It was a dark time for the family.

The centerpiece of Granny and Pawpaw's farm was a relatively spacious, white, wood-frame residence already on the property when purchased. It included a living room, dining area, and kitchen on one side, and two bedrooms, hallway, and bath on the other, with three fireplaces scattered throughout the home. The dining room and kitchen were separated by a swinging door, and a "shed room" was attached to the kitchen in back. It was typically used like a modern pantry, only bigger, but my grandparents converted theirs into a much-needed extra bedroom.

The best thing about the home to me was the large screened-in front porch, maybe twenty by thirty feet in size, which wrapped around the face of the house in a somewhat triangular fashion. Inside the porch were two doors on either end that led to the living room and master bedroom, respectively. In between the doors were several windows that looked into the dining area and kitchen. The porch floor was made of sturdy wood planks, and ceiling fans cooled it in summer.

The porch served as the usual gathering place for much of the year. Several chairs that rocked or not were positioned where folks could sit and talk, play cards, or simply rest. Sitting on the porch and enjoying people's company were part of life's pleasing routine. An ever-present companion was Uh Uh, the porch pooch, my grandparents' affectionate pet dog. Medium tall, thin, dark, and mixed, Uh Uh received his frivolous name from Granny for his odd-sounding bark.

From the vista of the front porch you could see a good bit of the farm. Directly ahead, within a semicircular dirt driveway leading from Sanford Road (now Lee County 11) to the house, were approximately ten acres planted in corn. Off to the left were the family garden, row crops, and the cotton fields I occasionally worked in as a boy. To the right were several barns and sheds.

An equipment hangar was located farthest in the distance, closest to the highway, housing tractors, plows, tillers, and tools. Not far away stood a storage barn with its adjacent pig pen, and a rectangular chicken coup next door. Nearest to the porch were two smaller structures, a car house and well house. Hidden from sight was the smoke house out back, used for curing ham, bacon, and other meats.

A similar veranda at the rear of the residence would have afforded a scenic view of the surrounding countryside. The small back porch astride the kitchen was not built to sit on. Here is where Granny hung clothes to dry, put tomatoes in the sun, shelled butterbeans, and churned her butter. I treasured it for the view.

The house was situated on the brow of a plateau, and looking outward from the rear of the home site offered a lovely panorama of pastures, fields, forests, and sky. Aside from fire tower hill, there was not a more picturesque spot in all of Beauregard. I often enjoyed sitting on a backyard fence post while gazing into the distance, dreaming of faraway places and far-flung plans.

As a boy I loved to visit the farm for a variety of other reasons as well. It was a veritable playground of animals, farm equipment, hiding places, and room to roam. A new adventure, it seemed, awaited every visit. Pestering the pigs, congregating among the cows, and chasing the chickens provided hours on end of childhood delight. Tending to the chickens was Granny's responsibility, and I enjoyed watching as she fed them, gathered eggs, and nurtured the bitties that were coming along.

To Granny also fell the gruesome task of selecting and preparing two or three hens for chicken dinner. The elaborate procedure first entailed killing the fowl by ringing their necks, then wetting them with scalding hot water so the feathers were more easily removed. After plucking the birds, Granny hung them upside down on a clothesline and cut open their necks to release the blood. Then she placed the poultry in a large pan, poured boiling water over them a second time, and let them sit for a while. Later she gutted the chickens, removing their insides, and sliced them into various pieces, cooking every part except the head and claws. It took at least two hens to feed her family, so fried chicken was a special occasion entrée. How Granny must have rejoiced when Colonel Sanders came to town!

The farm was a lot of fun for children, but it wasn't always the safest place to play. When I was four years old, I wandered a little too close to a circular saw Pawpaw was operating and almost turned into a small-scale version of a Cyclops. The tip of the saw blade entered my temple half an inch away from my left eye. The scar is still visible to remind me of a frightening brush with blindness.

The farm's storage barn was my favorite spot to explore, although the air wasn't the freshest with a pig pen and chicken coup nearby. Pawpaw kept the corn to feed the pigs in the barn, along with a favorite tractor he owned. When I was thirteen my older cousin Tommy showed me something else kept in the barn that I never knew was there, what he called "girly magazines." This was not long after the embarrassing revelation in Miss Wright's geometry class, so I was suddenly receiving a crash course on the fundamentals of the softer sex.

The magazines were well hidden under stacks of hay in the attic, above where the tractor was usually parked. According to Tommy, he was continuing a long-standing Long ritual passed down to him by older cousins, a barn tradition traced back to our uncles. The magazines showed me things I had never seen before, and it took quite a while to get them off my young mind.

One of the saddest days of my youth occurred in 1969 when I was fifteen. Pawpaw was visiting with mama when he received a phone call that his house was on fire! By the time we arrived a few minutes later, the structure was ablaze and there was no hope of saving it. Beauregard didn't have a volunteer fire department, and Opelika's was no match for the swiftness of the conflagration. Thankfully, Granny was also away visiting with my Aunt Jimmie Clyde, and no one was home to be harmed in the tragedy.

The farmhouse burned completely to the ground, destroying the entirety of the contents as well as copious good times on the front porch. Granny and Pawpaw were devastated, the cause of the blaze never determined. Pawpaw remembered hanging a shirt up to dry in front of a space heater. Granny recalled putting a penny behind a fuse to try and make it work. They eventually bought and moved into a mobile home on the property, but the old farm was never quite the same.

The fire is many years in the past, and Granny and Pawpaw have long been gone, but their heritage lives on at a fall family hoedown known as the "Collard Cookin'." It transpires every so often at my Aunt Jimmie Clyde's, next door to the old home place, and collards are actually cooked and served along with cornbread, smoked sausage, and a vast assortment of delicious Beauregard cuisine. There are hayrides and coloring contests for kids, country singing and square dancing for adults, marshmallow roasting and apple bobbing for all ages. What I enjoy most, however, are the stories that are exchanged—stories about Granny and Pawpaw, stories about Beauregard, stories about the history behind our lives.

****

A curious thing about living in Beauregard is that at an early age you must declare allegiance either to the Alabama Crimson Tide or the Auburn Tigers. That's the way it is in just about every household and hamlet throughout the state. After being taught our preferred names, the first words many of us learn are "Roll Tide" or "War Eagle." No doubt some poor kids have started life thinking those were their middle and last names respectively—Johnny Roll Tide or Jenny War Eagle. Actually, they are code words and rebel yells for the athletic teams of two institutions of higher education, the University of Alabama in Tuscaloosa, and Auburn University, located in its namesake village.

One might think that Beauregard, situated only seven miles from Jordan-Hare Stadium and the heart of the Auburn campus, would be staunchly in the Tigers' camp. Not so. My sense is that today most folks in the community shout "War Eagle," but this hasn't always been the case. During my youth the University of Alabama employed a legendary football coach named Paul "Bear" Bryant who beat the heck out of Auburn almost every year, and just about everybody else along with them.

The Bear's winning ways predisposed a majority in Alabama toward the Tide, including a goodly number of Beauregard families, and ours became a decidedly (crimson) red state. Coach Bryant passed away in 1983 and Auburn has since beaten its archrival more frequently. As a result, in recent years the state has trended a little more blue (and orange) in hue than in the past.

You grow up in Beauregard cheering for either the Tigers or the Tide; there is little middle ground. Passion for one team and hatred for the other are common and accepted. Dual support is not honorable. No self-respecting diehard says, "I hope Auburn wins except when they play Alabama," or vice versa. Among the rabid, rooting for one school means the other is your lifelong enemy, to be held in utmost contempt until your dying day.

You love one with your whole heart, soul, mind, and strength, while simultaneously loathing the other with every cell, gut, nail, and fiber in your being. You want your football team to go 14-0 and win the national championship (as, remarkably, each have done in recent seasons). You want that other school across the state to lose every game, and be humiliated in the process.

Such quirky fanaticism comes naturally in our neck of the woods and is akin to apocalyptic religious fervor. We're talking blood sport here, a Hatfield and McCoy rivalry like none other. The Red Sox and Yankees are sweethearts by comparison.

Usually you become an Auburn or Alabama fan because that's what your family is. You're born into it, like being Baptist or Catholic. Your loyalty is inherited, handed on by fiat, something you grow into and rarely question. The reason you live in an Alabama or Auburn family may never be known to you. It could stem from a long-ago forebear who graduated from the institution or worked there. It could be as simple as an ancestor liking one school's mascot or colors or coach, initiating the commitment passed down in the genes for generations.

What gets interesting is when Auburn and Alabama folks fall in love and decide to wed the lower caste. Such mixed marriages are frowned upon in our state, a social faux pas filled with serious repercussions. For one thing, the unequally yoked invariably suffer the perception of cavorting with the enemy, and often are held in suspicion as much as pitied by their collegiate comrades.

For another, couples who intermarry are assured a lifetime of marital stress. Friction in the relationship is automatically built in. Peace and harmony are more challenging. Holding the tongue, particularly when your team is doing well and the other isn't, becomes a never-ending battle.

Moreover, there is little relief from the rivalry's tension. Rarely is the school color difference ever out of sight or mind, appearing as it does with cherished logo on everything from shirts and hats to license plates and clocks. Alabama/Auburn is a year-round fracas, perhaps the number two topic of conversation after the weather.

It's enough to drive mismatched husbands and wives to their knees, praying for divine intervention on behalf of their significant other. Seldom do you see conversions, however. As much as you may yearn to share some sideline togetherness with your chosen one, school blood is thicker than matrimonial water. You will need to look elsewhere for your Tiger or Tide soul mate.

Intercollegiate marriages among the zealous are particularly hard on the kids. Hybrid children are constantly evangelized by one parent or the other. Mama will put her little tot in a crimson and white cheerleader outfit; daddy counters by teaching her to sing the Auburn fight song. Dad will offer junior an autographed football from his favorite team; mom answers with ice cream and cookies to celebrate her school's victory. Such crossbreeds occasionally descend into the sad state of utter confusion, blathering "War Tide!" or "Roll Eagle!" and eventually cheer for the likes of Georgia Tech, or in cases of extreme abuse, Notre Dame.

Life also gets sticky when your loyalty lies with one school and you or your children attend the other. That's what happened to my good friend Gary from Liberty. Gary has always been a devoted Alabama fan, but lo and behold, he ended up at Auburn. He graduated from one university and pulls like mad for the other. My sister Vicki and her husband were in a similar bind. They are both ardent Auburn fans—Joe an alum. But life has a sense of humor, and now they live smack dab in the middle of enemy territory, passing by the hated grounds of Bryant-Denny Stadium almost every day. They've even watched a couple of their progeny work on Crimson Tide diplomas, making mom and dad extremely proud—but a tad nauseous at the same time.

One of the biggest days of the year in Beauregard is Iron Bowl Saturday. That's when the Auburn and Alabama football teams meet in November to settle their annual dispute. It's called the Iron Bowl because for decades the two teams kicked off every year in the state's largest city, Birmingham, once renowned for its extraction of iron ore. For the past several years, however, the game has alternated between the two campus stadiums.

Life gets no more delicious in Beauregard than when your team whips the other one in the Iron Bowl. As the final seconds tick off the clock and your guys walk off the field victorious, you know you have bragging rights for the next 365 days. The other team and its legion of fans will now endure shame for an entire year, the butt of juvenile jokes about their athletes, intellect, and social skills.

Alabama people will humor themselves with talk about how Auburn's library once burned to the ground—and they lost both books. Or how the Tigers' football team was so sorry they had to buy a house—just to gain a yard. Auburn people will gush to tell about the Alabama quarterback who ordered a pizza after the game. When asked whether he wanted his pizza cut into six or eight slices, the Tide field general gave instruction to cut it into six—he didn't think he could eat eight.

No Tide fan wants to be the subject of such ridicule for having lost to that cow college in West Georgia. No War Eagle devotee wishes to be heckled by supporters of that elephant institute in East Mississippi. Dishing it out is a heckuva lot more fun than suffering indignity and scorn for fifty-two weeks. That's why, if offered a choice, Auburn people would prefer their team go 1-11, with the lone victory against the Crimson Tide, than 13-1, with the only loss to the tacklers from Tuscaloosa. It's the same way on the opposite side of the field.

If Iron Bowl Saturday is the most anticipated day of the year in Beauregard, the day after, Iron Bowl Sunday, is the most awkward. Less than twenty-four hours following the "War within the State," Auburn and Alabama folks get together for church. We do this despite the fact that we are sworn enemies and have just engaged in mortal combat.

The special virtue needed on this Lord's Day is grace, as in being a gracious winner or a gracious loser. I don't know which is easier—Beauregard people have trouble with both. Winners come into God's house with the swagger of Mick Jagger, showing more teeth than Jimmy Carter, and glad-handing more people than Billy Graham on his best Sunday. The losers, straggling in late and looking marginally better than road kill, are content to be mocked, do their Sabbath duty, and quickly return home to lick their wounds.

The game is the main topic of conversation, for which the preacher gives us all a proper tongue-lashing. "We're here to worship the Lord, not talk football!" you can almost hear him scold, although his words are more cordial, his tone much gentler. We dutifully shake our heads in affirmation, or mutter an inaudible "Amen" under our breaths, with the winning team's portion of the flock possessing an added twinkle in their eye.

We know the preacher's right, of course, but we just can't help ourselves. We'd absolutely bust if we didn't celebrate—or mourn—the biggest earthly event of the year, and the Lord knows we're only human. Anyway, we reason, He's the One who's blessed us with the greatest single rivalry in all of creation, His own personal scuffle with the devil the obvious exception.

On the day after the Iron Bowl, it may seem strange to sit on the same pew with your football enemy, call him "brother" or her "sister," and commit to loving them in the name of the Lord. Most of us do it, however, with surprisingly little anxiety or internal conflict. We may take our rivalry a bit too seriously at times, but we draw the line in church, fully aware that spiritual things are infinitely more important in the grand scheme of life.

We understand that in heaven we're all going to have to live together anyway, both Tigers and Tide in the Hallelujah Chorus. We just pray the Lord's not an Alabama fan. Or Auburn, as the case may be.

****

The Apostle Paul's comment to the Athenians, "I see how extremely religious you are in every way," could also be said of Beauregard. The barometer of religiosity in ancient Greece was the abundance of shrines and statues dedicated to various divine figures. Paul even says that he observed one altar with an inscription reading, "To an Unknown God." By claiming ignorance, evidently the citizens of Athens were seeking to protect their city from the wrath of any foreign deity who might feel slighted.

Athens had its altars; Beauregard has its churches—a plethora of houses of worship, virtually all of the Christian variety. There are churches on just about every highway, byway, and thruway—paved, gravel, or dirt—in the community. Brick churches, wooden churches, churches constructed of concrete; affluent churches, poor churches; churches of different shapes and sizes, colors and denominations—they are all here.

Beauregard especially has its share of Baptist churches. Some flippantly claim that Baptists are ubiquitous because of their propensity not to get along. As a card-carrying Baptist, that's a point I won't argue—

although it may be the only one. I have to shamefully confess that we Baptists are notorious for our squabbling.

We can't even agree on a simple thing like when we got started. Many are of the opinion that Baptists derive from the English Puritans of the seventeenth century, or the Anabaptist movement of the Reformation era. A few mistakenly believe the denomination originated with John the Baptist, just prior to the ministry of Jesus. Others facetiously trace our heritage back even further, to the early days of the Old Testament. They point to Genesis, where Abraham once told Lot, "You go your way and I'll go mine." Their quarrel, they say, sounds a lot like Baptists!

My first exposure to church life in Beauregard was actually with a denomination of a more agreeable reputation. After moving back to the community at age twelve, I initially attended Pierce Chapel United Methodist Church, partly for its proximity to our house— only a couple of football fields away—but also because my relatives had a history of worshiping there. Pawpaw's grandfather, Frank Long, was a Methodist minister who helped found Pierce Chapel in 1858. There have been Longs in the congregation off and on ever since.

To my youthful eyes, the Methodists didn't seem a whole lot different than the Baptists. They pretty much sang the same songs, preached the same sermons, read the same Bible, and talked about the same sins. The most noticeable difference was the confirmation ceremony some of my friends experienced. I wondered at the time if I should participate, for I, too, wanted to be a good person, do the right thing, and please the Lord.

The gospel seed planted at Liberty and watered at Pierce Chapel was nurtured considerably at a second church stop in Beauregard. When I was thirteen we started attending Union Grove Baptist, where we became fairly regular in our Sunday worship. Mama was Baptist and thought we kids should be brought up in the Baptist way of religious things. Many Sundays Granny and Pawpaw went along with us, despite their Methodist connections, and there we came under the influence of a ministerial marvel by the name of Paul Weekley.

Preacher Weekley, as he was affectionately known, held a staggering twenty-six pastorates in the East Alabama / West Georgia region during his lengthy sixty-five year career. Many of the congregations were half-time churches, and some he served more than once, including a couple of stints at Providence Baptist in Beauregard in the 1930's and '40's. He would step on too many toes at one place of worship and move on to another, only later to return once his former flock's feet quit hurting.

Granny and Pawpaw had known him for years. They were not customary churchgoers until late in life, and Preacher Weekley had often been after them to attend his churches. Every now and then he would visit the farm for this very purpose. Granny loved to tell about the time he called, spied her well-worn Bible sitting on a table, then turned to his wife Lois, declaring, "Look, honey, there's a little bit of heaven in this house!"

When I first saw Preacher Weekley at Union Grove, he looked as old as Methuselah to my young eyes. In his mid-seventies, the somewhat stocky figure he presented was topped by a big bald head that bore thick metal-frame glasses in front of a round friendly face. I still recall the first time I heard him preach. His younger brother Seth went to the front of the church to read the scripture before the sermon. Preacher Weekley then ambled up behind the pulpit to deliver the message, not carrying a Bible or using sermon notes at all. Afterward I learned that he was nearly blind and could not see well enough even to read from the Good Book.

Preacher Weekley, toward the end of his long and distinguished ministerial career.

Despite this handicap, he preached with passion and wisdom, rattling off verses of scripture from memory and making pointed application from them. Even though I was at least sixty years his younger, I found myself listening with keen interest and seriously contemplating the spiritual dimension of life, something he had spent a lifetime pondering. Ironically, God used this blind preacher to open my eyes to the sinful nature I possessed and the need of Christ to deal with it. He also affected the eyes of Pawpaw.

One Sunday following the sermon, Pawpaw started weeping during the final hymn of commitment. He held on tightly to the pew in front, obviously under conviction, but unable to move or control his emotions. A relative from my father's side, Ed Manning, came to his aid. He took my grandfather by the arm and escorted him down the aisle to the elderly pastor, who then led him to make a public profession of faith in Christ. My grandmother soon followed, and Preacher Weekley baptized Granny and Pawpaw a few Sundays later, the belated answer to prayers he had offered on their behalf years earlier.

Paul Weekley was a spiritual giant in our community, a hero of the faith whose life was a model of integrity and devoted ministry for the Lord. In my own religious journey, he functioned as a kind of John the Baptist—preparing the way for the coming of the Lord. In much the same role, he served as the forerunner to another man's ministry and to the arrival of our messianic age in Beauregard.

Chapter 2
"Brother Robert"

Beauregard is not only my Bethel, it is also my Galilee. There I heard the Lord's familiar call of "Follow Me!" and responded to His direction for my life. Beauregard is where I started a lifelong journey of faith in Christ and proceeded down the road of discipleship. Sowers like Preacher Weekley scattered the gospel seed, others cultivated it. It took root and began to grow under the Christ-like ministry of a man lovingly known as "Brother Robert."

Thirty-six year old Robert Lee Dismukes became pastor of Beauregard's Providence Baptist Church in the summer of 1968. Little could anyone have imagined the enormous impact this humble preacher would have upon the church and community over the next fifteen years. No one could have guessed that under his watch a dynamic movement of divine power would emerge, bringing the life and love of Christ into the hearts and homes of so many. Brother Robert was God's mover and shaker for our place and time, the spiritual leader of our messianic age.

There was nothing about his appearance or demeanor to suggest the immense influence he wielded. Slight of stature, almost diminutive, with skinny arms and legs and trunk, the physical package he presented looked somewhat fragile. It was surprising, therefore, when this slender figure of a man greeted you with big, strong hands that were firm, yet soft.

His face housed an easy smile, warm and friendly, with eyes that squinted and twitched behind ever-present glasses, looking at you pleasantly but intently, as if seeking to gaze deeply into your soul. Above his forehead, wavy black hair with gray edging was rapidly receding, thinning especially on the very top, making him appear a bit older than his years. He spoke with a gentle and pleasing voice, crisply articulating each syllable, as if carefully choosing every word. Listeners tended to leave with the impression they had talked with a person of spiritual wisdom and genuine concern.

Brother Robert's relatively weak physical presence was mainly due to diabetes, a disease he had borne since adolescence. To combat it, he gave himself insulin shots every day and constantly monitored his diet. Even so, the condition took an evident toll on his fitness, robbing his body of strength and function. He largely shielded the disorder from those outside his immediate family, and only in later years did I learn the extent to which he suffered while serving as our pastor. I never heard him complain about the disease or the extra burden it placed upon his ministry obligations; rarely did he talk about it. His focus was not on himself, but on Christ and the needs of his congregation. Those in his flock were so taken by his spiritual vitality that it was easy to overlook the physical ailment so obviously there.

In reflecting upon his ministry, and knowing what I do now about the New Testament, Robert's physical condition and spiritual character remind me a great deal of the Apostle Paul. This is a bold comparison to be sure, but whenever I read Paul's second letter to the Corinthians, Brother Robert comes readily to mind. There the Apostle makes numerous references to the poor state of his own health, at one point calling it his "thorn in the flesh." No one knows the identity of his malady, though many suggestions have been proffered. It could easily have resulted from the many hardships he suffered as a missionary of the gospel.

In this same letter Paul mentions that he was whipped on five separate occasions with the thirty-nine lashes, beaten three times with rods, and underwent "countless" floggings. He also says he endured a stoning, multiple imprisonments, and three shipwrecks, one setting him adrift at sea for a night and a day. The physical toll was doubtless substantial. References in the letter to being "afflicted in every way," the "outer nature wasting away," and "always carrying in the body the death of Jesus," are likely based upon personal experience.

That Paul was in pain—probably chronic physical pain—is apparent. He refers to his thorn as "a messenger of Satan to torment me," and on three occasions prayed God would remove it. Yet throughout his ordeal Paul remained faithful, paradoxically finding in his suffering the power of God for life and ministry. "Power is made perfect in weakness," he wrote, for "whenever I am weak, then I am strong." Indeed, he even celebrated the "treasure" found in his perishable "jar of clay," metaphors for the life of Christ so clearly evident in his mortal body. Rather than blaming God for his troubles and shaking a fist toward the heavens, Paul trusted God to know his situation and to provide grace sufficient for his needs.

This was the response I saw in Brother Robert, a biblical approach to unprovoked suffering that is sometimes referred to as "the cruciform life." It's a lifestyle that uses the cross as its paradigm, a symbol of sacrifice, selflessness, humility, and love. The cruciform life seeks to emulate the faithfulness of Jesus in going to the cross, accepting suffering—when necessary—as one's destiny, viewing it as a cathartic means through which God's will is ultimately accomplished.

Relegating the pursuit of prestige, power, and possessions to the way of the world, one focuses instead upon the attitudes and practices of Jesus, seeking to develop the mind-set of Christ. The Lord's words concerning true discipleship are taken seriously: "If anyone will come after me, let him deny himself, take up his cross daily, and follow me." Denying self, taking up the cross, and following Jesus every day were what Brother Robert was all about.

While likely not familiar with the terminology of the cruciform life, Robert certainly understood the concept. He simply preferred to put it in the language of scripture. A favorite Bible text he taught us to memorize was Paul's declaration to the Galatians: "I am crucified with Christ, nevertheless I live; yet not I but Christ lives in me, and the life I now live in the flesh I live by faith in the Son of God who loved me and gave himself for me." The Apostle took up the cross in his own life, dying to self in order to live for the Lord, and urged his readers to do the same.

Paul's phrase, "I am crucified with Christ," could well serve as Brother Robert's motto for ministry. He liked to express it in poetic form, so he encouraged us to memorize an anonymous prayer that meant a lot to him.

> Lord, bend that proud and stiff-necked I;
> Help me to bow my head and die;
> Beholding Him on Calvary,
> Who bowed His head for me.

What Jesus taught regarding discipleship and Paul communicated concerning the cruciform life I saw personally exemplified during the years of my youth and young adulthood. Robert's flesh and blood example I have taken with me all of my Christian life, even while falling far short of it. As Robert lived out his faith in Christ, the adversities he faced did not impede his commitment—they intensified it.

From him I learned that being Christ-like does not guard against the trials and tribulations of life. The so-called "prosperity gospel" is entirely bogus; troubles often descend especially upon those who are closest to God, as they did upon Jesus and Paul. Brother Robert taught us that the wisest among the saints look upon their sorrows and sufferings as opportunities to become more Christ-like.

A few years ago I began referring to these adversities as "Lulus." The word comes from a favorite story about a visitor to a psychiatric hospital who found a patient gazing blankly into the distance while rocking back and forth in a chair and repeating to himself one word: "Lulu...Lulu...Lulu."

"What's the matter with that man?" the visitor inquired of his host.

"Lulu was the name of a woman who jilted him, and he's never been able to get over her," the host explained.

The visitor proceeded on his tour of the facility and later came to a room where another patient was repeatedly batting his head against a padded wall while shouting the same name over and over again: "Lulu!...Lulu!...Lulu!"

"What's the matter with him?" asked the visitor.

"Oh," answered the host, "that's the guy who married Lulu."

From time to time life has a way of sending us "Lulus"—difficulties, problems, troubles—that test our confidence in the Lord's goodness and care. How we respond provides a useful measurement of Christian faith and character. Brother Robert showed how to handle life's Lulus with trust and courage and grace.

The Lord seeks to use our struggles to make us stronger and wiser, more attune to His purposes, and more capable of accomplishing His will in our lives. Paul, who surely would have earned a Ph.D. at the proverbial University of Hard Knocks, found the power to be more like Christ in—of all things—his thorn in the flesh.

So did Robert Dismukes. There are lots of reasons to admire this man who became my spiritual father, brother in Christ, and co-laborer in the vineyard of the Lord. But perhaps the thing I admire the most is that he modeled how to personalize the gospel, making it relevant and applicable to every facet of his existence, even the unpleasant ones. As mentor and friend, pastor and counselor, he shaped my life for Christ more than any individual I have ever known. So many others would say exactly the same.

****

The story of Robert's life begins in his native Alabama. He was born during the throes of the depression on June 29, 1932 in Houston County near

Dothan, located in the extreme southeast corner of the state. The Dismukes family included six boys—Earl, Wallace, Robert, Paul, Charles, and Wilmer, and one girl—Frances. Another sibling, Fred, the oldest of the eight children, died as a two year old. Robert's father, Mervin—better known as "Dizzy"—was a barber by trade, while Julia, his mother, experienced serious medical issues for much of her life. The family mostly lived on the edge of poverty due to their size, health problems, and the dire economic conditions of the time.

"Dizzy" and Julia Dismukes,
Robert's father and mother.

Dizzy frequently moved the family around the county in an effort to find affordable housing and enough tonsorial work to meet their needs. To compound their financial troubles, a frightening accident completely incapacitated him for a while. Dizzy's leg was caught in the spokes of a rolling wagon wheel, causing a severe break and leaving him crippled for the rest of his life. Some of the children went to work at a young age to ease the family's monetary woes—plowing gardens, picking cotton, gathering pecans, and the like.

By all accounts Julia was a sweet, unassuming woman who endured the misfortune of a debilitating form of asthma. In an age with no air conditioning and few paved roads, the hot and humid summers of the Deep South were especially harsh for Julia. Rendered periodically weak and sickly by the severity of the ailment, she found herself recurrently bedridden and unable to perform even the simplest of household chores. These she delegated to the children.

Robert's specific responsibilities included helping prepare the family's meals and ironing their clothes. Perhaps he was assigned domestic duties because of his relatively modest size. Robert was a smallish child, more skinny than trim, with a neck that appeared too long for someone of his body type. His most evident physical quality was squinty little eyes that often appeared to be jumping up and down, as if winking at you while he talked. Despite his slight dimensions, Robert grew to possess physical strength that belied his slender build.

On one occasion younger brothers Charles and Wilmer were playing with matches near a hundred gallon drum filled with kerosene, fuel used to burn coal for heat in winter. The drum always dripped a little kerosene from its spigot onto the ground, and it was this that Charles and Wilmer promptly set ablaze. Fortunately for them, Robert was nearby. As the fire began to rage, he frantically ran toward the conflagration and all alone dislodged the heavy drum from its stand, rolling it a safe distance from the fire. According to brotherly lore, it took three men to move the drum back to its base. Hidden muscle, a burst of adrenaline, and perhaps divine intervention apparently gave Robert the Samson-like strength that likely saved his siblings' lives.

The family eventually settled in the Rehobeth community south of Dothan, residing in a house high enough off the ground that their hogs could rest comfortably below. Robert and his brothers often watched the swine through cracks in the floor of their bedroom. The Dismukes family, like others in the area, raised farm animals on their small parcel of property, while also working a large vegetable garden to serve their voracious appetites.

The post-World War II era of Robert's teenage years was an idyllic time of peace and growing prosperity in our country's history. Baseball was still the national pastime and Robert's sport of choice. He regularly played outfield for Rehobeth High and the local American Legion squad. One unforgettable highlight was accompanying his legion teammates to Montgomery to meet the legendary Babe Ruth, who came through on a barnstorming tour shortly before his death in 1948.

At Rehobeth Robert also lettered in football and developed an avid interest in drama, winning the lead role in a couple of stage shows. Unlike today's high school generation—and even my own—Robert never acquired the regular use of an automobile, depending on others for the six mile trip to and from school activities, walking the half mile or so between his house and the main highway where he caught the bus or hitched a ride. The family's Chrysler Plymouth was strictly off limits.

*Football was only one of Robert's
many pursuits in high school.*

Robert was recognized by family and friends for
his good character, never known to dabble in the vices of
alcohol, drugs, or sexual promiscuity. He was not beyond
mischief, however, and occasionally bent the rules in the
interest of a good time. He loved to tell how he and best
friend Arthur Powell, who later served as best man in his
wedding, once played hooky from school. They decided
to catch a city bus to take them on their adventure of
truancy. The boys hadn't gone far when they
discovered—to their utter dismay—that Arthur's mother
was on the very same bus! She spotted them and
promptly escorted the two delinquents back to Rehobeth,
with proper tongue-lashing and threat of future
punishment.

A much more serious moment in young Robert's
life occurred when he was diagnosed with Type 1
diabetes. Rehobeth's principal, W. T. McNeal,
personally brought him home one morning after he
complained of not feeling well. No one else was present

at the time, and family members who arrived in the afternoon found Robert unconscious. The family physician, Dr. Hasten, came quickly and made the stunning diagnosis. The disease would afflict him for the rest of his life and soon affect his availability for military service. While siblings and friends left home to fight in the Korean conflict of the early fifties, Robert remained in Dothan.

Following graduation from Rehobeth High School in 1951, eighteen year old Robert vaguely decided upon a career in the business world. With no firm long-range plans, he enrolled at the Riley Business School in Dothan as a way of getting started on something. The business courses served as preparation for the work he was doing when three decisive events transformed his life. In fairly rapid succession, Robert came to know the Lord, his future wife, and his life's calling.

****

After one year at business school, Robert took the position of clerk for a Dothan attorney by the name of Robert Ramsey, whose office was downtown. There he busied himself with such duties as preparing deeds, composing abstracts, and typing contracts. He could often be seen walking to the courthouse or the post office in typical 1950's attire of white shirt, bow tie, dark pants, and saddle shoes. One of those walks ultimately led to an encounter with the Lord.

Through the years Robert mostly attended the Methodist church of his family, but never made a deliberate and public profession of faith in Christ. His salvation experience occurred in December of 1952, when a high school acquaintance named Edwin Worthy talked to Robert about the need of receiving Christ and becoming a Christian. Edwin was a personable young man on fire for the Lord, making him bold in his witness and quick to share his faith. For some time he had prayed for Robert, targeting him as a top mission project.

On a Tuesday afternoon Robert ran into Edwin at the post office not far from Ramsey's law practice. They began chatting on the steps, with Edwin asking if he had thought any more about accepting Christ as Savior. Robert replied that, indeed, he had been giving the matter serious consideration. Edwin once again witnessed to his friend and invited him to attend a young people's event later that evening at his church. Robert promised to go, kept his promise, and at the meeting Edwin led him to faith in Christ.

The church was Headland Avenue Baptist and the event was known as the Bible Lover's Club. Every Tuesday night older teenagers and young adults came together to study the Bible, share testimonies, sing, pray, and enjoy each other's company. The club was started by the church's previous pastor, Reverend Arthur Zbinden, as a way of deepening commitment to Christ on the part of his youth.

Brother Zip, as he was fondly known, served Headland Avenue for eighteen years and possessed a special passion for the spiritual welfare of young people. His zeal for soul winning, prayer, and helping teenagers stay on the straight and narrow was evident to all. When youth saw him coming in his big blue Chevrolet sedan, they instantly knew why he was there—he wanted them to know Jesus and become like Him. He was also one of those no-nonsense kinds of pastors who didn't put up with going to movies or attending dances, two spiritual taboos of his day. A favorite saying was that he had never seen a dancing foot and a praying knee on the same leg!

Under his ministry God moved among the young people of his church. Brother Zip taught them well how to pray and how to witness, and one youth who soaked it all up was Edwin Worthy. Edwin prayed for Robert, faithfully witnessed to him, and now was excited to see the lawyer's clerk become a new brother in Christ and begin the process of discipleship. Robert was one of a number that Edwin personally led to Christian faith as he went about sharing the gospel and inviting people to his church.

Edwin eventually made the gospel his full-time business as he went on to become pastor of several churches in Alabama. There were, in fact, many young men the Lord called to the ministry from the Bible Lover's Club in and around 1950. Charles, Edwin's brother, also became a pastor, as did Bob and George Zbinden, sons of Brother Zip, who followed their beloved dad in doing the Lord's work. Another set of brothers, Sigurd and Wayne Bryan, went on to distinguished careers as religion professors at Samford University in Birmingham and Baptist Bible Institute in Graceville, Florida, respectively. Jim Bruner served both as a pastor in Georgia and as an executive at Mercer University, a Baptist school in Macon. One could add to the list the names of Johnny Boyd, Richard Brackin, Thomas Kennedy, Bobby Moore, Hilton Olive, George Palmer, James Underwood, and Malcolm Wade.

Robert was among the last of the Dothan "preacherboys," as they were known, to give his life to Christian ministry. They were a tightly knit group, and frequently socialized after church at Rainbow's Restaurant or Tom's Drive-In. They went out together witnessing and soul winning, bringing more and more Dothan youth into God's kingdom. Youth for Christ, the Christian young people's organization where Billy Graham first came to prominence, was in its heyday, and the preacherboys held evangelistic rallies in Dothan and surrounding towns under its banner.

The Dothan "preacherboys" get together at Mrs. Worthy's. Robert sits in front, wearing glasses. Edwin Worthy also sits in front, second from right.

Through the years, as the young men went their separate ways to follow the Lord's calling, they stayed in touch via correspondence and by doing revivals and Bible conferences in each other's churches. When returning to Dothan at Christmastime, reunions were held at the home of a lady who took special interest in the group. Annie Worthy, mother of Edwin and Charles, hosted an annual holiday gathering for food and fellowship. There they caught up on current news, reminisced about good times, and shared future plans.

Mrs. Worthy is remembered as a beloved saint at Headland Avenue—friendly to a fault, generous with time and money, and completely supportive of those doing the Lord's work. In distinct contrast to his wife and three children, Edwin Worthy, Sr. did not attend church or even profess to be a Christian. He also didn't want anyone talking to him about it. He was happy to support God's house by extension, holding fast to the spiritual security blanket of his family members' rich faith.

Mr. Worthy made a good living running a junkyard, and often employed his two boys and their friends to help out. Among other tasks, the young men extracted spare parts, compressed batteries, and brought in more junk. With the preacherboys working for him, a wife praying on his behalf, two sons in the ministry, and a daughter married to a preacher, Mr. Worthy didn't stand a chance of escaping the conviction that he needed the Lord. Thankfully, his story has a happy ending. George Zbinden, the preacherboy who married Mr. Worthy's daughter Jane, finally succeeded in introducing the keeper of junk to the treasures of Christ.

The good times experienced at Mrs. Worthy's Christmas gatherings were the inspiration behind a reunion the Dothan preacherboys organized in later years. Jim Bruner, George Palmer, and Bob Zbinden initiated the first in 1987 at the old Headland Avenue Church (now Greater Beulah Baptist Church) with about forty in attendance, and the get-together has been held semi-regularly ever since. The numbers attending have necessarily declined in recent years, but those who are able eagerly come to laugh, to cry, and to remember.

****

The Sunday after attending his initial Bible Lover's Club meeting Robert joined Headland Avenue Church, professing publicly his faith in Christ and requesting baptism. The church's new pastor, Reverend Henry Nettles, was overjoyed to see the twenty year old walk down the sanctuary aisle and indicate his recent decision. In the congregation that Sunday happened to be a young lady who would factor enormously into Robert's life.

Shirley Ann Griggs was the youngest of five children born to J. C. and Lillie on February 9, 1937, coming along late in their lives. Though thrilled to have another child, the financial burden of providing for an additional family member strained their meager budget during the latter years of the depression era. After World War II began to rage, J. C. decided to start a floor covering business to help provide for the family, as well as to have jobs waiting for two sons when they returned from the war. Customers were few at first but he stayed with it, and despite limited education and scant resources, within a few years he achieved success as the owner and operator of Griggs Floor Covering.

Shirley's parents, J. C. and Lillie Griggs.

The Griggs family was Baptist and members of Headland Avenue, which they attended regularly except for the first Sunday of every month. That Lord's Day was typically reserved for J. C.'s home church, Oaky Grove Baptist, located north of Dothan between Headland and Abbeville. When Shirley was seven, she was baptized at Oaky Grove, though she didn't become a Christian for another six years. Her actual conversion occurred during revival services at Headland Avenue when the recently turned teenager personally received Christ as Savior and Lord. It was then that Shirley realized she had not understood the meaning of the earlier baptismal ceremony, and was soon re-baptized as a believer by Brother Zip.

Two years later when Robert joined her church, Shirley's eyes lit up. This was not the first time she had noticed the handsome young man with dark curly hair. After classes at Dothan High, Shirley often went downtown to her father's business, located near the courthouse complex and not far from Ramsey's law office where Robert worked. Growing bored with the carpet and tile, she habitually wandered down the street to Cash's Drug Store where many of her friends hung out. In the 1950's, pharmacies with soda fountains were popular gathering spots for teens, a safe place to see and be seen. Shirley liked doing both and went to Cash's to eat a bite, drink a soda, and pass the time.

Teenage Shirley, hitching a ride aboard her father's delivery van.

On occasion she saw Robert there as well, when he stopped on his way back to the office from the courthouse, or perhaps after work. They never spoke directly, though secretly Shirley wished they would. Since she was almost five years younger than Robert and lived in an age that frowned upon the forwardness of females, she kept the attraction to herself. Now, seemingly out of the blue, here he was joining her church! She couldn't help but wonder if there was something providential going on.

Robert also began to notice Shirley as he started attending worship, Sunday School, and other activities at

Headland Avenue. He joined the church during the
Christmas season, and two months later, by Valentine's
Day, he had asked her for a date. She turned sixteen only
days before he called, inviting her to go with him to
Marianna, Florida to attend a weekend Youth for Christ
rally. Some of the preacherboys were leading the event,
one of many they participated in at various churches
throughout the southeast Alabama, southwest Georgia,
and northwest Florida triangle.

Robert agreed to drive two of the preacherboys,
Johnny Boyd and James Underwood, to the Saturday
evening service using his father's Chrysler sedan. Each
of them had dates, and Robert wanted Shirley to be his.
After getting permission from her parents, she readily
accepted. She sat in the front of the car with Robert,
while the other two couples filled up the rear. To allow
Shirley to sit close to Robert, they piled all of their jackets
and sweaters in the front seat against the passenger side
door.

From that moment on Robert and Shirley were a
couple. Their dating life centered upon Headland
Avenue, and over the course of Sunday and Wednesday
church dates, Tuesday night Bible Lover's Club meetings,
and weekend Youth for Christ events, their romance
blossomed. They found themselves falling deeply in love.

Their passion for one another was at no time more
evident than when they were apart. An initial separation
occurred the following summer when Shirley left for a
week to attend a youth conference at Shocco Springs
Baptist Assembly in northern Alabama. She received a
letter from Robert the very first morning—he had sent it
before she left Dothan. In fact, he mailed two letters

before her departure, and she enjoyed correspondence from him each day she was away.

Not only did Robert send daily letters, but he also dispatched several telegrams, boldly declaring his love and the loneliness he felt without her. One tender Western Union message is dated August 6, 1953, exactly one year before their wedding.

> DEAR HONEY I SURE AM LONESOME
> HURRY UP AND COME HOME AND PLEASE
> WRITE AND LET ME KNOW IF YOU HAVE
> BEEN GETTING MY MAIL PS I LOVE YOU
> LOVE =ROBERT..=

A few months later Robert decided to take a trip as well. He traveled to California with Dizzy to see older brother Earl, who was now living and working out West. The Golden State fascinated Robert, and he spontaneously decided to remain with Earl and not return to Alabama with his dad. He figured he could find a better job there and save more money for his anticipated marriage to Shirley. She still lacked almost two years of high school, he reasoned, and he could set aside a lot of cash in that amount of time. By the wedding date, perhaps there would be enough to make their home in California like his brother.

Being 2500 miles away from Shirley, however, soon changed Robert's mind. He started missing her terribly, along with his family and friends back home. Added to his homesickness was the inability to secure the well-paying job he envisioned. Robert's "California dreaming" was short-lived, and he quickly returned to

Dothan, to Shirley, and to his clerk's position with Robert Ramsey.

It was not long afterward that he asked Shirley to marry him. They had talked about it many times, and more or less assumed they would wed since the early days of courtship, but Robert wanted to make it official. So after attending a basketball game at Dothan High on a late autumn evening, he drove to a favorite spot and proposed, presenting her with the engagement ring she had already selected.

Shirley knew the proposal was coming, if not that night then soon. She mentioned to Robert that she didn't want to get the ring at Christmas or on her birthday in February. Whatever day he chose, she wanted it to be a special day for them, a time she could forever mark as the day she agreed to marry the man of her dreams, a romantic day, a day indelibly etched into the canvass of their lives. Their day was December 1, 1953.

The two lovers displayed a lot of courage in making their plans to marry. Shirley was so young, only a junior in high school. Robert didn't really have anything to offer, except his love. Convincing her parents to consent to their marriage in the near future might prove difficult, they agreed. Winning them over would not be easy.

In their favor was the fact that Robert had recently moved to Shirley's neighborhood. Robert's mother Julia died from asthma complications not long before they started dating. A few months after the funeral, Dizzy began seeing a widow, Mildred Hayes, who lived across the street and three houses down from Shirley. Mildred's husband died suddenly in an ammonia fire at the Borden ice cream plant in Dothan, leaving her with six children, all still at home. When her boys needed haircuts, Mildred took them to Dizzy, which is how they met and started dating. Marriage came quickly, and they decided that Dizzy and his children should move in with Mildred and her kids, a fifties version of the Brady Bunch.

This pleased Robert and Shirley immensely. Since neither owned a vehicle, the move conveniently facilitated the amount of time they could spend together. Robert could now walk to her house, which he did almost every day. There they talked and listened to music or studied Shirley's homework. Often they asked her dad for the keys to the family car so they could "get something to drink." They just wanted to get away, of course, to be alone, with freedom to express their love for one another. After returning, Robert would kiss her goodnight at the front door, their romantic finale often serenaded by a noisy neighbor, Mr. Bottoms, who sat on his porch grunting and spitting tobacco juice into the night. They paid him no mind; nothing could spoil their happiness together.

With Robert's constant presence in the Griggs household, their affection for him grew stronger by the day. He gained their confidence, and soon the young couple secured J. C. and Lillie's blessing to marry. They liked Robert and were happy for Shirley, but worried about the timing of the marriage. Approval for a summer ceremony was given on one condition: Shirley must promise to finish high school. That was no problem for the couple, and they wed on August 6, 1954. Shirley was seventeen, and Robert had turned twenty-two.

Robert and Shirley, on their wedding day.

****

Robert and Shirley spent their wedding night in Chipley, Florida as they made their way to the white sandy shores of Panama City Beach. The PCB of the early fifties was quite different than it appears today, with oceanfront high rises as far as the eye can see and summertime masses blanketing the area. Laid back, not crowded, seemingly a million miles from the real world, here it was easy for the two of them to focus on each other and their dreams for the future. Those dreams were still unclear; they only knew they would share them together.

After a brief honeymoon, the newlyweds returned to Dothan in time for scheduled youth revival services at

Headland Avenue. Robert was asked to fill the role of youth pastor for the event, a responsibility that involved assisting in the worship services and counseling young people who made decisions during the week. His selection revealed the level of confidence the church's leadership placed in Robert. Even though he had not announced a call to ministry like other young men in the church, he was enlisted to serve as a key member of the revival team.

Since his conversion less than two years earlier, Robert had become very active at Headland Avenue and in the Bible Lover's Club. He was also prominent in the church's Royal Ambassadors ministry to boys. The RAs met on Wednesday nights to study the Bible and engage in various ministry projects. The boys of the church had come to love and trust Robert, making him an excellent choice to serve as the revival's youth pastor.

No doubt the Lord was also at work in his selection, for at that time God was dealing with Robert about his career choice. What vocation best suited him? What did the Lord want him to do with his life? He had just gotten married; that part of the equation was filled in. The next big step was to find his life's calling.

He had begun thinking and praying about it in earnest prior to his marriage. Now, as he helped conduct the revival services with prayers, scripture readings, announcements, and counseling, Robert felt a certain comfort level with worship responsibilities. People in the church noticed it, too, and mentioned to Shirley how natural Robert looked before the congregation. She paid them little attention, too newly married to think much about it.

On the final day of the revival, Robert and Shirley were at home in their new rental apartment, relaxing and chatting about nothing in particular. Robert picked this moment to surprise his new bride with the question he was struggling with in the privacy of his heart.

"Shirley, what would you say if I told you the Lord might be calling me to preach?" he offered.

She laughed softly, not picking up on how seriously he intended the question, and replied with a perfunctory, "I don't know, honey; what do you mean?"

"Well, I think God might just want me to be a preacher," Robert continued. This time he gained her rapt attention.

"Robert, you must be teasing me!" she responded, with an incredulous tone to her voice. Undaunted, he went on.

"Haven't you noticed how preoccupied I've been lately? It's been weighing on my mind throughout the revival. I just can't get away from feeling that I should be a preacher."

The conversation was difficult for Shirley to absorb, occurring barely a week after their wedding. Finally convinced of how earnest he was, she suggested he discuss it with the revival's evangelists, Johnny Boyd and Bobby Moore, two of the preacherboys.

Robert left immediately to find them. Shirley remained in the apartment, nervously awaiting his return. At last he came back and shared his decision to surrender to the ministry.

"I have a peace about it," he told her. "I really believe this is what God wants me to do."

Initially Robert was reluctant to make the decision public because so many young men in the church had committed themselves to ministry. He didn't want people to get the idea that he was simply keeping up with his friends. Despite this pause for concern, the conviction about his call was so strong that he decided to go ahead and announce it during that evening's service.

"Okay, but before you do I'd feel better if we told mama and daddy first," Shirley suggested. She didn't want her folks finding out secondhand about such an important pronouncement in their lives.

Shirley didn't know how her parents would react. Neither did Robert. When they went over and Robert shared about his call to preach, Mr. Griggs simply looked at him and said, "That's real fine son; you do what you feel led to do. But I'll tell you right now, it's no gravy train!" What Shirley took as her dad's slight disapproval, she later understood to be only a father's valid concern.

Robert took his place in the revival service with more of a sense of belonging in the pulpit. At its conclusion, he announced to the church his call to ministry, news welcomed enthusiastically by the congregation, and especially by the other preacherboys. Later on, in a special service of recognition, he was licensed to preach by Headland Avenue, indicating the church's approval and recommendation to others regarding his call. Two noteworthy signatures on the license were those of Robert's father-in-law, who happened to be serving as the church's clerk, and Headland Avenue's interim pastor at the time, Dr. Arthur Steinbeck. Dr. Steinbeck was president of Baptist Bible Institute in Graceville, Florida, and would soon offer valuable assistance to Robert and Shirley.

The newlyweds intended to remain in the apartment until the following spring when Shirley was set to graduate from high school. However, with Robert's sudden career decision, they moved out after only a month and lived with Shirley's parents in order to save money for his future education. While Shirley finished her senior year, Robert continued to work at the law office and in volunteer ministry at the church. He also began receiving preaching opportunities. The first came at the invitation of an older minister and family friend named Ewell Henry.

Reverend Henry served as pastor of two churches in and around the Bascom, Florida area, and he asked Robert to preach at one of them. Shirley went with Robert for his first sermon, delivered at the Bascom Baptist Church in the fall of 1954. They were both quite nervous about the occasion. Robert planned a message about making Christ the captain of our lives, using the Gospels' account of Jesus asleep in the boat with frightened disciples who awaken Him to calm a ferocious storm.

Since this was his first sermon, Robert had no idea how long it would last. There was so much he wanted to share that Shirley was afraid he might get longwinded. Having no watch or clock to go by, they decided to arrange a predetermined signal to indicate it was time to bring the sermon to a close. She was to scratch her nose and he would know to end the homily. After about half an hour of sermonizing, Shirley scratched, and pretty soon Robert sat down.

Things went well enough that Reverend Henry asked Robert to preach to his other flock at Mount Olive. The Mount Olive folks liked the young preacher, and thereafter Reverend Henry invited him to fill the pulpit on several occasions. Following one such service on a

Sunday night in March, Robert became violently ill to the point that he nearly died. He experienced severe complications from diabetes and spent the next ten days in the hospital, much of it in a diabetic coma.

Shirley stayed faithfully by his side, only leaving to attend her senior classes. Each morning as she reluctantly left the hospital to go to school, she feared it might be the last time she saw her husband alive. She prayed fervently for the recovery of her new spouse.

"Lord, we've been married now for only a few months. We love each other so much! We both want to serve you together here on earth. Please, Lord, just let us have 25 more years together."

The future would show that God granted Shirley's desperate prayer request, and awarded her a little bonus time as well.

****

Upon Shirley's graduation from Dothan High School in May of 1955, the couple decided to move to Birmingham so Robert could attend Howard College. Howard, now part of Samford University, was a Baptist liberal arts school with a program in religious studies that catered to young ministers. The plan was for Robert to earn his college degree in preparation for full-time ministry while Shirley worked to pay their expenses.

After arriving in Birmingham, they lived in the vacant apartment of Headland Avenue friends Richard and Alec Brackin until they could find more permanent quarters. The Brackins attended Howard, and Richard also served on staff at one of Birmingham's leading churches, Central Park Baptist. They were conveniently house-sitting the residence of their pastor, Dr. Wayne Dehoney, while he was on summer sabbatical, leaving their apartment temporarily free. Shirley quickly found a job as secretary at Vulcan Printing and Lithographing through the assistance of another Dothan acquaintance. Their connections were paying nice dividends, their plans apparently coming together as they moved down the track of training for pastoral ministry.

Those plans were momentarily derailed when Robert was unable to pass the college entrance examination and gain admittance to Howard. Crushed and humbled, but still trusting God for their future, Robert and Shirley said goodbye to the Brackins and took themselves home to Dothan.

Privately, Shirley began to doubt that Robert possessed the attributes necessary for a successful career behind the pulpit. In her view, his public speaking skills were more than a little suspect. He talked slowly and deliberately, and didn't always use the best grammar. There was little charisma to his presence before a group, and it now appeared he would go lacking in academic credentials. With all of this in mind, she wondered if he should continue to pursue ministry as a vocation.

Robert had no such doubts. No matter how lacking in educational pedigree or oratorical skill, he was firmly convinced that God had called him to be a minister of the gospel. The Lord must have another path for him to get there.

That path proved to be through Graceville, Florida, only twenty miles southwest of Dothan. Located there was Baptist Bible Institute, better known as BBI (now The Baptist College of Florida), which had not yet begun its fall term. The school existed for the primary purpose of training ministers.

The institute's president, Dr. Arthur Steinbeck, took a special interest in Robert and Shirley. He had been the interim pastor at Headland Avenue a year earlier when Robert was called to preach, and now promised to help the young couple if they decided to enroll at BBI. Following a quick visit to the campus, it didn't take long to make up their minds to come, and Dr. Steinbeck delivered on his promise.

His connections enabled Shirley to land a job as secretary at Graceville High School. He also found them an apartment close to campus. The apartment's owner, Irene Carter, was especially kind and understanding, actually lowering their rent a time or two to assist them. Robert and Shirley saw the doors open wide to Graceville, just as they had seen them shut tight only a few days before in Birmingham.

Shirley, on the steps of their
Graceville apartment.

Feeling certain that this was where the Lord wanted them provided a much needed boost of confidence, and they settled into life in Graceville with a sense of comfort and security. Robert took delight in the intense Bible courses he found at the new school, preparing for the day he would preach and teach from scripture regularly at a church. Shirley enjoyed getting to know the staff and students at the high school, making new friends especially among those who came to Graceville for the same reason she did. There wasn't a lot to do in the sleepy little town, so most weekends they returned to Dothan to be with family and friends. The arrangement of spending the weekdays in Graceville and weekends in Dothan was perfect for their situation and needs.

They were not in Graceville long, however, before another health crisis erupted. The high school was only a couple of blocks from their apartment, but most days Robert met Shirley after classes to drive her home. One Monday afternoon he didn't show up as planned, and she immediately feared something was wrong. They owned no phone, so she briskly walked home, first noticing that their Chrysler was parked in the yard.

She tried to stay calm as she made her way to the entrance of the apartment, and finally was relieved to see Robert lying on the bed through a window. Upon entering the front door, she expressed her displeasure that he didn't pick her up as planned.

"Robert, why didn't you come and get me?" she asked. Her voice roused him, and she instantly knew from his response that something was terribly wrong.

"Becauuuse" he cried hoarsely, as if gasping for air. Right away she recognized the symptoms of an insulin reaction. His pillow was soaked, his eyes glazed over, and he was acting like he wanted to talk but couldn't.

Eighteen year old Shirley was scared to death, fearful that she again faced losing her husband. At first she was unable to recall exactly what to do for a diabetic attack. Her mind raced in panic mode. Finally realizing that his blood sugar level was too low, she found some sugar, coated her finger several times, and repeatedly thrust it into his mouth. Next she ran through the neighborhood seeking help, but couldn't find anyone at home. In frantic fashion, she hurried to the Graceville funeral home nearby and asked if they could possibly take him to the hospital in Dothan.

They could. The funeral home sent a hearse to the apartment where they picked Robert up and sped to the hospital. Shirley kept feeding him a little sugar all along the way, and soon he began to show signs of coming out of it. When they arrived at the infirmary, he received a shot of glucose, and shortly afterward he was fine. Dizzy took them back to Graceville the same evening.

This was the second medical emergency in six months for Robert and Shirley. There would be similar episodes throughout the course of their marriage. Understandably, this caused Shirley to be vigilant regarding her husband's eating habits and behavioral tendencies, constantly monitoring his lifestyle and prodding him to take care of his physical needs even as he focused upon the spiritual.

After being in Graceville a few months, Robert was recommended to be the pastor of a church, Pine Level Baptist in Louisville, Alabama. Robert was interested in pursuing the opportunity, and to his delight found the church was not averse to breaking in an inexperienced preacher. The small congregation was in the process of building a new sanctuary and needed a new shepherd to go along with it. The exterior of the facility was finished, but interior work still needed to be done before it was worship ready.

Robert and Shirley were asked to travel to Louisville for what's known as the "trial sermon." He auditioned by preaching during the morning worship service, and then went outside with Shirley to wait in the car as the congregation voted on extending a call. Several anxious minutes later an older member of the church emerged. Ola Hovey—"Miss Ola"—delivered the good news that the church had voted to hire Robert as pastor for $35 per week. He accepted, and Pine Level became his first pastorate.

*With Bible in hand, Robert is ready to preach
at his first pastorate, Pine Level in Louisville.*

It's doubtful that a man of the cloth could inaugurate his ministry with a better flock. The folks at

Pine Level were not demanding, got along well, and were supportive of their pastors. Comprised largely of plain, country people who took pride in their church and community, they sought to faithfully serve the Lord on their little plot of earth. A special mission of their church, they felt, was sometimes helping along still wet-behind-the-ears preachers like Robert. Though the salary was small, extra touches like providing meals, sharing vegetables, and remembering birthdays and anniversaries enabled the congregation to show love for their pastor and his wife.

Louisville was in Barbour County, approximately seventy miles to the north of Graceville and about fifty above Dothan. Robert and Shirley soon established a routine of leaving school on Friday afternoon, spending the night in Dothan with Shirley's folks, then driving to Louisville on Saturday morning and staying overnight there with a couple who lived near the church. They ate meals with different families according to a carefully arranged schedule the church devised to feed the preacher and his wife for the entire time they were on the field.

After church on Sunday evening, they drove to Dothan to spend the night, and then awakened early Monday morning to travel back to Graceville so Shirley could be at work on time. Robert had no Monday classes, but devoted the day to catching up on his studies. The new pastor's dedication to his first congregation was shown not only in weekend ministry, but also by his presence at Wednesday night prayer meetings—something not required in his job description. Robert drove from Graceville to Louisville and back to lead the mid-week service for no extra compensation. He worked the little church like it was a big church.

The ensuing months brought major changes for the Dismukes. After finishing up their first year in Graceville, they decided to move to the church field in Louisville for the summer. Robert had no classes and Shirley was out for the extended school break. The church was thrilled and promptly found them an apartment to live in. The couple enjoyed it so much that by the time September rolled around, they didn't want to leave. They loved Graceville, and Robert was benefiting considerably from his studies at BBI, but his heart was in pastoral ministry. Shirley wanted to begin her college education, too, something she could not accomplish in Graceville.

They decided to remain in Louisville and change schools. Both would attend Troy State College (now Troy University), about a twenty mile commute from Pine Level. It would not provide Robert the ministerial training he desired, but appeared to be a better overall fit for their situation. Again the church was delighted, and so were Shirley's parents. They offered to help with finances, and on Monday mornings Shirley usually found in the mail a letter with the Griggs' return address, the envelope stuffed with money to help pay for her college expenses.

Robert continued his studies at Troy while caring for the flock at Pine Level by living among them. Shirley found part-time employment as a bookkeeper at the Midway Lumber Company in Louisville, traveling to Troy with Robert for classes in the mornings and working at the lumber company in the afternoons.

The time in Louisville was a happy one. The excitement of being newly married, coupled with the adventure of embarking upon their life's work at a church

that showered them with affection and appreciation, made
the earliest years of marriage and ministry exceedingly
pleasing for Robert and Shirley.

****

Despite their contentment in Louisville, after two
years of service at Pine Level Robert and Shirley decided
the time was right to leave. Members at Banks Baptist
Church in Troy heard about Robert and invited him to
become their pastor. It was a half-time church, meeting
two Sundays of each month. Another half-time church in
Troy, Old Lebanon Baptist, was also looking for a pastor.
Things fell into place for Robert to lead both
congregations should he so choose.

He and Shirley talked it over and prayed about it.
The opportunity to expand their ministry was inviting.
Troy was an attractive town, more like Dothan than either
Louisville or Graceville. It would certainly make their
lives easier educationally and financially, they reasoned.
Perceiving no major obstacles and sensing the leadership
of the Lord, they agreed to move to Troy. They did so
with heavy hearts, knowing they were leaving behind a
faithful and loving congregation to whom they would
always be indebted.

A major concern was what the change would
mean to Robert's youngest brother, Wilmer. Wilmer
often came from Dothan to visit, and in the process met a
young lady named Sylvia, with whom he had fallen in
love. He decided to live with Robert and Shirley in
Louisville and attend high school there. With Robert's

move to Troy, it appeared that Wilmer would have to leave Louisville as well.

A solution to the problem was soon in the offing. Pine Level called Ewell Henry, the minister who first gave Robert opportunities to preach, as their next pastor. He had led a revival at Pine Level during Robert's tenure, and the congregation turned to him when they needed a new preacher. Reverend Henry learned of Wilmer's plight and promptly invited the teenager to reside with him. Wilmer lived with the new pastor for more than a year while he finished high school in Louisville. The arrangement paid rich dividends as Wilmer and Sylvia's young love blossomed into a lifetime of marriage.

After departing Louisville, Robert and Shirley spent the next three years in Troy, residing in a house three blocks from campus. While this was a considerable convenience, the move actually increased the busy pace of their lives. Taking a full schedule of classes and caring for two churches didn't leave a lot of time for leisure. They were obligated to be at one church or the other a minimum of three evenings a week, including Sunday worship and two separate prayer meetings on Wednesdays and Thursdays. There were also visitation nights, youth services, denominational events, Bible study courses, revivals, weddings, and funerals, among other ministry duties. Added to the workload was how Robert attempted to lead each congregation as if it were a full-time responsibility.

Robert, outside their rental home in Troy.

The two churches were in communities on opposite sides of Troy. They were also on different ends of the spiritual spectrum. Robert preached the first and third Sundays of each month at Old Lebanon, a congregation much like the one he left at Pine Level. It possessed a sweet spirit, was full of love and hospitality, and eager to hear and support their young pastor. On the second and fourth Sundays, he preached at Banks, a congregation whose leadership didn't seem to take its Christian commitment to heart. Like Ephesus of Revelation, in the estimation of Robert and Shirley, Banks had lost its first love.

A significant bone of contention was the church's tradition of raising money through barbeques, fish fries, bake sales, and the like. Robert was against it. He didn't believe in church fundraisers, thinking that a church should support itself and its ministries through the unencumbered tithes and offerings of its members. Fundraisers were not God's way but man's way of providing money for the church, he felt.

Robert's disapproval did not prevent the fundraisers from occurring. They continued, but Robert was seldom involved. On one memorable occasion, however, somebody in the church mentioned that a fundraiser was coming up.

"Preacher, we're going to be cooking barbeque Friday night. Why don't you come and join us?"

They likely didn't expect their minister to appear. In almost three years of ministry at Banks, Robert had never attended a fundraiser. Crossing them up, he decided to go. On a cold Friday evening, he slipped into corduroy pants and a heavy coat, and planned to spend part of the night with members of his flock.

It wasn't long before he returned home.

"Robert, what happened?" Shirley asked, surprised to see him back so soon. He looked as sad and discouraged as she had ever seen him.

"Shirley, if I had another church to go to on Sunday, I wouldn't ever go back to this one," he answered.

When Robert arrived at the barbeque, they were cooking in back of an old abandoned building. A church member returning to his vehicle saw Robert drive up and began chatting with him, strongly hinting that the pastor might want to leave. Robert walked around to the back anyway, and what he found filled his soul with anger and grief.

"Shirley, it seemed like every man in the church was there with a beer in his hand. You would have thought lightning had struck when they saw me walk up. They began to scatter like ants."

It broke his heart to see the church music director, Sunday School superintendent, several deacons, and other members of Banks engaging in an activity that to him was the way of the world, not the way of Christ. To see them doing it in the name of the church he led was almost too much to bear.

After the barbeque episode, Robert believed it was time to go elsewhere and began praying for the Lord to lead the way. He soon received a telephone call that initiated the next phase of his ministry.

****

While living in Troy, Robert received inquiries from other churches who wanted to gauge his interest in becoming their minister. He politely discouraged their advances, believing that he and Shirley should complete their education first. After three years in Troy, they were both close to receiving college degrees—Robert lacked less than a year, Shirley a little more.

Robert looked forward to the day when he could serve a church full-time. He missed the daily contact and care for a specific congregation, such as he experienced at Pine Level. Shirley wanted to settle down in a parsonage or home of their own and start a family. But it seemed prudent to wait on all of this until they were finished with their studies. The frustrating experience at Banks, however, caused a reassessment of their plans.

Three weeks following the barbeque Shirley was studying and Robert was washing dishes when they received a call from an old friend, Joe Gwyn. Joe was pastor of Louisville Baptist Church when Robert was at Pine Level, and now he was serving at Girard Baptist in Phenix City, about seventy-five miles northeast of Troy. His wife Nell was from Headland Avenue, and the two couples had become good friends during their days together in Louisville. Joe related how a neighboring church in Phenix City, Pine Grove Baptist, was looking for a pastor. Was Robert interested?

"Funny you should ask, Joe," replied Robert. "Just last night Shirley dreamed that we were going to another church, and now you call!"

"That is a coincidence," Joe responded. "Maybe the Lord's trying to tell you something." Joe then asked if Pine Grove's search committee could meet with him. Robert was willing.

The committee was favorably impressed with the twenty-six year old preacher and his wife. In their discussions Robert mentioned his hesitation about leaving Troy before earning their degrees. The committee understood but suggested they could finish their education by commuting to nearby Auburn University. The possibility eased his concern, and believing the Lord had opened the door of opportunity, they moved to Phenix City in March of 1959.

Going to a new church in a new town with the prospect of living in a nice house and starting a family was exhilarating for the young couple. Nonetheless, Robert and Shirley entered this particular community with more than a little trepidation. In 1959 Phenix City was still reeling from its sordid past, an era rife with gambling, drugs, prostitution, racketeering, and the criminal underworld. It was definitely no Mayberry.

In much of the forties and fifties, organized crime controlled the city and its leadership. Preying off the soldiers of nearby Fort Benning and a stream of out-of-town visitors, vice and violence ruled the streets. Less than five years before the Dismukes' arrival, Alabama

Attorney General nominee and local lawyer Albert Patterson had been brazenly assassinated outside his office as he campaigned to remove the mob from Phenix City and crack down on corruption. Subsequently, martial law was imposed and a massive cleanup begun.

Despite its reputation, Robert and Shirley found Phenix City to have its share of model citizens, many dedicated to the Lord's service. The church proved to be a very active congregation, keeping Robert busy to the point that he didn't feel he could neglect his ministry and attend to his studies. He enrolled at Auburn the first summer, but sensed a few members resented his absence from the church field, so he didn't go back. He would never complete his degree.

The same was true for Shirley. Upon arriving in Phenix City, she found a shortage of teachers in the schools. Though not having her degree in hand, she was hired to teach fifth grade at Girard Elementary on an emergency teaching certificate, a position she held for the next three years. As long as she continued to pursue a degree in education, she could teach on the certificate. Shirley attended Auburn for two summers, until the most significant event in her marriage occurred. Like Robert, she ended up having the equivalent of about four years of college work, but stopped just short of completing the bachelor's degree requirements.

The incident that led Shirley to suspend her degree plans and discontinue teaching at Girard was the adoption of their first child. He came in a special way, with the hand of Providence all over his arrival.

After church on a hot August evening in 1962, Shirley told Robert she didn't feel up to staying for the weekly youth fellowship. Robert had started a dedicated youth ministry at Pine Grove that included a get-together every Sunday night after worship. Though she regularly attended, Shirley felt more tired than usual on this particular night. Their eighth wedding anniversary the next day was in her thoughts, as was another matter that had weighed heavily on her mind for several weeks.

She hitched a ride the two or three blocks to their home and took a moment to make herself comfortable, turning on the television to relax. The telephone suddenly rang.

"Shirley?" asked the voice on the other end.

It was Dr. Harold Jarrell, a legendary obstetrician and gynecologist in the Chattahoochee Valley area of Georgia and Alabama. He doctored hundreds of women and delivered thousands of babies, including my own first-born.

Immediately recognizing his voice, Shirley responded in an excited tone. "Dr. Jarrell, I hope you have some good news for us!"

The physician had performed surgery on Shirley a year earlier, and in going back for her annual check-up in July he surprised her with talk of adoption. She had shared with him previously about her intense desire for a child, but they never spoke of the possibility of adoption.

Adoption was something the Dismukes hadn't thought was a viable option. There were too many marks against their eligibility: their income was low, they didn't own a home, Robert had diabetes, and Shirley was only twenty-five. They figured it would be difficult to gain the state's approval, so although open to the idea, especially with the problems they were encountering in having a biological child, they never pursued it. Dr. Jarrell, however, was suggesting it was a distinct possibility.

In fact, after discerning her keen interest on that mid-summer morning, the good doctor went on to tell her something else.

"Shirley, I have a baby that's due in a few weeks. The mother says she doesn't think she can keep it. I would love to see you get that baby. Go home, talk with Robert about it, and if the two of you want to adopt, let me know soon." He often worked closely with the Alabama Department of Human Resources to find good homes for children in such instances.

Shirley rushed to the church to tell Robert, who was equally enthused. She immediately called Dr. Jarrell to tell him they were very much interested. The physician cautioned that getting the child was a possibility, not a certainty, but that he would be in touch. That was a month ago. Now he was on the other end of the telephone line!

"It's a little boy, Shirley, three days old," explained the physician. "I know you and Robert want a baby. Y'all talk about it and pray about it, and if you decide you want him, meet me at my office first thing in the morning."

Shirley hung up the phone and was ecstatic. She had long dreamed of having a child, especially these last few years. Now, on the verge of beginning her ninth year of married life, it appeared that her dream was about to come true. She couldn't wait to tell her husband the wonderful news, but he lingered at the church fellowship longer than usual. She knew he would share her excitement—they had spent a lot of time the past month joyously discussing the possibility and praying over it.

When Robert finally arrived home, Shirley met him at the door with eyes moist and a huge smile upon her face. He guessed instantly what it meant. There followed great rejoicing, not a few tears, and not much sleep in the Dismukes house that night.

Early the next morning they were at Dr. Jarrell's office before he was. After talking with him and getting the particulars about the baby and his mother, they spent the rest of their eighth anniversary at the Alabama Department of Human Resources filling out paper work, and at a lawyer's office working on legalities. It all happened in whirlwind fashion—less than 48 hours. By the following afternoon, a Tuesday, they were at the hospital picking up their son, born five days earlier on August 2, 1962. They named him David Kidron, after the famous Old Testament king and brook.

The new parents faced the formidable task of quickly assembling furniture, clothes, food, and other items that their baby would need. With the help of family, friends, and church members, this was accomplished in short order. The pastor's wife at neighboring Auburn Heights Baptist, Jimmie Ruth Caughron, brought a bassinet over to the parsonage the day of the baby's arrival. Many of us would get to know Jimmie Ruth years later through her sign language ministry to the deaf.

While Jimmie Ruth was visiting, Shirley's principal from Girard Elementary, Robert Bryan, happened to drop by, completely unaware of recent developments. He was selling encyclopedias during the summer, and wanted to know if she and Robert would like to make a purchase before the new school year began.

Of course it wasn't the most convenient time to listen to a sales pitch, but she invited him in anyway, not feeling she could turn her boss away. Immediately he noticed the new-born and asked innocently, "Whose baby's that, Shirley?"

"He's mine, Mr. Bryan!" she answered with pride.

He paid her no attention, thinking she must be joking, and proceeded to extol the merits of owning a set of Britannicas. Jimmie Ruth's presence apparently made him assume the baby belonged to her, but when Shirley's friend left without the infant, the part-time encyclopedia salesman was bewildered and again asked about the child.

"Shirley, now really, whose baby are you keeping?"

"I told you, Mr. Bryan, that's my baby!" beamed Shirley.

Seeing his skeptical look, Shirley then told the story of the adoption, even showing him the hospital papers she had received earlier in the day. Finally persuaded that little David did indeed belong to his fifth grade teacher, he extended congratulations and suggested it was all the more reason to buy a set of encyclopedias.

Shirley asked the principal not to say anything about the baby to others at Girard just yet, fearing word might get out to the school superintendent and his staff. She was unsure at the moment what to do about her job. She wanted to stay home with the baby, but didn't know if they could afford it. Since she and Robert had yet to make a decision, Mr. Bryan promised to keep it to himself and left without a sale.

A little later he phoned.

"Shirley, there's really no point in trying to keep this a secret," he told her. "Everybody in town is talking about it!"

Shirley and Robert subsequently decided that she should not return to the classroom. After three years of teaching other people's children, she would now devote exclusive attention to one of her own.

She loved being a full-time mom, and Robert loved being a full-time pastor. Pine Grove was his first church without doubling as a college student, and he put his heart and soul into it. The needs and demands of the largest of his four flocks enabled Robert to hone his pastoral skills.

It was during this period that he developed one of the signatures of his ministry—a devotion to youth camps and retreats. It began when he made an initial visit to the Baptist Retreat Center in Ridgecrest, North Carolina. At one of their conferences, Robert was introduced to R. C. Johnson, who oversaw the Juvenile Rehabilitation Program in nearby Columbus, Georgia, a youth ministry of the Columbus Baptist Association of churches.

Robert returned from Ridgecrest enthused about the program, particularly the retreats they sponsored that sought to help problem children. He decided to volunteer at their summer camps, giving up part of his vacation time to help out. Soon he became heavily involved in the ministry, seeing firsthand the positive impact it made in the lives of teenagers. From this point on he was a firm believer in the camp experience as an effective means of reaching young people with the love of Jesus Christ.

The first four years of the pastorate at Pine Grove were challenging but fruitful, a happy and rewarding time for Robert and Shirley. By contrast, year five was tumultuous and discouraging. Despite general spiritual and financial health, with new ministries started and contributions at an all-time high, dissatisfaction with Robert began to creep in. He had already stayed longer than any pastor in their history, so perhaps discord was inevitable.

A focal point of controversy was a new sanctuary the church voted to construct. The excitement such a project evokes soon gave way to general disappointment, not least to Robert and Shirley. To save money, the congregation hired a contractor who had little experience in church construction. To further complicate things, he was diagnosed with cancer in the midst of the venture, making him unavailable much of the time.

The final product was a sanctuary that looked more like a warehouse than a 1960's church, and much of the membership was exceedingly displeased. To compound their discontent, the Building Committee decided to add a basement late in the process. Somehow this threw the structure out of line, causing the steps to end up awkwardly high, among other problems. Unhappiness reigned in the new house of the Lord.

When things go wrong on a baseball team, the easy thing to do is to blame the manager, even though he never threw a pitch, stood in the batter's box, or ran the bases. The same is true with churches. Pastors often simply follow the game plan of their committees and congregations, but find themselves in the line of fire when problems arise.

Disenchantment with Robert gradually grew more pronounced, with complaints increasingly heard. He was faulted for the new building and criticized for purchasing a new car. Disapproval was registered for time away at the camps, for focusing too much on youth, for lackluster sermons and uninspiring worship. Mumbling and grumbling became prevalent. Robert was giving it his all, but it wasn't enough to satisfy.

He faced a crisis, the low point of his ministerial career. Robert felt that for the church to move forward and resume its growth they would probably need a new pastor, and he believed the church's leadership felt the same way. The sense was unmistakable that his remaining ministry at Pine Grove would not be very productive.

Personally, it was an unsettling time for the couple, a troublesome and nervous stretch of days. They now had a one year old to care for, debts to pay, and only Robert's income to live on. The fear was real that he could face dismissal. If this should happen, they worried about its effect upon the on-going legal adoption of David, not to mention their future in ministry at other churches.

Robert experienced a kind of crossroads in his ministry that probably most pastors go through at some point or another. He knew it was best to move on, but had nowhere to go. Once again he looked to the Lord for an open door, and the Lord would not disappoint.

****

Jenny Smith and Shirley Hendricks were case workers for the Alabama Department of Human Resources who came to know the Dismukes through their responsibilities in monitoring David during the adoption process. Jenny and Shirley both lived in Hurtsboro, a small rural hamlet about thirty miles southwest of Phenix City, and rode together to and from their jobs. They were

co-workers, carpoolers, friends, and active members of
the same church, a church in need of a pastor.

The Lord used this connection to bring Robert and
Shirley out of the pressure-cooker that developed at Pine
Grove and into the next chapter of their ministry. First
Baptist Church of Hurtsboro issued Robert a call to
become their pastor in March of 1964. It would prove to
be an excellent match.

The following four years in Hurtsboro were
probably the happiest of their lives. They fell in love with
the little town, and the town fell in love with them.
Hurtsboro was typical tiny-town America—Deep South
style. There were two downtown churches, Baptist and
Methodist, competing for the allegiance of the white
citizenry. In an age before Wal-Mart, the post office,
café, grocery, pharmacy, and hardware store served as
informal meeting places during the week. Robert was
delighted that he could leave the church office and walk
to all of these venues, allowing him to make impromptu
visits with various members of his congregation. The
slower pace of life permitted more time to study for his
sermons and cultivate his prayer life. Shirley noticed his
spiritual life deepening, which motivated him to be
faithful in evangelism and church visitation.

It was an idyllic time for Shirley, as well. Taking
care of a young child enabled her to experience the
indescribable joys of motherhood. The pastor's house
was located next door to the church, and she loved
leaving it to stroll up and down the city sidewalks with
David, running into various church members and
acquaintances, carrying on conversations with little
concern for time. Gregarious by nature and always
loquacious, the laid-back Hurtsboro lifestyle suited

Shirley to a tee. Her penchant for friendly banter was the perfect complement to Robert's more reserved and studious nature.

In Hurtsboro they were able to add a new member to the family. They had talked and prayed about adopting another child for several months when suddenly things fell into place. Myrtle Prior, director of the ADHS in Phenix City, was aware of Robert's work with juvenile rehabilitation in the area. She came to Hurtsboro to visit the Dismukes, and more specifically to ask if they were interested in opening their home to foster children.

Robert and Shirley worried about the potential effects upon David, since foster children would only stay in their home temporarily, and told Miss Prior they thought it best to decline the opportunity. Then Shirley used the occasion to reveal that their interest lay elsewhere.

"We've been talking about trying to adopt another baby," she casually mentioned to the director.

"Oh really?" responded Miss Prior, who went on to discuss the possibility. "You've already had one adoption, so it could prove difficult to get another child. But let me see what I can do."

It wasn't long before she called back, indicating she could help. Shortly thereafter, five month old Susan Ashley, born September 25, 1965, joined the Dismukes family.

Miss Prior filled the same role Dr. Jarrell did three years earlier. Robert and Shirley were firmly convinced that the Lord used both to provide them with precious little children who were the answers to their prayers.

*The Dismukes, at home in Hurtsboro--an
exceedingly happy time in their lives.*

Robert was thirty-one years old when they moved
to Hurtsboro, and just hitting his stride as a minister. He
consciously sought to model the Christ-like life. As
Christ's representative to the town, he prayed, he visited,
he preached, and he evangelized. God blessed and First
Baptist started growing rapidly under his spiritual
direction. People were getting saved, joining the church,
and making decisions for Christ nearly every week. The
spirit of revival gradually swept through the community.

One of the most influential men in town, Frank
Ellison, caught fire for Christ under Robert's ministry.
Frank was a cattle farmer and a man of considerable
physical size, with a shock of white hair on top of his
head. He had a presence about him that made you stand
up and take notice, and later in life became a tireless
worker for the Gideons, a Christian businessmen's
organization. Frank started tithing and giving large

donations to the church, enabling some of the new ministries Robert envisioned, particularly among the young people.

As pastor he invested large chunks of time in the youth of Hurtsboro, starting with Sunday evening fellowships after church, expanding them to additional nights during the summer months. He enjoyed interacting with this age group, having fun through games, skits, songs, and practical jokes, but always mixing in times of Bible study and prayer. Church members like Frank saw the positive effect he was having upon their children and built an activity area beside the parsonage. Here they could play volleyball, basketball, and other youth-oriented pastimes.

They also provided financial resources so their pastor could take his young people to summer camps. Robert felt that what he saw working with juvenile rehabilitation would work equally well or better among church youth. Get teenagers away from home, remove the distractions of everyday life, give them ample amounts of fun, food, and fellowship, provide opportunities to focus upon the Lord, and young lives will benefit socially, morally, and spiritually, he believed. This was a recipe he thought God would honor and anoint to reach young people for Christ.

Hurtsboro's initial youth retreat took place at a primitive facility known as Camp Friendship, outside of Ellaville, Georgia. With Spartan quarters that were devoid of hot water, isolated deep in the woods and beside a lake, it was an apt setting for concentrating upon the non-material, more important things in life. Camp Alabama in Autaugaville was another hideaway to which he took the group. The refuge that took on special significance, however, was a site near Navarre Beach, Florida called Camp Ada. Robert only camped there once while in Hurtsboro, but ensuing years would see Ada become an annual rite of pilgrimage.

After being in Hurtsboro for a couple of years, Robert began to be courted by several church search committees, with whom he flirted but never said "I do." People in congregational circles were beginning to hear about Robert and learn how God was using his ministry in a special way. A committee from Catoma Baptist in Montgomery tried to persuade him to become their pastor. They invited Robert and Shirley over to tour their facilities, meet their leadership, eat in their homes, and preach a Sunday sermon. Subsequently, Catoma voted to issue a call. But Robert didn't feel quite right about going—they had been in Hurtsboro only a short time and loved it—so he decided to stay put.

A committee from Talaweka Baptist in Tallassee heard him preach and asked him to come for "a look-see." Robert and Shirley went, toured, and ate, but decided to remain in Hurtsboro before the trial sermon. Months later the Talaweka committee tried their luck again with Robert. They came a second time to Hurtsboro and found the church packed, with the only available seating at the front upon a deacon's bench that conspicuously faced the congregation. Everyone at First Baptist knew the reason for the strangers' presence, but resisted the temptation to stick out their tongues or make ugly faces in their direction. Once again Robert didn't take Talaweka's bait.

A committee from Bethel Baptist in Odenville near Birmingham called. Robert and Shirley went to look it over, did the usual routine, and decided to refuse their offer. Years later the Odenville church once more was without a pastor and again contacted Robert to inquire about his interest in coming. After Robert politely said no, the church's representative, who was also a member of the earlier search committee, responded, "Well, preacher, how about let's do it this way. You just call us whenever you get a hankering to move."

In the summer of 1968 a call came from a pulpit committee to whom Robert could not say no. Their church was Providence Baptist in Lee County, just outside of Opelika and Auburn. Going to this church made no sense from a human perspective. Robert and Shirley were quite happy in Hurtsboro, with a congregation that adored them and a ministry that was successful by every ecclesiastical standard of measurement.

Providence, on the other hand, had just undergone a split, with the former pastor and several members leaving to start a new church nearby. Providence was also in substantial debt, having just built a new sanctuary and Sunday school complex, and could not offer the salary Robert was making at Hurtsboro. Compared to other congregations that had wooed him, Providence paled in comparison. Yet, inexplicably, Robert felt drawn to the church in Beauregard.

****

The search committee from Providence courted Robert aggressively, playing up the many ministry possibilities of a church with new facilities in a growing area practically on the doorstep of Auburn University. Robert, Shirley, and their children went to visit, meet several prominent members, and see the surrounding community. Robert agreed to preach a trial sermon, was offered the job, and asked to make a decision by a certain date. He and Shirley talked, prayed, and studied over it for several days. Shirley couldn't get excited because she didn't want to leave Hurtsboro. Robert couldn't make up his mind, feeling tugged in both directions.

As the deadline approached, Shirley concluded, "Honey, you just go ahead and tell them how you feel led, and I'll go along with it."

Robert continued to pray for guidance. On the day of decision, when the committee chair called his office needing an answer, he intended to decline their invitation and stay in Hurtsboro. It made little sense for him to leave. Yet, still, the pull was there. He would later say that the "no" he planned to tell Providence somehow came out a "yes" by the time he finished the phone conversation. He told them that he would indeed come to Beauregard and be their next pastor.

When Robert returned to the house to let Shirley know of his decision, he found her with David in their bedroom sitting on the bed. With nervous trepidation Shirley asked about the answer he had given.

"Well, what did you tell them?" she said in a subdued tone.

"I told them we'd go," responded Robert, matter-of-factly.

Shirley immediately exclaimed, "Robert, you told them the wrong thing!"

She began to cry, and then David, almost six, started crying, too. Robert cried as well when reading his letter of resignation before the congregation the following Sunday. In fact, he was compelled to leave the sanctuary, compose himself, and return to finish it.

Leaving Hurtsboro was an emotionally draining experience for the family. They felt such a special bond there, a sense of acceptance and security. It was a great place to work, to attend church, to raise a family. They would miss the town and its people terribly. Added to all of this was the knowledge they were heading into a situation that had just undergone turmoil and hard feelings, something they experienced firsthand almost five years earlier in Phenix City.

Robert felt like he was doing the right thing, but it was the harder path, and he felt responsible for putting his family and church through such a sorrowful parting. For Shirley, it was an especially depressing time, having to leave the home she so enjoyed and cherished. Although several members at Providence attempted to make her feel better about the move, they were largely unsuccessful in lifting her spirits.

On their final day in Hurtsboro, Shirley finished packing and loading their belongings. She took the cleaning woman, who had been scrubbing the parsonage as the family moved out, to her home. After she returned, Robert went on ahead with a truck filled with their possessions. She then put David and Susan in the car for the short trip to Beauregard, just twenty miles to the north.

As she drove out of town, Shirley impulsively stopped at one of her favorite haunts, the Hurtsboro Dairy Bar. She wanted to linger a little longer and make a final memory. A man named Kizzie Hall came up to her while she and the kids were eating, put his big lumberjack arms around her, and said, "We sure are gonna miss y'all!"

He started weeping, and then Shirley began weeping, too. She wept all the way to Providence.

Chapter 3
"Providence"

Numerous churches dot the landscapes of our lives, a variety of religious names, denominations, structures, and symbols on display all around us. There are so many houses of worship, in fact, that we often become oblivious to their very presence. They are a passing blur amid the Krogers, Wal-Marts, McDonalds', and two story homes of our everyday existence.

For those in relationship with the Lord, however, there is often one temple that towers above the rest, a sanctuary where God has visited our souls in a fresh and memorable way. For me, that special place is Providence.

Decidedly plain by Westminster Abbey or National Cathedral standards, Providence Church nonetheless possesses an austere grandeur to my spiritual eyes. There are no stained glass windows, ornate carvings, or colorful icons to make the spirit soar. Organ pipes and golden candelabras are absent from the premises. Yet within the ordinary wrappings of red bricks and gray mortar and white steeple, Jesus may be found just as surely as He was in that unadorned manger of two millennia ago.

Churches, of course, are not the only occupiers of sacred space. Hallowed ground may be inhabited by rock or bush or patch of road, just as it was for the biblical heroes Jacob, Moses, and Paul, respectively. But more times than not, a holy site includes a building dedicated to God, an earthly shrine that's especially revered if it's also where a heavenly pilgrimage was begun. Providence serves to commemorate the spot where my own heart was first "strangely warmed."

The faces inside the church are mostly different now. Many of those I once knew well have gone on to meet their Maker. The generation of my youth has scattered here, there, and yonder. The building remains, a monument of memories, a testament of individual stories and collective experiences of the Lord God's workings in our lives.

I'm thankful that today the structure still stands in all of its unpretentious glory. I can attend worship and sit in the same pew where I publicly responded to the gospel those many years ago. I can enter the Sunday School rooms where the Bible was opened and read and taught to my young and inquiring mind. I can walk behind the pulpit where I initially attempted to wax eloquent with sermon.

Nostalgia of place is a prevalent emotion in the scriptures and an ever-growing presence in my own life. For some reason hard to explain, tangible spiritual roots are more meaningful the older I become. The nomadic soul longs for visible evidence of the invisible realities which have impacted personal experience. Maybe that's why Jacob went back to Bethel. That's surely why, every once in a while, I long to go home to Providence.

The line Judy Garland made famous is no less true in the spiritual realm: "There's no place like home." Revisiting my home church is a joyful trip down memory lane where I reconnect with the religious path first taken decades earlier. It's there, as a teenager, I entered through the strait gate and headed down the narrow road that leads to eternal life. At Providence I learned the meaning of serious discipleship and found the call of God upon my life.

It's also where I came to know Brother Robert and Miss Shirley, the Aquila and Priscilla of my younger years. Like the famous biblical couple, they opened hearts and hearth to me and others of my little circle, showering us with Christian hospitality and "explaining the way of God more adequately."

Without them, Providence would be just another place of worship on the religious horizon of our lives. But because of their faithful witness, there we met Jesus, and Providence became the ecclesiastical home of our messianic age.

****

On Tuesday, July 30, 1968, the Dismukes family arrived in Beauregard to begin Robert's pastoral ministry at Providence. It had been emotionally trying to leave Hurtsboro, a safe haven of warm friendships, material comforts, and spiritual success. Their new destination, by contrast, presented a host of challenges that made the transition to another congregation personally and professionally demanding.

Their new church traced its roots to the year 1884 and a small group of founding members whose names and number have not survived. Providence was born on a plot of ground located on Lime Kiln Road, just down from the old Chewacla Lime Works and Spring Villa Park. The congregation now worshipped in its third sanctuary on the site, a modern brick building erected three years previously, succeeding the wood and block structures of earlier generations.

Unpretentious, yet glorious, Providence Church.

The new complex included a worship center that seated approximately 350, along with three floors consisting of class rooms, choir rehearsal area, nursery accommodations, and office space. The membership took on $100,000.00 of debt to finance the larger facility, an obligation that in recent months had become increasingly burdensome due to declining attendance and contributions in the aftermath of a painful divorce from their former pastor.

Providence's unadorned sanctuary.

The Reverend Thomas H. Preston came to Providence as chief shepherd in early 1963. The record shows he was an effective leader during his five year tenure. Sunday School attendance and church financial receipts set new highs, and the congregation quickly outgrew its modest facilities. His most visible legacy was overseeing the construction of the new building that served the needs of the faith community for decades to come.

Something happened, however, during his final year of service to interrupt the cumulative success he enjoyed. According to witnesses, after participating in an out-of-town religious conference, Reverend Preston came home a somewhat different preacher. More animated and emotional in the pulpit, he augmented his new style with eyebrow-raising descriptions of encountering an angel while attending the recent event.

Congregants also listened with alarm as his sermons took on a harsher, more political tone. On one occasion he blasted the deacons, referring to them as "demons," and proceeded to lock horns with influential church leaders. He repeatedly voiced support for controversial Alabama governor and 1968 presidential candidate George C. Wallace. Although most parishioners likely agreed with him at the ballot box, they wanted their preacher to stick with the Bible.

Complaints about the pastor's unconventional behavior grew strident. Donations fell, as did attendance at Sunday and Wednesday services. When the board of deacons confronted their pastor about congregational dissatisfaction, he declined to make substantive changes and eventually was asked to resign. Upon his refusal, the deacons called for a special church conference where a vote for dismissal passed. Reverend Preston left in April of 1968 to start a new ministry in Beauregard.

Personally, I was grateful that Reverend Preston continued to reside in our little community. I had never met the man, but his daughter Marilyn was a classmate at Beauregard High. We boys constantly vied for the attention of the petite brunette with dark brown eyes and movie star smile who later became Lee County's Junior Miss. Three years after her dad's departure from Providence, I was all smiles when she said yes to my stuttering invitation to attend Scott Preparatory School's inaugural junior-senior prom.

Fairly bursting with pride, I escorted the Beauregard beauty to the dance, receiving the much cherished thumbs up or nods of approval from my buddies. They whispered in my ear their verdict that she was "a fox," which was like a steroid shot to my fragile ego. Never having danced in my life, I managed to fake it pretty well that evening in order to sway cheek-to-cheek with the lovely Marilyn. It turned out to be the most intimate moment we shared, but produced in me one of those sensational feelings that last a lifetime.

When Marilyn's father resigned the pulpit at Providence, he took some of its membership with him. A loss of families, of course, meant less church income, lower attendance, and more responsibility for those who remained. There were also hurt feelings to overcome, along with the embarrassment and guilt that inevitably accompany fissure in the body of Christ.

It was an awkward time for a fresh pastor arriving on the scene. Robert was well aware of the turmoil of the past several months, but he didn't want to dwell on it or make the ruckus a matter of public or private conversation. "Let's just love one another and move forward for the Lord" became his mantra to those who insisted on bringing up the subject. His positive attitude seemed to catch on and take hold, helping quickly heal the wounds of his new flock.

Church membership was not the only downsizing encountered by the Dismukes when they arrived at Providence. The church parsonage, or "pastorium" as it's sometimes called in Baptist life, was less roomy and comfortable than their home in Hurtsboro. There was only one bathroom, and no carpet, central heating, or air conditioning in the residence. Robert also took a reduction in salary to come to the new congregation, believing that money should not be the deciding factor in where God leads. Consequently, the family budget was extremely tight with two adults and two small children living on his $100.00 weekly income.

The "pastorium" where the Dismukes resided in Beauregard for 14 years.

Despite being paid less, the new pastor found himself working harder than ever. As the church's only salaried staff member, he was expected to provide leadership and service in virtually every area of congregational life. Wearing the multiple hats of good shepherd, gospel preacher, worship leader, youth director, missions coordinator, and Sunday School administrator consumed more hours than were available. Robert even performed the church's secretarial duties, handling such tasks as recordkeeping, correspondence, and bulletins. On a typical Saturday he typed the Sunday programs, cranked out copies on an old mimeograph machine, made sure they were neatly folded, and placed them in the sanctuary for worshippers to peruse the following morning.

Robert, in the church office at Providence.

The church he inherited possessed tremendous potential, but currently struggled on several fronts, particularly in those areas Robert deemed keys to success. In his mind the formula for building a great church included vibrant music, a growing Sunday School, and an exciting youth program. He immediately rolled up his sleeves and went to work, seeking to revitalize and develop these three important ministries of the church.

Providence's music department was in especially poor health, with the choir barely functioning and no regular pianist available for Sunday services. The church could not afford to hire outside help, so a lay member, Valeria Brown, directed the music and sought to resurrect the choir. With Robert's public encouragement, in a few weeks she had a pianist and twelve to fifteen musicians regularly occupying the choir loft on Sunday mornings.

Before his first year concluded, Robert led the church to hire an Auburn University student, Donald Hart, from nearby Phenix City, to serve as pianist and music director. He not only led the sanctuary choir, but helped start youth and children's choral groups as well. Donald was only a part-time summer worker, but represented a giant leap forward for the congregation. From this point on, Providence would hire professional church musicians to lead its music ministry.

Over the course of Robert's career at Providence, the church's music program underwent a dramatic transformation. Within ten years, more than 150 people were involved each week in making a joyful noise to the Lord. An exceptional ministry gradually developed that achieved recognition throughout Alabama. Under the tutelage of such leaders as Hart, Larry Evans, John Jordan, Paul Johnson, Carlos Golden, and most especially Dr. Thomas R. Smith, Providence became synonymous with excellence in church music. Smith, an Auburn University music faculty member, brought his devotion and expertise to Providence in 1974 and continued to serve as church music director for several decades.

Sunday School was a second area of concern for the new pastor. Attendance declined more than 12% from the previous year, and baptisms had dropped to a low of only seven. To Robert, a church's Sunday School program was its lifeblood, an essential vehicle for spiritual health and growth. The twin goals of evangelism and discipleship are met, he believed, when its classes invite outsiders to join and then "rightly divide the Word of truth." He immediately began promoting Sunday

School as the church's most effective means of reaching the community for Christ.

Less than two months after arriving, Robert embarked upon the first of many Sunday School enlargement campaigns. It began with a week-long series of meetings he held with teachers and officers. Here he personally prepared leaders for an upcoming six week "Reaching New Heights for Christ" promotion that kicked off the new church year in October. It paid handsome dividends, climaxing with 163 in Sunday School on November 10. Afterward the sanctuary was almost full, and three professions of faith were made during the worship service. The church went on to average more than150 in Sunday School for the month of November, the most in its history.

At the conclusion of a second Sunday School campaign in March, entitled "Forward for the Lord," an attendance goal was set at 200 on the fifth Sunday of the month. No information survives about whether the goal was reached, but on the following Sunday, April 6, the bulletin shows there were 214 in Sunday School, likely a new high water mark for the congregation. Records are spotty for much of Robert's inaugural twelve months at Providence, but what is known is that the Sunday School averaged 160 for that 1968-69 church year, a 25% increase, with 65 individuals baptized by the new pastor.

The ensuing years brought several more Sunday School emphases with catchy slogans like "Lift High the Cross," "March Forward," and "Sunday School Roundup," along with attendance goals the congregation was challenged to meet. Most of the time they fell short, but Robert kept raising the bar and attendance continued to climb. In his third year as pastor, a typical Sunday's turnout eclipsed 200 a week, and two years later it had more than doubled from where he started to an average of 257. After eight years of ministry, average Sunday School attendance reached its pinnacle at 330 in 1975-76. Yearly baptisms averaged 48 in number over that same span. The pastor dreamed big, the congregation responded, and both realized the Lord's abundant blessing and the church's immense potential for reaching the community for Christ.

Youth ministry was a third need at Providence requiring ample attention. Other than regular Sunday classes, there wasn't an ongoing youth program when Robert arrived. As at Hurtsboro, he felt led to devote a disproportionate amount of time to the young people of the church, believing that a large youth group brings enthusiasm and growth to the congregation as a whole. He promptly continued his practice of holding a "Youth Fellowship" after the Sunday evening service. There were only a handful of teenagers at first, but the ones who came enjoyed the refreshments, games, and songs their new pastor provided. He also started a "Junior Fellowship" for the younger boys and girls, who met for an hour prior to Sunday night worship.

Besides these regular Sunday activities, Robert held special youth events at appropriate times throughout the year. In the early fall he scheduled a Saturday night "Singspiration" where they roasted marshmallows, sang, and shared around the campfire at a local pond. He and Shirley chaperoned occasional Friday night lock-ins at the church, housing boys in a large classroom and girls in the nursery after they had enjoyed each other's company for much of the evening. Banquets at Christmas and Valentines, backyard fellowships, trips to Six Flags and

Calloway Gardens, as well as numerous recreation and Bible study nights were all part of that initial year.

Robert believed in involving young people in the church's worship as much as possible. In September he instituted "Squad Night," a time when Beauregard's football players, coaches, and cheerleaders were recognized during the Sunday evening worship hour. In January he did the same for the basketball team. He held a youth-led Sunday worship service in December and another in August. A weekend youth revival with a student evangelistic team from Samford University took place in May.

In late spring Robert convinced the church to hire a part-time summer youth worker, and Shelton Harden, a student at Samford, became Providence's first paid youth director. He and fellow staff member Donald Hart assisted the pastor in working with young people in the church and community. Donald oversaw the music end of things, developing a youth choir and ensemble to sing in the Sunday services. Shelton planned and supervised other youth activities, while also recruiting young people to participate. Robert felt teenagers needed Christ-like examples that were nearer their own age. Donald and Shelton fit the bill perfectly, providing influential role models for the impressionable youth of Providence.

During the first year of his tenure, Robert also led the congregation to convert the old block sanctuary into a youth house, and then secured donations of a ping pong table, board games, and several pieces of furniture to supply it. It was re-christened as the Providence Youth Center. Church youth now had their own place to hang out, and the frequency of their fellowships increased to include most Friday and Saturday nights. In Robert's eyes, the Center expanded his opportunities to help young people grow in the Lord, something soon to become the signature of his ministry at Providence.

****

The first time I encountered Brother Robert was not at church, as one might expect, but at Beauregard High School in the spring of 1969. I had often seen him around the campus, and by that time probably most students knew who he was. Robert believed that a pastor should be out and about among the flock and community he served, not holed up in his office or at home. He made himself visible and available to people, a habit that significantly contributed to his success as a minister.

Several months before our meeting, but only a few weeks after his arrival in the community, Robert made an appearance at the school gym. My friend from Liberty, Gary Dennis, was standing in the foyer along with a couple of ninth grade buddies. Robert entered and immediately struck up a conversation, sharing his name, asking theirs, shaking hands, and making small talk. He had come to set up "Squad Night" for the football team at the church. After inquiring where he might find their coach, he bid the group goodbye and proceeded in the direction they pointed. When he left, Gary asked about the slender and slightly balding man and was told that he was the new preacher at Providence.

About a week later Gary saw Robert once again on school property, this time in the gym's parking lot. Robert waved, called Gary's name, and asked how he was

doing. To a skinny, gangly, fourteen year old lacking
self-confidence, it was a big deal when the new pastor
remembered your name. Robert understood that it was an
important matter to young people, and constantly worked
at memorizing the names and faces of those he met.

When the spring months rolled around, Robert
began showing up on Beauregard's baseball field, not just
for games but for practices as well. I noticed him several
times from my shortstop's position as he sat in the
bleachers or roamed behind the backstop and benches.
He often yelled encouragement, applauded when we did
well, and called out our individual names in support. He
loved baseball, but that was not the primary reason for his
presence.

Before the school term was over, our ninth grade
class planned an end-of-the-year trip to Six Flags over
Georgia near Atlanta. The amusement park was fairly
new, having opened just two years earlier, and we were
excited by the prospect of riding a couple of its initial
roller coasters, the Georgia Cyclone and Dahlonega Mine
Train. Adult chaperones were needed to escort and
supervise thirty rambunctious teenagers whose hormones
were hitting their prime.

"How about the new preacher at Providence?"
someone suggested. Robert was contacted and readily
agreed. Although he had no family on the trip, and
despite the fact that it would be a long fourteen hour day
in the company of frequently silly and smart aleck kids,
he wanted to go for the opportunity of impacting some of
them for Christ.

He succeeded with at least one in the group.
Somehow I was assigned to ride with Robert, and as I sat
in the back of his Chevrolet Caprice, it was somewhat

surprising that he knew my name since we had never conversed. His easy, comfortable manner almost made me forget that he was a clergyman, and that I'd better mind my "Ps and Qs" on this occasion. He laughed with us and even told a joke or two, much to our delight. Once or twice along the way he turned the conversation to the things of the Lord, and we grew quiet and respectfully listened while he shared about his experience of coming to know Christ. He was careful not to preach a sermon, but to speak for only a moment or two about what Jesus meant to him.

Perhaps no one else in the car listened closely to what he was saying, but I heard him loud and clear. At the time I was attending Preacher Weekley's church, and the Lord was using the blind preacher's sermons to convict me of sin and my need of salvation. Now another pastor, one much younger and more relatable, was sharing about what had happened to him when he became a Christian. I realized something was missing in my life that both Preacher Weekley and Brother Robert possessed and felt deeply about.

It would be another four months before the spiritual void in my heart was filled by Christ, but the Six Flags trip was a major step in that direction. There I heard a personal testimony about what it meant to ask Jesus into one's life. There I met Brother Robert, who later led me to faith in the Lord. And there I saw firsthand that being a committed Christian and having a lot of fun were eminently compatible, both modeled superbly by the little preacher from Providence.

****

Summers for Robert brought the opportunity to focus upon what he did best—youth ministry. In his mind, kids who were out of school were especially available to engage in the things of the Lord. This not only meant a week of Vacation Bible School, but also opportunities for camps, mission trips, Bible studies, recreation nights, lock-ins, and excursions to various parks and pools. Virtually anything wholesome that attracted young people to the church was fair game for Robert.

The main event of his first full summer in Beauregard was the initial Providence youth camp. Summer retreats were a staple of Robert's ministry to teenagers since his days in Phenix City. He led several during his time in Hurtsboro, and was convinced they would effectively serve as a springboard for summertime outreach and discipleship at Providence. With staff members Donald Hart and Shelton Harden assisting, the first of fifteen annual youth camps commenced in June.

Robert believed that camp was one of the most valuable spiritual tools at his disposal. At camp, youth were free from the distractions of the outside world and able to focus their attention upon Christ. Getting them away from home and school and community—and into the isolated vacuum of a campground setting—allowed them to think more seriously about the Lord and His will for their young lives. Robert had seen numerous young people impacted for good and for God by spending time in the wilderness, and this motivated him to go back year after year.

Not only did Robert's ministerial sense tell him that youth camp was a wise investment, his heart echoed it as well. He genuinely loved going on retreats. It was not a chore, but something he looked forward to, eagerly anticipating the experience months in advance. Like an enthusiastic traveler taking an exotic vacation, Brother Robert delighted in planning the details of each camp's itinerary. His goal was to keep things lively and fun, yet focused upon Christ.

Robert spent an inordinate amount of time developing each camp's individual spiritual emphasis and program. Whether the week's theme was "I Have Decided to Follow Jesus," "His Way, Mine," or "Heaven Came Down," preparations must be made to coordinate everything with the particular topic selected. Hours were given choosing scripture passages, spiritual songs, and discussion topics to be used during times of corporate worship, personal devotionals, and group activities. Robert studied several Christian film catalogues in order to select just the right movies to fit the camp's agenda.

It was also necessary to allot plenty of thought and effort toward enlisting suitable worship leaders, Bible study teachers, and adult chaperones for the trip. More importantly, time had to be set aside to pray for the upcoming week, lest all his erstwhile plans be done for naught. In his prayer times Robert asked the Lord to touch specific youth, to anoint the films, Bible studies, and other elements of the program, and to use him and other leaders as vessels of service during the week.

Robert loved the camp experience despite its many hassles. The main aggravation concerned fluctuating numbers of potential attendees. He usually faced an early reservation deadline and needed to know—

weeks in advance—how many youth were going on the trip. Each year he encountered the same problem of vacillating commitments from his young people, promises that hinged on other plans or someone else's decision. It was easy to get discouraged by the ambivalence or fickleness he experienced, but Robert saw too much positive about camp to let the emotion linger.

Camp also brought along many personal inconveniences. His other pastoral duties did not disappear the week he was away serving the youth. There were still Sunday's sermon to preach, the sick to tend, a church to run, all of which he must begin to catch up on the Saturday following camp. Camp week took a toll on him physically, as well, with long hours and a large group of juveniles to supervise. Nevertheless, Robert received a ministerial rush from the whole camp experience that more than made up for its numerous demands.

By this time in his ministry, Robert had settled upon one particular retreat center as an ideal location for summer camp. Its name was Camp Ada, found in the Florida panhandle on Santa Rosa Sound, east of Gulf Breeze and nestled along the inlet about four miles west of Navarre, a site owned and operated by the Pensacola Bay Baptist Association of churches. Robert first utilized the facility while in Hurtsboro and became a regular customer during his tenure at Providence, taking scores of youth and adults each year, most often during the early days of June.

If there is soil outside of Beauregard where the seeds of our messianic age were chiefly sown and bore fruit, that place, no doubt, was Camp Ada. Except for Providence Church, its ground feels the holiest underneath my feet. Like the Garden of Eden before the fall, communion with the Lord came easy there. The spiritually adept could almost hear His voice amid the palm trees and see Him walking beside the gulf water.

While Ada may have possessed mystical parallels with the paradise of Eden, lavish and opulent it was not. Creation's salty water, sandy beach, and semi-tropical landscape were awe-inspiring, but the man-made facilities were decidedly simple and plain. A central cafeteria and dining hall served as the camp's nerve center, while also doubling as sanctuary, classroom, theater, and group meeting area. A portico and breezeway connected to adjacent barracks, two cabins each for boys and girls, each lodge containing 20-25 bunks and a woefully inadequately bathroom. A small recreation room separated the male and female accommodations.

The beach was only a short walk down a beaten path that lay at the back end of the property. Off to itself, on the way to the water, stood a large screened-in pavilion that could be used for outdoor worship or Bible study. It overlooked the white sandy shore and emerald-colored water extending from the Gulf of Mexico.

At the front of the camp, alongside the main entrance from U.S. Highway 98, were found two separate stand-alone cottages. The first, nearest the roadway, was home to Camp Ada's on-site overseer, for many years an affable soul named Wayne Orcutt. He and his family were the permanent residents who managed the property and handled our meals in the cafeteria. The smaller cabin, closest to the dormitories, is where Robert and Shirley resided for the week. There they could more easily monitor his diabetes and care for their children. Typically, Robert utilized it only for sleep and rest purposes, preferring to mill about, mingle, and make himself available to the youth.

Simple and serene from initial appearances, Camp Ada packed a spiritual wallop for the many that came from Providence. When first riding into Ada, more often than not, we turned up our noses at the bare-bones facilities, military-style quarters, cramped bathrooms, and generally primitive surroundings. We loudly complained that we missed our four-channel TVs, our hi-fi stereos, our Jack's hamburgers. But before the week was done, with few exceptions, there lingered little desire to leave Ada and return home to the luxuries of our lives. Sometimes I wish we never had.

****

A highlight of camp week was the trip down to the Florida coast. We would leave Providence early on a Monday morning and remain at Camp Ada until lunchtime Friday. In the early years we rode there and back in the lap of non-luxury, aboard the epitome of un-cool—a 60 passenger Blue Bird bus long past its prime. It was affectionately nicknamed "the Old Blue Goose," and was painted, appropriately enough, a splendid shade of sky blue topped with white.

From the trip's first mile, there was never any question as to who was in charge—Brother Robert positioned himself in the front seat opposite the driver. He gave direction along the way regarding such things as when to make a restroom stop—someplace near Montgomery, and where to eat lunch—always the Dairy

Queen in Brewton. Between these two interruptions we serenaded one another in song, usually of the spiritual variety. Sometimes, however, pure adolescence kicked in and tunes like "Great, Green Gobs of Greasy, Grimy, Gopher Guts" gushed out.

Full of anticipation, emancipation, and suspense, the Old Blue Goose carried us along toward our week of adventure. The anticipation and emancipation we felt need no explanation. The suspense concerned our means of transportation—namely, how far down the road would the Goose get this year before breaking down? Prior to pulling out of Providence's parking lot, we always said a special prayer for the old bird, and then prayed intermittently all along the way. I'm sure Brother Robert prayed "without ceasing." If the Goose made it to Brewton and to lunch at the Dairy Queen, we counted it a favorable response to our persistent petitions.

One year we traveled only as far as the Tuskegee exit on I-85—about twenty miles—before the Goose gave up the ghost. It would not go another inch. Robert didn't know what to do. Here he was on the side of the road with a bus load of teenagers and Camp Ada still five hours away. In a day before cell phones and easy communication, he hopped in the truck that carried our luggage and backtracked to Opelika looking for help. There he contacted several area churches, but no one had a bus available to loan.

After waiting on the edge of the interstate for about two hours, we finally spied Robert pulling up behind the Goose in another bus—of the black and white striped variety. We couldn't believe our eyes. On the side of our substitute means of transportation were written the voluminous words, "LEE COUNTY JAIL." Robert had somehow managed to corral a prison bus! We inmates dutifully boarded, and the jailhouse wagon took us all the way to Florida without further incident. We encountered plenty of strange stares along the way, especially when a few yo-yos among us unfolded the "JESUS SAVES" banner and hung it out the windows!

When we finally arrived at Camp Ada and entered the grounds, the superintendent and his family didn't know what to think. They stood perplexed until they saw Robert emerge from the bus and heard him explain what had happened. To their great relief, he was not bringing a bunch of juvenile delinquents into their nice Christian camp. Some of us, however, surely acted the part.

The breezeway at Camp Ada, with the Old Blue Goose behind. Little David Dismukes is ready for the beach.

After claiming our luggage and finding a bunk, camp week began with an orientation session in the dining hall. There we were given a printed program that outlined each day's schedule, described expected and non-acceptable behavior, and introduced the camp's theme and key Bible verse(s). Generally, mornings were reserved for Bible study, music, and worship, with sessions often led by young guests. The afternoons consisted of recreation, free time, and small group discussion. Evenings were for practicing and performing skits, watching Christian films, and sitting around a glowing campfire down by the water—the day's climactic event.

Robert wanted camp to be enjoyable and entertaining, but without the provision of televisions, radios, stereos, or other media distractions. Involving us in skits, songs, discussion groups, and recreational endeavors were all efforts on his part to make our week a pleasant experience. He believed that if we were having a good time, we would be more apt to focus on the higher purpose for which we had come.

With this in mind he devised a short, interactive group activity held immediately before the evening meal that he called "Fun Time." After everyone cleaned themselves up following the day's leisurely pursuits, we gathered under a covered breezeway in front of the dining hall for a few minutes of amusement led by Robert. Ordinarily this consisted of practical jokes cloaked in the guise of homemade games. We loved seeing our beloved pastor play the role of duplicitous trickster, and Robert reveled in acting out the part. We also watched with delight as good friends were thoroughly duped and made to look the fool.

An annual Fun Time ritual was meeting King Bobo. To play the part, Robert chose a camper the size of an offensive lineman whom he dressed in royal clothes, paraded in front of the group, and introduced as the world famous King Bobo. He then sat him on a makeshift throne positioned in the center of the breezeway.

Meanwhile, several campers new to the Ada experience were ushered into the dining hall prior to Bobo's arrival. They would be given the special privilege of personally meeting the camp's illustrious ruler.

Each was blindfolded and brought out individually with great fanfare and shouts of encouragement. As they stood before the king, hearing the cheers of their fellow campers but seeing nothing, Robert explained that before meeting His Royal Highness they must get down on hands and knees and bow three times in his honor, while thrice making the acclamation, "Hail, King Bobo!" Lastly, they must kiss the king's magic ring.

Another unsuspecting victim pays homage to King Bobo, much to Robert's delight.

King Bobo wore no shoes, and his feet were exceedingly filthy from a special anointing of Ada dirt and water, much of it encrusted around his big ugly toes. With unique style he conspicuously wore a regal ring on the second toe of one of his repulsively muddy feet, which was plopped cross-legged directly in front of the unsuspecting kneeling teenager. After bowing and kissing, and while still prostrate before the king, each humble camper's blindfold was removed by Robert. The first image he or she saw was the ring on the nauseatingly gross foot of the noble King Bobo!

Howls of laughter erupted as the lowly subject grimaced in horror and inevitably began to spit the presumed dirt from their mouth and to wipe their unclean lips, while also uttering inaudible unmentionables as they looked around in shame and disgust. To add injury to insult, they beheld Brother Robert hovering above them with a rascally grin upon his face. A measure of confidence in their trustworthy pastor was soon restored, however, when the next victim was brought out. Then was revealed the secret known to everyone else—they had not kissed the muddy, grubby foot of King Bobo after all, but a separate ring that Robert held out in his hand.

Another Fun Time treat was the funnel trick. Robert liked to demonstrate his skill at putting a cone-shaped funnel inside his belt buckle, placing a quarter upon his forehead, holding his head back, and then dropping the quarter neatly into the shaft. As with Bobo, several new campers were taken into the dining hall beforehand and brought out to the breezeway one by one. Robert displayed his skill and offered the quarter to the teen if he or she could ring the funnel two out of three tries.

All who watched voiced support, calling the young person's name and urging them on toward success. Should they miss, Robert told them to concentrate, hold their head back a little further, or make sure their aim was straight. Then, on each contestant's second or third try, Robert took a cup of water and promptly poured it down the funnel, much to the surprise of the unwary participant and to the utter merriment of satisfied spectators.

Taking our cue from Brother Robert, we campers were good at creating our own fun times at Ada. Beds were routinely short-sheeted, and crabs somehow found their way into bunks. Youth in slumber occasionally awoke with toothpaste atop their noses, while those showering sometimes received an extra splash of cold water. And, of course, there was always the need to make sure no shaving cream occupied your swim suit. Pranks galore and laughs aplenty made retreat week all the more enjoyable—and memorable.

After much amusement, each day appropriately concluded on a serious note with a Christian film and worship service, the latter held by the water's edge. Following the movie, we quietly made our way to the sandy shore, seeing in the distance a lonely fire burning amid the surrounding darkness, beckoning us forward. Logs serving as beach seats encircled the blaze. As we sat around the campfire, the service began with the singing of familiar choruses and spiritual songs. Next came a time of sharing, where individuals talked about their relationship with the Lord.

Different youth and adults tended to testify about how the Lord had spoken to them through a Bible study, sermon, movie, or small group session. Those who shared sometimes became emotional. Occasionally, confession of sin took place. People often talked about getting right with God, or unloaded their burdens about family members and friends who did not yet know Him. Brother Robert brought the campfire service to a close with his words of wisdom and a chorus. Many times he also issued an invitation to salvation and surrender.

*Robert stands beside an evening
campfire on the beach at Camp Ada.*

On the final night of camp, we found candles placed on the logs where we sat for the Thursday evening commitment service. After a time of singing, Robert took his candle and lit it from the fire. He spoke about what the week had meant to him and what he saw going on in our lives. Then he encouraged us to come forward and light our own candles, sharing the personal promises we had made to God during our time together at Ada.

Numerous decisions for Christ were registered during these nocturnal sessions on Santa Rosa Sound. As we sat under the stars around the glowing embers, the Lord reached down and touched our lives in a special way. Year after year God used the sparks from Ada's campfire to help ignite a spiritual conflagration, flames that would long burn within the hearts of Providence's youth.

****

In June of 1969 as Robert prepared for Providence's first trip to Camp Ada, he was pleased to find among those registered two young men for whom he had been praying. Brother Robert by no means neglected ministry to the distaff members of his congregation, but felt he could especially relate well to the guys. He was also convinced that when young males took up the cause of Christ, young females were sure to follow.

One of those he personally invited to camp was fifteen year old Gary Dennis. Gary was already a Christian and member at Liberty on the other side of Opelika, where his family had long been involved and where we first met. Liberty's youth group was small, with most of its participants enrolled at Beulah High School. Gary went to county rival Beauregard, and with several friends active at Providence, he began attending youth functions there. In time Gary wanted to join Providence, but his parents did not approve. He decided to talk to Brother Robert about it, and Robert counseled him to follow his parents' wishes and stay at his home church.

"You can be a part of anything and everything we do here at Providence," he told Gary, "and we'll think of you as one of our own. You don't have to be a member here for that. But there's a need at Liberty for someone like you who's committed to the Lord. Why don't you keep going to your church on Sundays and be a light for Christ there, and then come and be with us at Providence other times as much as you can."

Robert was not concerned about padding his church's statistics, but in building the Lord's kingdom and developing young men like Gary into kingdom people. Gary decided to take Robert's advice and remain at Liberty, but over the course of the next few years he also became an integral part of Providence's youth.

Gary was in the process of developing the athletic build that eventually helped make him a star football and basketball player in high school. Ultimately standing 6'3" and weighing 215 pounds in his prime, he was an imposing presence who often reminded me of James Arness' Gunsmoke character Marshall Dillon, particularly with regard to his appearance, demeanor, and voice intonation. One of the smartest students in our class at Beauregard, with rugged good looks to go along with a muscular physique, it was easy to envy all Gary had going for him. Yet, somewhat surprisingly to a pair of outside eyes, self-doubt and insecurity would not leave him alone.

Three Beauregard lovelies surround Gary, including my future prom date Marilyn Preston, on his right.

Before entering college Gary lived all of his life in the same house in Beauregard with his parents, Sydney and Gertrude, and two older sisters. Sydney—also known as Dewey—worked at the West Point-Pepperell cotton mill and later at the Uniroyal tire plant as a mechanic. He met his future wife when she moved to Opelika from south Alabama shortly after graduating from high school. Gertrude found employment at the same Opelika Manufacturing textile plant where my mom first worked, and was introduced to Sydney through her first cousin. They married after a brief courtship.

Two offspring later, Sydney and Gertrude bought approximately seventy-five acres on the northern end of Beauregard and began building the home where Gary was born. It consisted initially of material salvaged from old barracks found at a vacant World War II prisoner of war camp located a couple of miles down the road. The house was expanded through the years into the residence where Gary grew up.

Gary almost didn't live to be a toddler. As a thirteen month old he inhaled part of a peanut hull that blocked off one lung. Simultaneously he developed a severe case of pneumonia, becoming deathly ill from a tragic combination of the two events. Doctors in Opelika advised his parents to rush him to Ponce de Leon Infirmary in Atlanta—his best hope lay in their specialized medical personnel and technology. Sydney and Gertrude experienced every parent's worst nightmare when hearing the urgent words, "We need to get him there in a hurry."

The Dennis' jumped into their 1943 Chevrolet and sped as fast as possible toward Georgia's capital city, located a hundred miles away. They drove too fast, and thirty miles up the road a state trooper sounded his alarm, turned on his emergency light, and stopped them for speeding. Sydney quickly explained the situation to the lawman, and the understanding officer promptly offered his assistance. The patrolman hopped back into his squad car, turned his siren on again, and escorted them the remaining seventy miles to Atlanta. In a day before interstates, they raced up U.S. 29 through every Georgia community from LaGrange to College Park in what surely approached record time.

At the hospital Gary was immediately x-rayed and operated upon. They successfully retrieved a peanut hull about half the size of a pinky fingernail. It and the pneumonia had completely closed off oxygen in one lung and considerably lessened the supply in the other. The doctors soon announced that the baby should be fine, but it had been a close call. Had they arrived a day or so later, he might not have survived. Gary's parents thanked the good Lord profusely, and Mama Dennis offered up her only son for future divine service.

Gertrude was raised in a Methodist household, but Sydney was Baptist, so she changed denominations when they married. She liked the fact that he was the song director at Opelika's Second Avenue Baptist Church. Later they joined Liberty, where he served as deacon and she as Sunday School director. Liberty is where they chose to provide their children with a spiritual foundation, and a fond memory for Gary is standing next to his dad in worship, listening to him sing the great hymns of the Christian faith.

His father was not beside him the day he gave his heart to Christ, however. Sometimes it was necessary for Sydney to work on Sundays and at night. Since Gertrude didn't drive, he always arranged for someone to take the family to church when he couldn't make it, as he did in the summer of 1965 during revival services. Eleven year old Gary had thought about his soul's salvation for quite awhile, but was somewhat timid as a child. He was too frightened to walk down the church aisle and stand before the congregation at the conclusion of the worship service, the usual Baptist manner of indicating a desire for salvation, baptism, and church membership.

Gary often pondered spiritual things in the stillness of his bedroom before drifting off to sleep, sometimes reading the King James Bible his parents had bought him. He started in Genesis, but soon the "begots" got him, and he became frustrated and quit. Nevertheless, he continued to sense God's tug upon his heart and to voice a persistent prayer each night at bedtime: "Lord, please help all the Christians to be better Christians, and please help me to be one, too."

The Lord answered his child-like prayer during Liberty's revival. Gary, uncharacteristically, found himself sitting upon the front row, and the evangelist—local pastor N. S. Harden—preached a rousing sermon on the fiery flames of Hell, an especially pertinent message considering the hot July temperatures and the lost people in the pews. Gary listened attentively, and once again the Lord pulled at his heartstrings, asking for a response. On this night, instead of needing to walk thirty or forty feet past eight or ten pews of people, there were only a few steps to navigate. When the invitation was issued, Gary went forward, took Pastor Bob Schoonhoven's hand, and indicated he wanted to be saved.

After Gary arrived home that same evening and was in the bed asleep, his father returned from work and learned from Gertrude what had happened earlier at their church. Sydney went into the bedroom and awakened his young son. He gave Gary a big bear hug and told his only boy how extremely proud of him he was.

Gary thus embarked on a lifelong voyage with Jesus, though his spiritual boat didn't sail very far the first couple of years. Reverend Schoonhoven attempted to talk to the pre-teen a few times about growing in the Lord, but his words were slow to sink in and find relevance. Gary tried reading the Bible again from time to time, but continued to have difficulty getting past the "begots," with the "thees," "thous," and "sayeths" also giving him trouble.

That problem was remedied during his first teenage year when the Dennis family enjoyed a summer vacation at the Alabama coastal resort of Gulf Shores. One day it rained and they found themselves stuck inside, unable to enjoy the beach. Love of reading and boredom caused Gary to pick up a paperback lying on a nearby coffee table. Thumbing through its contents, he noticed unusual drawings of stick people that whetted his curiosity. He began reading and soon realized that it was the Bible! What's more, he could readily understand it.

The version of the Bible he chanced upon was the recently published *Good News for Modern Man: the New Testament in Today's English,* a colloquial, modern paraphrase of the scriptures. It was the first time Gary had encountered a new translation of the Bible, a rendition that made sense to him; he was finally reading the Holy Book in a language he could easily comprehend and enjoy. Gary went home and purchased a copy of *Good News* for himself and began reading it regularly. He also decided to make a deliberate effort to apply what he read to his daily life.

Another seminal moment occurred about that same time when Gary's mother suddenly started hemorrhaging from ulcers and was rushed to Lee

County's hospital. Gertrude required nine units of blood, and for a while it wasn't known whether she would live or die. At home, Gary knelt down on his knees and prayed in desperation.

"God, if you will let my mom live, I'll do anything for you. I'll serve you all my life. I'll even go to Africa if you want me to!" Living in Africa was the worst fate he could think of at the moment.

By the next morning doctors had managed to stop the bleeding, and after fifteen days in the hospital, Gertrude came home and gradually returned to health. The commitment Gary made to God, however, did not go away, but clung to his mind and reverberated deep within his soul. He had promised himself to the Lord's service, just as his mother had offered him up for that purpose more than a decade earlier.

A year or so later, Brother Robert came to Providence, and it was under Robert's ministry that Gary's commitment found strength and direction. Their relationship began to blossom at Camp Ada during Providence's first youth camp where Robert explained and modeled the Christ-like life in a way that Gary grasped and was ready to pursue. At Ada he started gaining a clearer understanding of the deeper disciplines of the Christian faith, and soon surrendered himself wholeheartedly to the Lord's work, wherever that might take him—even to darkest Africa.

****

The other individual Robert was pleased to see on his camp roster was a relatively tall, lanky, fair-haired boy by the name of Billy Duncan. Only fourteen at the time, Billy was already establishing himself as a budding prep star in the area. Playing wide receiver and backup quarterback on Beauregard's varsity football team, as well as small forward on the junior high basketball squad, coaches salivated over his natural physical talent and uncommon athletic potential. They were not the only ones drooling over Billy. His inherent good looks, sports prowess, and engaging personality drew the girls like a magnet, leaving also-rans to fight among the spoils.

Billy proudly displays his trophy for winning the popular Ugliest Man on Campus contest.

If Gary resembled Gunsmoke's James Arness, Billy called to mind Butch Cassidy's Sundance Kid, played by Robert Redford—same blond hair, handsome face, and leading lady's persona, minus the mustache. Many of us guys would gladly have exchanged physiques with either Gary or Billy. Next to them, we felt like Marshall Dillon's faithful sidekick Festus, or worse, Harry Longbaugh's toady card-playing opponent Mr.

Macon. We couldn't begin to measure up, not in the venues that counted most to a male teenager—on the ball field and in the dating arena.

Born in the Five Points neighborhood of Opelika, Billy came to Beauregard as a third grader. He lived every kid's dream when his folks moved into a house across the street from the DuBose Dairy Bar, with the Blue Top Grocery alongside. Raising a girl and three boys—Billy was the second oldest child and senior son—Frank and Frances Duncan were typical of working class couples in the early 1960's, scraping by from week to week while trying to save enough to purchase some land and build a family home.

Frank was tall and lean with crew-cut hair, and possessed perhaps the deepest base voice in all of Beauregard. When he spoke, you knew you were talking to a man's man. A hardworking, no-nonsense kind of fellow, he was deeply devoted to his children, all the more because he knew what it was like to grow up without a father—his dad tragically murdered when he was only two years old.

He subsequently experienced a rough home life surrounded by promiscuity, drinking, and gambling. As a young married man, Frank came to Opelika from Sylacauga looking for work, intending to leave behind the destructive lifestyle of earlier years. Past demons would not let him go, however, and he gradually fell back into the hard-drinking and foolish-gambling ways of his adolescence.

By contrast, Frances provided the parental model of stability and propriety, and served as the early spiritual leader of the Duncan household. A slightly built woman with a feisty look emanating from exceedingly dark eyes, she faithfully took her brood to the old Southside (now Central) Baptist Church in Opelika, where the Reverend B. S. Ward held court. Billy's earliest religious memories are of attending this church, standing under the large oak trees that graced its grounds, and sitting through various versions of Sunday School, Vacation Bible School, and Sunbeams missions programs.

By 1968 Frank and Frances had saved enough to buy an acre of land within sight of Beauregard High, along Marvyn highway between the school and Lloyd's Grocery. There they commenced building a house at about the time Brother Robert began his ministry at Providence. Passing by one afternoon, the new pastor noticed Frank working and decided it was a good time to get better acquainted. Robert continued to stop by in the weeks ahead, checking on the house's progress and encouraging the soul of Frank Duncan.

He and Frances had begun taking their kids to Providence shortly before Robert's arrival. Deacon Joe White and his wife—also named Jo—had invited them to attend, and mother and children were in the congregation for Robert's first sermon as pastor. As Billy shook Robert's hand on that August Sunday morning, what he didn't know was that the new preacher was already familiar with him. Donella Nipper, an English teacher at Beauregard and a committed Christian, was a good friend of the Dismukes in Hurtsboro. Months earlier she had asked Robert to pray for a certain seventh grader in her class who needed the Lord, someone she felt could be an enormous positive influence on fellow students. That boy was Billy.

Robert prayed and continued to pray after meeting the young man, with his petitions magnificently answered the following spring. During a March 1969 revival, guest evangelist John Rigby preached a message entitled, "Ten Things in Hell That Are not in Heaven," a proclamation that especially caught Billy's ear. The sermon was disturbing, not least because he had begun to slip into some "unheavenly" thoughts and behaviors he believed were displeasing to God. In fact, Billy began to seriously question whether he really knew the Lord at all.

He had walked the aisle and been baptized at Southside as a nine year old, assuming he was saved at that time. But Reverend Rigby's message caused a reexamination of this supposition, and he left the revival service pondering his soul. Later Billy expressed his doubts to Robert, who encouraged the teenager through prayer, scripture, and conversation to further contemplate his salvation. Over the course of the next two months, Billy came to the realization that he was not heaven-bound after all, that his experience of five years earlier was more about church membership than a relationship with Jesus Christ.

During a May weekend youth revival led by an evangelistic team from Samford University, Billy's quest for spiritual clarification found closure. Upon hearing the gospel at the Saturday night service, he went down Providence's church aisle, took Brother Robert's pastoral hand, and professed faith in Christ, receiving Him as personal Savior and Lord.

Thus began Billy's pilgrimage with God, and so also began a transformation in the Duncan household. Not long after Billy's born again experience, his dad made a similar commitment to the Lord. Frank was converted and baptized along with his oldest boy, becoming a loyal church member and later a deacon, leaving his worldly pursuits forever behind. In the ensuing years, Frank would also serve as an anchor of godly support for Billy, as well as for other young men at Providence.

When the calendar changed to the month of June, Billy found himself far more enthusiastic about attending Providence's first youth camp. He would now be going with a higher purpose in mind than simply to have fun at the beach. He would go as a new Christian, eager to learn about his Lord.

****

I didn't join Billy, Gary, and the other Beauregard young people at Robert's inaugural Providence youth camp. At that time I didn't attend Providence at all. Reverend Paul Weekley's Union Grove church was my place of Sunday worship.

For me the summer of '69 consisted mostly of two pursuits—baseball and groceries. Playing, watching, and listening to as much baseball as I could absorb was the primary pleasure of my life, and had been since I was old enough to carry a bat and glove. When not engaged with the national pastime, I could be found working as a part-time bagboy at the Big Apple Supermarket, a gig that provided my first taste of earning a regular paycheck.

The Big Apple was a longtime fixture in downtown Opelika. Mention it to any Lee County native born before 1970 and the northeast metropolis of the same (nick)name is an afterthought, at best. Milk, bread, and potato chips come first to our minds.

Its goofy logo of an oversized apple, with the emboldened words BIG APPLE—the latter term beneath the former—printed on its red peel, was a familiar sight around the store and in the Wednesday afternoon editions of the Opelika Daily News. The food market was one of three major chains to shop for groceries in the city, competing with the A & P and Kwick Check for customers' patronage.

The familiar logo of my teenage employer.

The Big Apple occupied a prime location in Opelika, at the corner of Avenue B and South Seventh Street. Of the three supermarkets, it alone was situated on the downtown side of the railroad tracks, close to retail shops and businesses that formed the hub of the city. Perhaps for this reason, or maybe because of a larger base of customers, it prided itself as the leading grocery in town.

My mom worked directly across the street as a telephone operator at the local South Central Bell office. As I looked through the huge glass plate windows that formed the front of our store, and out beyond the spacious Big Apple parking lot, I could see her three story red brick building in the distance and feel a measure of comfort that mama was close at hand.

I had bagged groceries for about a year when my eyes began to gaze upon another sight in her general direction that stirred a much different emotion. Standing tall between the Big Apple and South Central Bell was a wooden utility pole upon which I had left an indelible impression. One afternoon during break time, I walked from my place of employment over to my mother's and decided to take her car for a spin—without her permission. She would never know the difference, I reasoned.

While turning the corner of Avenue B and South Seventh, the utility pole impeded my uneven path. The sickening sound of metal bending soon gave way to the awful realization that what was done could not be undone, at least not without mama finding out. The collision left a sizeable dent on the passenger side car doors of her 1968 Chevrolet Impala, along with a swath of blue paint and chipped wood on the pole.

One of the worst moments of my young life was interrupting my mom with the disturbing news that her first-born had just wrecked her fairly new car. After making sure I was alright, she was not pleased. Several Big Apple paychecks later, I was able to atone somewhat for my misdeed. Fortunately, prior to the accident I had received a small wage increase on my sixteenth birthday, enabling me to help pay for the damages a bit sooner.

At the Big Apple Bud McCollum ruled as manager. He had run the produce section when he and my father were co-workers there years earlier, and their connection is how I landed my first job as a fifteen year old. Bud was a big man, somewhat tall with a waste size in the forties. His customary attire consisted of an ill-fitting white shirt with a black bow tie, black pants, and black shoes. While friendly with the customers, he could come across as stern and demanding, although usually fair and understanding, with his employees. I normally bagged groceries on the store's busiest days, Thursday through Saturday, and tried my best to stay on the good side of Bud.

On Tuesday nights Bud was the bossiest. That's when, after the 5:30 closing time, every bagboy was expected to come in for a couple of hours to sweep, mop, and wax the floors. Bud watched us like a hawk, making sure each speck of dirt was removed and every square inch of linoleum thoroughly washed and shined. Cranky from the long day, grumpy at having to work late, and chewing on the stump of a cigar, he played the overbearing taskmaster to perfection. Dubbed "Bud Butt," we delighted in the dual interpretations of our epithet.

Usually two to four bagboys—there were no "baggirls"—worked at any given time. Dressed in a neat oxford shirt with a white apron tied around our wastes, we mastered the art of stacking various groups of groceries in their appropriate brown sacks. No need to ask, "Paper or plastic?" The former was the exclusive grocery carrier of the day.

Meats, dairy products, produce, and other perishables, along with glass goods, toiletries, and cleaning supplies, must be housed in separate sacks. We were particularly careful with eggs and loaf bread, the two main sources of customer complaints. Patrons did not take kindly to returning home with cracked eggs and mashed bread, and neither did Bud. So we carefully checked the eggs before inserting them in a bag and always placed the bread on top.

Bagboys were only paid the minimum wage—$1.30 an hour when I started—but could increase their earnings significantly through tips. Most were of the nickel and dime variety, and many customers gave nothing. A good tip was considered to be a quarter or more. Occasionally, well-to-do shoppers tipped fifty cents or even a dollar.

In our store bagboys worked all four of the cashier lanes on an as-needed basis, and usually took turns waiting on the customers. When a particularly good tipper arrived, our adrenaline level grew markedly. We watched our prey excitedly as she wandered around the store, while also eyeballing one another to see who else was keeping tabs on the nearby source of additional revenue.

To be in the right position when the celebrated shopper was ready to check out was a key to receiving perhaps the day's biggest bonus. Timing was critical, and often luck reigned. Even if everything went perfectly and you could almost feel the extra treasure in your pocket, a senior bagboy might come along, wave you off, and steal your customer away.

Bradley Mangram was the worst. Mangram, as he was called, had risen through the ranks to become Bud's pet bagboy, and took advantage of his status at every opportunity. He was a master at the art of sycophancy, telling Bud what he wanted to hear while simultaneously tooting his own horn. Eddie Haskell had nothing on this fellow.

Mangram could spy a big tipper from six grocery aisles away. He openly gawked and let the rest of us know without equivocation that she was his customer, and we'd better steer clear. If not, he'd report us to Bud, accusing us of dereliction of duty or some other bogus crime. We acquiesced, knowing he had Bud's ear. Luckily, Mangram was often too busy talking to the manager or hiding in the stockroom to employ his bullying tactics.

I continued to bag groceries for Bud through much of my high school career, the workplace becoming something of a second home. A decade or so later, sadly, the familiar old store ceased to be stocked with hamburger buns and cans of vegetable soup, the big red apple adorning its façade taken down. Succeeding years have seen hand-me-down clothes and discarded furniture items lining its assorted aisles, with the sign out front reading "GOODWILL." More recently, neighboring First Baptist Church purchased the property to accommodate its parishioners' parking needs. Now the building is gone, with only traces of its glorious past left behind.

These days, whenever I drive along Avenue B and stop at the traffic light on South Seventh, I look to the right and scan the lot I roamed so regularly as a teenager. Inward vision propels me to a time when I am once again pushing a buggy full of food and following a customer to her automobile. I pick up the brown sacks topped with groceries and carefully position them onto the vehicle's rear floorboard and empty back seat. I happily receive an unsolicited gift for my services and head toward the store with a feeling of satisfaction and mission accomplished.

Back inside, I return the buggy to its stall and take my place behind Jane Long's cashier's counter, ready to reload. While waiting for the ketchup and dinner rolls to be checked, my eyes wander over to Mangram, who is pleasantly passing the time of day with Bud near the manager's office door. A little smirk arises upon my face as I reach into a pants pocket and cradle the half dollar tip I have just received.

Suddenly, I'm brought back to the present by the sound of another vehicle pulling up from behind. Looking into the rear view mirror and then at the green traffic light, I decide I'd better move on. Turning the corner, I smile as I avoid the utility pole and relish bygone days at the Big Apple.

****

The Big Apple provided a steady source of spending money for a high school student and was an excellent means of initiation into the workaday world of society. But in my young mind, it was basically a boring job that took time away from life's amusements—chief among them, the world of sports. My passion was baseball, a diversion I pretty much lived for during the summer.

There is never a time I don't recall being in love with the game. How it came to hold such fascination, I can't say; there were no rabid fans in my family spreading their infatuation. Maybe it was the sport's untimed and unhurried pace that so suited me. Perhaps it arose from the various skill levels on display—running, catching, throwing, and batting, all of which must be honed and harmonized for success. Or its appeal could have stemmed from the luscious green playing fields or larger-than-life superstars. However my enthusiasm originated, baseball constituted a large measure of my early identity, and is something I have continued to enjoy through the years.

As a child I hit rocks with a stick for hours on end, converting the dirt road that passed in front of our Jim Walter house into my own personal "rockpark." Pretending to be the next Mickey Mantle, I would play out an entire World Series in a single afternoon, always blasting the walk-off, game winning homer in the bottom of the ninth inning of the deciding seventh game.

When winning the Series on one occasion, I hit the rock a bit too far and it shattered the back windshield of our 1956 Ford Fairlane. The "Oh Yes!" of victory quickly collapsed into the "Oh No!" of defeat as the agony of reality set in. Upon hearing the unnerving sound of disintegrating glass, my father came running out of the house faster than Maury Wills could steal second base. My punishment was severe, but I gained a degree of satisfaction in believing that, like the Mick, I could sock'em an awfully long way and create quite a commotion.

Transferring my hitting prowess from the dirt road to the diamond proved a challenge. Playing for the Hawks and Mules in the Opelika Dixie Youth League, I tended to bat toward the latter end of our lineup— sometimes dead last—and was usually happy not to strike out. Slugging existed only in my dreams.

When we moved to Beauregard, the driveway at our new house was not suitable for practicing offense, so I switched to working on throwing and catching instead. There was a large propane gas tank situated in the middle of our back yard, and I loved to spend considerable chunks of time bouncing a tennis ball off its front side. Defense became my specialty and shortstop my position.

Since I couldn't hit like Mickey, Clete Boyer, a slick fielding, light hitting infielder for the New York Yankees, replaced him as my favorite player. I could relate to Clete's struggles at the plate, while also admiring his grand ability with the glove. Although I might not be the next Mickey Mantle, I reasoned, perhaps I could at least be another Clete Boyer. My sights were firmly set on the big leagues.

The first major league game I ever saw was via a big box, tiny screen television positioned in our small Jim Walter living room. The little black and white screen seemed satisfactory at the time, the gargantuan models of today as incomprehensible as smartphones and tablet computers. I sat mesmerized as a five or six year old while watching the likes of Mighty Mouse, Bozo the Clown, Popeye the Sailor Man, and a charismatic baseball announcer by the name of Dizzy Dean.

Ol' Diz called the games on Saturday and Sunday afternoons on the local CBS affiliate, WRBL in Columbus, one of only three or four stations we could receive off our housetop antenna. Folksy and funny, dressed in string tie and Stetson hat, the 6'2" and 250 pound Dean was part baseball expert, part comedian, and part salesman. I never knew him as a Hall of Fame pitcher for the St. Louis Cardinals; I only remember him as the country showman who made me laugh and enjoy the game of baseball.

No doubt he caused numerous educators to cringe with his rural diction and heavy abuse of the English language. According to Diz, pitchers "throwed" the ball and batters "swang" at it. Runners "slud" into bags and returned to their "respectable" bases. Gutsy players possessed "testicle" fortitude, and everyone around was known as "podnah." A highlight of the telecasts was his twangy rendition of the classic railroad ballad, "The Wabash Cannonball."

Dizzy was the major spokesman for Falstaff beer, one of the sponsors of his "Game of the Week" broadcasts. He hawked it shamelessly, influencing at least one little underage member of his audience. "When I get old enough, I'm gonna drink Falstaff beer, just like Ol' Diz," I proudly proclaimed as a seven year old to anyone interested. I even attempted to convince my dad, who always loved a good brew, to convert to Dizzy's variety, but Carling Black Label was more his taste. Perhaps to compensate, one day he brought home some Ol' Diz brand charcoal briquettes to use on our grill.

As the 1966 baseball season got underway, I turned on our TV in April but couldn't find Dizzy Dean's distinctive voice on WRBL. Instead, Curt Gowdy was calling Saturday's "Game of the Week" over on WTVM. "Where's Ol' Diz?" I asked family and friends, but no one seemed to know. I promptly fired off a letter to CBS Television headquarters in hopes of getting an answer.

To my amazement I soon received a reply from New York explaining the business of TV and baseball. NBC had signed an exclusive contract to nationally televise the major leagues for the next several seasons and had hired its own play-by-play man. CBS was sorry, but Dizzy Dean had been booted from the booth. There would be no more "sluds" or "podnahs," no more "Wabash Cannonballs." Watching baseball was not quite as much fun without its premier entertainer.

One or two TV games a weekend were not enough to satisfy my baseball appetite—the smorgasbord of games on cable and satellite still in the distant future. Until 1966 it was Ol' Diz or nothing on our tube, so I also warmed up the radio almost every summer evening. With no team in the South, it was often a challenge to find a game to listen to on the AM dial. The weather must cooperate, and often more static than pitches came through the small speakers in my bedroom.

I had the best luck tuning in St. Louis Cardinals games on their 50,000 watt flagship station, KMOX. I hung on virtually every word of their two Hall of Fame announcers, Harry Carey and Jack Buck. Different as day and night—Harry: blue collar, verbose, easily excitable; Jack: more buttoned down, reserved, and dignified—they formed a dynamite booth combination. Their respective signature calls, "Holy cow!" and "That's a winner!", delighted my baseball ears.

When I couldn't get the Cardinals, I moved the dial over to Pittsburgh's KDKA to hear the Pirates' Bob Prince, or to WLW in Cincinnati to listen to the old lefthander, Joe Nuxhall, sign off by "roundin' third and headin' for home." I came to enjoy listening to baseball on the radio as much as watching it on TV.

Both became a lot easier in the spring of 1966. That's when the Milwaukee Braves headed south to Atlanta, and we Southerners finally had a lineup of our own to cheer for. Softening the blow of losing Dizzy Dean was the gift of a whole team, along with their lead radio and television announcer, Milo Hamilton, a future Cooperstown inductee himself. Milo's soothing radio voice came through loud and clear 162 times a year, and the Braves televised around twenty-five of those games.

To my great delight even Ol' Diz joined Milo for a few Braves telecasts in 1967-68.

While listening to Milo, Harry, Jack, and the others, a future plan began to emerge in my teenage mind. If I couldn't make it to the major leagues as a player, I decided I wanted to announce the games instead. I would go to broadcasting school and become a sportscaster, with the dream of someday joining Milo and the Braves.

****

The summer of 1969 saw Neil Armstrong and Buzz Aldrin astound the world by walking upon the surface of the moon, generating enormous enthusiasm and pride among Americans. It also witnessed an astonishing feat in the world of sports. The lowly New York Mets, who had never finished higher than ninth place in their short eight year history, won the World Series, a remarkable rags to riches story that captivated the nation.

There was also special excitement for baseball fans in the Deep South as the Atlanta Braves won their first National League division title. With Henry Aaron, Rico Carty, and Phil Niekro leading the way, Milo kept his listeners enthralled by calling twenty-four more victories than defeats, including ten of the last eleven to claim first place. Clete Boyer, my old hero from the Yankees, played third base for Atlanta that season, making the team's accomplishment sound even sweeter. Unfortunately for the Braves, they ran into the Miracle Mets and never made it to the Series.

The Braves march to the playoffs was a venture into baseball heaven for their many devoted fans. Thoughts of another kind of heaven, however, were on my mind as Atlanta's successful season drew to a close. God began to deal with me about my eternal destiny, and five days before the Braves clinched the pennant, Brother Robert introduced me to the Lord.

On Sunday mornings during that unforgettable summer, I attended Preacher Weekley's church with mama, two siblings, and my grandparents. The blind preacher's messages had taken on added interest since Robert shared Christ with me during the previous spring's trip to Six Flags. I listened more attentively and understood more readily the significance of the elderly pastor's words.

While I worshipped at Union Grove, Gary, Billy, and other young people enjoyed a number of spiritual and recreational activities under the leadership of Brother Robert and his two college-age assistants. The glow of June's Camp Ada remained fresh in their souls for awhile, but began to wane as summer advanced toward its inevitable conclusion—perhaps one reason Robert planned an early fall revival. Some of Providence's youth invited me to attend the late September crusade.

Thursday evening was "Bring a Friend Night," and it was also the first time I set foot in Providence Church. I sat with classmates on the next to last pew, among the seventeen that lined the left side of the auditorium. I don't recall much about the worship service except for the invitation at its conclusion. The evangelist, David Causey of Geneva, Alabama, implored members of the audience to give their lives to Christ, voicing a special appeal to the young people present.

A few friends left their seats and made their way up to the platform area, where Robert stood waiting to receive any who came forward. The personal testimony he had casually related on the Six Flags trip raced through my mind, as did the regular Sunday witness of Preacher Weekley and the message of that evening's evangelist. I knew I needed Christ and sensed an urgency to talk with Robert about it. With much trepidation, I stepped out into the center aisle and began walking toward the front of the auditorium. It eased my anxiety considerably to see a reassuring smile on the face of Brother Robert, and to have him take my hand and welcome me joyfully into his presence.

After the service he escorted me upstairs to a Sunday School room where several youth were praying. There he shared the plan of salvation, and I willingly prayed the sinner's prayer. Those in the room, including Gary and Billy, hugged and congratulated me for the decision I had made to receive and follow the Lord.

The occasion of my conversion included no lightning bolt experience, just a simple prayer of sincere faith. I knew comparatively little about the Bible or the church or spiritual things. I only knew that I needed Jesus, and I invited Him to come into my heart to reign as Savior and Lord. I believe He did that evening, and so began a lifelong journey "toward the mark of the high calling of God in Christ Jesus."

Forevermore I will celebrate September 25, 1969 as my spiritual birthday. On that date I joined Brother Robert and Miss Shirley, Gary and Billy, and the vast company of those who share the common bond of "Christ in you, the hope of glory." The messianic age now dawned in my own life as the Son arose in my heart. B.C.

became A.D. I met the Lord at Providence, and seeking Him soon became my most intense desire.

Chapter 4
"The Seekers"

One of the great things about coming to know the Lord is the blessing of belonging to a family of fellow believers. Jesus not only calls us into relationship with Himself, but connects us to those who have also heard His invitation and decided to "go with Him, with Him, all the way." The messianic age is meant to be shared, a truth grounded in the very nature of God.

The Christian model of God is distinctly different from the monotheism of its distant cousins, Judaism and Islam. The deity revealed in the New Testament is a social being—Father, Son, and Holy Spirit, related together in perfect unity.

I make no pretense of completely understanding the biblical doctrine of the Trinity. My human brain can't ultimately fathom the paradoxical reality of "Three in One." Analogies like H_2O, a singular substance that appears in the different forms of ice, water, and steam, are helpful, but ultimately inadequate. Only God can fully comprehend Himself.

What my finite mind can perceive is scripture's claim that humans are created in God's image, and—like their Maker—are fundamentally social beings. The *imago Dei* strongly suggests that we are created for relationships of both the vertical and horizontal dimensions. Each individual stands in need of God *and* community in order to arrive at existential health.

The Trinitarian principle manifests itself in the ministry of Jesus as He surrounds Himself with a small cadre of disciples. Theoretically, the Lord could have performed His ministry without them—sharing His message, performing His miracles, dying on a cross, and ascending back to heaven—free from the bother of frequently selfish and immature followers. According to the Gospel record, the first group of believers was more of a hindrance than a help.

Such a course of solitary action, however, is strictly out of biblical character, for God desires the companionship of His creation. Jesus chose the Twelve "to be with Him" says the scripture, an indication of the Lord's primary purpose for coming. "In Christ, God was reconciling the world to Himself" is the concise way Paul sums up the divine mission. The Thirteenth Apostle's emotive metaphor vividly illustrates the Lord's loving intention toward His prodigals. Originating deep within the heart of the Triune God is the longing to bring together a community gathered around Jesus Christ.

Christendom's First Family constituted a motley band of pioneers that included four fishermen, along with a tax collector, zealot, doubter, traitor, and four less distinguishable personalities, all united by their initial commitment to follow Jesus. The most familiar names among them were Simon Peter, his brother Andrew, siblings James and John, Matthew, Thomas, and Judas Iscariot. Women also joined the entourage, with Joanna, Susanna, sisters Mary and Martha, and another Mary from Magdala among those specifically identified.

The Gospel writers portray this diverse cast of characters as mostly D and F students, frequently misunderstanding the identity, mission, and teaching of their Lord. The disciples start out well, leaving fishing nets, tax office, and nationalistic crusade to hit the road with Jesus, but quickly degenerate into a tragicomedy of discipleship errors. Strikingly, they largely come across as clueless dunderheads, while appearing before the reader as alternately faithless, selfish, ambitious, and disloyal.

The obtuseness of the original apostles is at times astonishing. Early in the ministry they are chided for failing to perceive even the simplest of Jesus' instruction. "Do you not understand this parable? Then how will you understand all the parables?" their Lord laments, perhaps seeking to motivate His underperforming pupils.

Later their lack of discernment causes disappointment to surface again. While voyaging with Jesus, the disciples panic during a ferocious storm, oblivious to the power of the One who can still the wind and the waves. Soon they hear the remonstrative words, "Why are you afraid? Have you still no faith?"

On another boat ride they wonder aloud where they will get their next meal, despite having witnessed the miraculous provision of food for more than nine thousand people! The Bread of Life points out the absurdity of their anxiety, rehearsing a litany of facts about the feedings and concluding with the reprimand, "Do you not yet understand?" When their vessel arrives safely at shore, the Lord and His cerebrally challenged crew head northward toward Caesarea Philippi. There the human leader among the Twelve sinks to new depths by voicing the devil's "cross-less" temptation and is promptly rebuked with the razor-sharp words, "Get behind me, Satan!"

Even more disconcerting is the disciples' decidedly "unsaintly" behavior. On one occasion they play their version of "king of the mountain" by arguing about who should be considered the greatest. On another, two followers greedily lust for thrones next to Jesus when He comes into His kingdom, a reign apparently envisioned in terms of lavish riches and world domination.

On the night before He dies, Jesus' closest friends are in need of caffeine when they nod off three times after being asked to watch and pray. Fittingly, all awaken early enough to high-tail it out of Gethsemane as soon as Jesus is arrested. One coward attempts to save face by returning, only to pose two-faced, spewing lies, curses, and denials. To top off a series of embarrassing mishaps, another of Jesus' inner circle receives blood money to plot his Lord's demise and then betrays Him with a deceitful kiss.

By choosing to air so much of the disciples' dirty linen, the biblical authors set before us examples of how *not* to follow Jesus. Unlike the Twelve, Christians should be full of understanding, faith, loyalty, and selfless service. Perhaps we are meant to see something of ourselves in the "rumbling, bumbling, stumbling" attempts to be Christ-like on the part of the earliest believers. They serve as rude reflections of discipleship gone wrong, sounding the alarm to all who have made a commitment to obey Jesus as Lord.

Whatever the reasons for showcasing the "warts and all" character of Christ's first followers, the Gospel story ends with many of the Twelve overcoming their missteps and embodying the true sense of the term "disciple." Etymologically, the word means "learner," and later church history testifies to their maturation in the things of God.

Impetuous Peter evolved into the bold preacher of Pentecost and a brave missionary in the book of Acts.

John the fisherman—and erstwhile co-regent of Jesus—is credited with a magnificent Gospel that bears his name, as is the case with his colleague Matthew. According to Acts, John's brother and co-conspirator James died as a martyr for Christ at the hands of King Herod Agrippa I. Ancient traditions trumpet Doubting Thomas' distinguished service for the Lord in Syria and India, as others do Andrew's ministry in Russia and Greece.

The unrefined ensemble that initially surrounded Jesus encountered great difficulty in advancing toward spiritual adulthood. There were numerous starts and stops, spurts and sputters. As such, they mirror Christian discipleship of every age. The follower of Jesus does not automatically know how to follow when taking his or her first steps. Although the Twelve experienced the distinct advantage of the historical Jesus in their midst, personal discipleship had to be individually learned and put into practice. So it is today for believers who possess Christ's words and deeds in the sentences of scripture, not to mention His Spirit in their hearts. It's a "slow go" for most of us. The fiery darts of our lion-like Adversary must be constantly dodged, the glamorous enticements of sinful human nature ceaselessly resisted.

The group of young believers I was privileged to join at Providence, while perhaps not as starkly dense or disloyal as the first disciples, was nevertheless similarly dilatory. Like our Gospel forbears, we initially amassed low scores on the religious aptitude portions of our discipleship exams. Resembling Peter, we had to learn to step out of our boats, overcome our fears, and exercise the kind of faith that keeps us from sinking down to the depths of the world around us. As with the Twelve, we required more schooling in "the law of Moses, the prophets, and the psalms." Akin to disciples elsewhere, there was the recurring need to "lay aside every weight, and the sin that clings so closely" and fix our eyes on Jesus. Additional training was necessary if we were to "live by the Spirit" and "not gratify the desires of the flesh." Thankfully, God sent Brother Robert, Miss Shirley, and Providence church to patiently offer their guidance.

Here, doubtless, is a primary reason for the centrality of family in the kingdom of God. Families by definition are comprised of relationships—liaisons that ideally provide love, support, companionship, and maturation. Family members are there for one another, offering strength and encouragement, helping loved ones to cope with life's struggles and celebrate its triumphs. Healthy families cultivate responsibility, accountability, and discipline. Families learn together, grow together, succeed and fail together. The Family of Faith is no different. The Church shares both foibles and feats while providing wisdom and energy for the task of following Jesus.

Disciples of Jesus Christ are not called to be solitary saints or redeemed recluses—Lone Ranger Christians are oxymoronic at best. The context of discipleship is always the society of the saved, the "fellowship of kindred minds…like to that above." It is the local church family that assists the development of the soul, advancing commitment to Christ through its worship, work, and witness.

My initial spiritual family went by the names of Gary and Billy, Jimmy and Tommy, Sharon and Judy, Marcy and Dianne, among many others. Young in age, sincere in heart, eager to grow, but devoid of knowledge and experience, we began to seek the Lord in earnest by seeking His will for our lives under the tutelage of Brother Robert. We came to be known as "the Seekers," a group of new believers excited about our relationship with Christ, who took seriously the biblical admonition that became our namesake motto: "Seek the Lord and His strength, seek His face continually." What the Lord did in and through the Seekers is the most marvelous memory of our messianic age.

****

The decade of the 1970's opened with the winds of change swirling across the social fabric of America. Small gusts were visible in the long hair and miniskirts that tended to dominate fashion. The era's signature iconoclasts, self-styled "hippies," helped usher in the blustery conditions of rebellious, free-spirited—sometimes reckless—behavior. Whirlwinds swooped down, wreaking havoc and destruction through the epidemic of recreational drugs, the decadence of the sexual revolution, and the unpopularity of the Viet Nam War.

Most tempests remained remote distractions to the residents of Beauregard. An enormous exception lay in a raging—though morally necessary—hurricane that struck our schools and nearby restaurants, theaters, and sporting events. Full-blown racial integration came ashore in the Deep South, rocking the very foundations of life in Dixie.

For our small community this meant the merging of two previously segregated black and white schools,

Sanford and Beauregard, respectively, with students in grades one through three and ten through twelve attending the latter, and four through nine the former. Like many area parents, my folks announced that their children would not return to Beauregard in the late summer of 1970, but attend a private school instead.

Several Hornets' classmates transferred along with me to Scott Preparatory School, a new all-white educational establishment in Opelika. A goodly number enrolled at other non-public institutions in the region: Lee Academy in Auburn, Macon Academy near Tuskegee, and Glenwood School outside of Phenix City. Many remained where they were. To my great chagrin, our prospective Beauregard "Class of '72" was suddenly ripped asunder by what may have been the stormiest gale to hit Southern society since Sherman's Union Army.

Amid historic cultural revolution, the religious reorientation I experienced began to work itself out in theory and practice. Like the earliest believers, I soon discovered that there is no fast track to discipleship, no shortcut down the narrow road. As a new-born babe in Christ, I needed to drink plenty of plain spiritual milk before eating solid biblical food; I must learn to sit up and crawl before walking steadily with the Lord. Clarity of understanding and the discipline to run well the race of "faith, hope, and love" are only gradually attained.

The first year of my Christian pilgrimage was spent getting acquainted with the Lord and acclimated to the people and programs of Providence. I began eagerly attending Sunday School, worship, and choir, as well as activities at the church's youth center on Friday and Saturday nights. Along with others my age, I participated in special events like the state youth convention, world mission conference, and weekend youth revival, each leaving a positive imprint upon my spiritually maturing mind and heart. Summertime trips to Florida for camp and to Ohio for mission work served to enrich commitment to Christ while solidifying my standing in Providence's youth group.

Ten weeks and two days after celebrating my first spiritual birthday, and about three months after changing schools, Brother Robert approached me before the Sunday morning worship service.

"Jerry, could I see you in my office for a minute?"

By this time he and I enjoyed a warm relationship full of affection and trust. Still, my mind couldn't help but wonder if I'd been caught talking during his sermon or engaging in some other transgression deserving of pastoral rebuke. With only slight hesitation I complied, and followed in the general direction he was heading.

When we entered the small pastor's study located only a few steps from the sanctuary, I was pleased to see two of my friends already inside. One was Billy Duncan, fifteen and in the tenth grade at Beauregard, although within weeks he would transfer to Macon Academy. Since his conversion a year and a half earlier, Billy had taken a leading role among the young people at Providence, something that came quite naturally. He was a faithful participant at youth events, served on the youth council, and spoke at the Youth Sunday worship services. His star had rapidly risen at church, much as it did on the football field and basketball court.

The other person standing there was sixteen year old Barry Jones. Barry had come to Christ a year earlier, three months after my own conversion. In appearance he often reminded me of the Peanuts cartoon character

Charlie Brown—same stocky build and large round head. He was more like Charlie Brown's best friend Linus, however, in his sharp intellect and penchant for philosophical musings. Barry was generally regarded as the smartest person in our class, vying with Gary and me for top academic honors. Among the three of us, soon he alone would remain at Beauregard, though not for long, choosing to bypass his senior year for early college admission.

I especially liked Barry because we shared a passion for the game of baseball. Like me he was an infielder, and also an occasional catcher for his older brother Bobby, a more than adequate southpaw pitcher. All of us enjoyed playing the sport together in the recreational leagues of Opelika, as well as for our beloved Beauregard Hornets. Barry's mom was an avid baseball fan too, and sometimes took us to see the Detroit Tigers' minor league farm club, the Rebels, in nearby Montgomery.

Barry loved baseball as much as I did.

Barry and Gary were close friends, and it was Gary who shared with him about the Lord. During our final year together at Beauregard, Gary placed Barry's name near the top of a prayer list of classmates who needed salvation. Brother Robert was also praying for Barry, and during the 1969 Christmas season he led the tenth grader to receive Christ. On the night of his conversion, Robert brought Barry to Gary's house so he could personally inform his good friend that his prayers had been gloriously answered.

In the year since becoming a Christian, Barry joined Billy and me at the forefront of Providence's youth, and now we found ourselves in our beloved pastor's office wondering why we were there. With only a few minutes to spare before the worship service, Robert stood behind his large church desk and got right to the point.

"Fellows, I believe you are three of the finest young men we have at our church, and I appreciate each one of you and your faithfulness to the Lord."

We smiled at the complement, glad that our pastor thought so highly of us. We also recognized that flattery often precedes the request of a favor. Sure enough, Robert was not finished.

"Lately I've been thinking about how the Lord might use you and the rest of our young people this next year. Do y'all think you could meet with me on Monday nights for awhile to talk about it, and to pray and study the Bible together?"

We looked at each other for a second or two, as if to detect interest in the proposal, none of us wanting to be the first to commit or decline. We immediately sensed, however, that we all felt the same way. On the one hand, we didn't really want to come to church another night during the week. We were already heavily involved in church activities, as well as with school, athletics, and part-time jobs, not to mention assorted family obligations. On the other hand, we loved Brother Robert. He had led all three of us to the Lord, and we didn't want to disappoint him. If he felt we needed to meet on Monday nights, we would accommodate him.

After only a moment of reflection, we simultaneously began to shrug and shake our heads affirmatively, agreeing to meet our pastor in his office the following evening at 6:30. Walking toward the sanctuary and to the eleven o'clock service, we had no inkling of the significance of the divine appointment just made.

****

The group that came to be known as "the Seekers" held its first meeting on December 7, 1970. Our small contingent went by no particular moniker at first; the name would evolve over the course of the following months.

Starting that first Monday night, Brother Robert met with Billy, Barry, and me every week for what turned out to be a no-frills class on discipleship. In our roughly ninety minute sessions, he typically selected a short passage of scripture to read and discuss, with the goal of applying it to our lives. Often the Bible study led directly to a topic especially relevant to teenagers—dating, family relationships, career choice, and peer pressure, for example.

After a lengthy period of instruction and dialogue, time was set aside to pray for our church, particularly the youth, and to voice personal and group concerns. We concluded with what Robert called a "love circle," in which we stood facing each other and holding hands. Sentence prayer was offered and vows were renewed to live for the Lord until we met again. Our circle usually ended with the singing of a short spiritual song or hymn, followed by back slaps and hugs all around.

Our Monday evening meetings were the sweetest times of fellowship I'd ever known and kept me coming back for more week after week. The personal training we received by a dedicated and experienced Christian pastor proved invaluable. Brother Robert taught us how to study the Bible, how to pray, how to witness, and how to make Jesus the Lord of our lives. Through these sessions we began to "grow up in every way into him who is the head, into Christ."

We had only gathered for a couple of weeks when Robert gave us a reading assignment. He passed out copies of the book *In His Steps* by Charles Shelton, and asked us to read a few chapters before the next week's meeting. Over Christmas I started turning the pages of this inspirational classic and found that I could not put it down. I became absorbed in its story of a small group of believers who made a remarkably simple commitment that dramatically transformed their lives. They pledged that for one year their every decision would be prefaced with the question, "What would Jesus do?" Then they promised to proceed as they felt He would, regardless of the personal hardship it brought.

The group was led by a pastor like ours, the Reverend Henry Maxwell, and included a diverse collection of church members. Among them were Edward Norman, a newspaper owner and editor; Rachel Winslow, a professional singer; Virginia Page, a wealthy young socialite; Milton Wright, a department store owner; and Alexander Powers, a railroad supervisor. How the Lord profoundly changed them and their community— through uncompromising obedience to a Christ-led life— both fascinated and challenged me.

Since by this time I was planning on a media career, the issues faced by newspaper editor Edward Norman especially caught my eye. "How would Jesus run a daily newspaper?" was the personal question he struggled to answer. More specifically: "Would the Lord print stories that did not uplift the human spirit?" "Would He accept advertising that promoted unseemly lifestyles and unhealthy habits?" "Would Jesus publish a paper on Sunday?" Edward Norman wrestled with these and other decisions as he sincerely sought to manage his enterprise as if Christ were doing it. He often found it necessary to make costly choices that ran counter to standard business practices.

Of course the import of reading this fictional account was quite clear. What if a group of real-life disciples—like us—made the same kind of vow and kept it? What could the Lord do with individuals—even those still wet behind the ears—who were totally sold out to Jesus? Long before the WWJD movement crazed Christendom, Robert challenged his three protégés to undertake a similar commitment of radical obedience to Christ, allowing Him to direct each and every area of our lives in the new year of 1971.

First and foremost this included our schools. As classes resumed following the Christmas break, we were enthused but apprehensive about practicing before peers our passionate brand of dedication to the Lord. This was especially true since we would find ourselves attending separate schools—three different mission fields from Robert's perspective—with few if any teenagers who shared the same level of purposeful devotion to following Jesus.

Added to our anxiety was a suggestion by Robert that involved the Good Book: he asked us to consider taking our Bibles to school. He proposed that we carry the scriptures with us as much as possible each school day, placing it with our textbooks and setting it upon our desks when attending class. Hiding it in phones or laptops was not an option in the technologically scrawny seventies.

We found the idea peculiar, though not surprising. We knew how much our pastor loved and valued God's Word. Next to Jesus, we assumed it was the most important thing in his life. In point of fact, it was impossible to think of Brother Robert without the Bible coming to mind. If he wasn't reading, teaching, or preaching from its pages, he was quoting its verses or consciously living by its wisdom. The initiative, strange as it seemed, was completely in keeping with his character.

There were also eminently practical reasons for Robert's unusual request. Taking our Bibles to school made a statement—without saying a word—about the seriousness of our discipleship. Seeing the Bible on top of our other books was a constant reminder to our own hearts of the lordship of Christ, while it also served as a bold witness to others regarding God's call upon their lives.

Wearing the Bible on my sleeve was an intimidating experience for a shy teenager. The first morning I walked into eleventh grade homeroom with the Holy Book under one arm was nerve-racking to the point of nausea. Though the inaugural junior class at Scott Prep numbered less than twenty, it felt like two hundred sets of eyes were watching my every move.

My stomach was in my throat as I took a customary seat toward the back end of the classroom. The green-jacketed King James Version I had owned for years fit inconspicuously under the bulky English composition and political science texts I used each morning. At the outset, no one seemed to notice the extra book I toted around from class to class. As the day wore on, however, it didn't escape the sharp-eyed attention of my chief spiritual nemesis and principal academic competitor, an immensely talented young woman named Julia Tatum.

Headmistress

My high school nemesis, the
exceptionally gifted Julia Tatum.

Julia, aptly dubbed "headmistress" by the editors of our senior class yearbook, was born into a prominent and affluent Opelika family, doubtless the source of her aristocratic ways. Self-assured, self-possessed, and self-designated as queen of our class—if not the whole dadgum school—Julia was an enormously engaging personality impossible to ignore. Tall, attractive, and brainy, she had few qualms about flaunting body, intellect, money, and charm in order to get what she wanted.

What Julia most wanted was adulation—she absolutely adored being adored. Naturally cocky, loud, and boisterous, she was automatically the star of every class, the life of every party. Ceaselessly she craved the spotlight, particularly when it shined upon a good time. Cyndi Lauper's musical mantra, "Girls Just Wanna Have Fun!" perfectly fit Julia. Recurrently naughty, risqué, and potty mouthed, when the Bible warns about the "lust of the flesh, the lust of the eyes, and the pride of life," Julia was unquestionably within its sights.

We were in chemistry class when Julia finally spied the extra volume in my collection of texts. Chemistry was taught by an Auburn University professor, Charles Neely, whose unstylish crew-cut and horned-rimmed glasses were a constant source of student derision. Dr. Neely often ran late, as he did on this particular afternoon, giving Julia the ideal opportunity to ferret out my buried treasure and bring it to everyone's attention.

"Jerry Ray! Is that a BIBLE you have there?" she called out in an incredulous tone, plenty loud enough for all to hear.

She proceeded to help herself to my green-covered edition of the scriptures, opening it up and checking it out, with a gaze of disbelief upon her face.

"What the hell are you doing with a Bible in chemistry class?"

By this time the other students were all starring at me with the same question, curious to know my answer. Unlike Julia, I hated being the center of attention, especially when put on the spot. Normally reserved and slow-witted, I had already compensated for my limitations by planning a rehearsed response. There had been little doubt that it would be Julia who discovered the Good Book, or that she would expose it in mocking, disparaging fashion.

"I need it to help me point out all your SINS, Julia!" I declared, with a sly grin upon my face.

To my great relief, Julia let out one of her patented ear-splitting cackles, and everyone else laughed and played along. She retorted that her sins were not all listed in the Bible, to which I heartily agreed. As Dr. Neely finally arrived, Julia placed the Bible on top of my other books as if it were a crown, a position it faithfully occupied for the remainder of my high school days.

Though our personalities clashed and we had different social and spiritual stations in life, over time Julia and I developed a healthy respect for one other, though never admitting it publicly. I greatly admired her many gifts and boundless zest for life. I often wished I could be as confident of my abilities and as gregarious in a crowd as she. I couldn't help but wonder how much good the Lord could accomplish through someone of her charisma, and privately prayed that He would get hold of her heart. In personal conversations Julia hinted of her own appreciation for my steady commitment to Christ. I knew she valued my academic ability, especially when I edged her out for valedictorian of our class.

Julia and I remained on opposite ends of the spiritual spectrum during our brief tenure at Scott. The religious dynamic became a familiar running gag anytime we were together: the sinner and the saint; the prodigal and the preacher; the "hello" and the halo. Julia egged it on far more than I, though I enjoyed playing along. It came to a celebrated climax not long before graduation.

Some fiendish soul hatched the impish idea of casting us as protagonists in our senior class play, a spoof of "Romeo and Juliet" cleverly re-titled "Jerreo and Juliaet." Written and staged by members of Mrs. Johann Kucik's Shakespeare class, the parody portrayed us as spiritually mismatched lovers. The main plot revolved around how I, with green Bible in hand, sought to convert Julia from her numerous devil-prone ways. In one memorable scene we embraced in a passionate kiss, evoking howls of laughter from our delighted audience. Yet as we looked into each other's eyes on that supremely awkward occasion, I distinctly recall seeing a measure of esteem that had been almost two years in the making.

****

After meeting on Mondays for a few weeks, Brother Robert suddenly proposed enlarging our circle by adding a fourth member to the group. The individual he had in mind was well known to us all—our good friend and Christian brother, Gary Dennis. Although Gary was not a member of Providence, Robert believed—and we heartily agreed—that commitment to the Lord was what mattered most in our venture, not church affiliation. Gary was probably more dedicated than any of us, so we unanimously approved our pastor's suggestion and invited him to join our little band, which he promptly accepted.

Evangelism was at the forefront of Robert's ministerial heart. Hence it wasn't long before he began to school us in the art of verbally witnessing to others about the Lord, with the goal of leading them to experience salvation. Soul winning, as it was called, was a time-honored method of propagating the faith, and Robert wanted to be sure his four charges knew how to go about it properly. He recognized that the best means of reaching young people for Christ was through the testimony of their peers.

Robert devoted three or four sessions to instructing us on the plan and rationale for Christian salvation, using the book of Romans—the so-called "Romans Road"—as his textbook. We memorized several verses of scripture that were especially applicable, and practiced sharing them with each other in a role-playing format. In addition, we rehearsed our personal testimonies of coming to faith in Christ as preparation for doing it with others outside the group. When we felt ready, Robert sent us out two-by-two into the community to give our witness.

Sometimes we went out witnessing at the conclusion of our meetings; on other occasions we met at an appointed time later in the week. Individuals we visited were often those for whom we had spent time praying. Robert frequently asked one or two of us to accompany him to the homes of our friends, where we helped encourage them in the Lord. Cold turkey or blind witnessing, as we called it, was more fun, if also more intimidating. That's when we'd go to a favorite spot— such as Midway Plaza, a popular shopping center in Opelika, or Pasqualles Pizza, a trendy college hangout in Auburn—to share the gospel and leave religious literature with strangers.

By the time February rolled around, we had been meeting together for two months but still had no specific name to identify who we were or what we were about. "Brother Robert's Monday night Bible study and prayer group" is basically how we referred to ourselves, having to pause to catch our breath each time somebody asked. Once Robert saw the earnestness of our commitment and the way God blessed our meetings, however, he began thinking seriously about an appropriate name. The discipleship group to which he had belonged as a young man in Dothan was known as "The Bible Lover's Club." Our meetings were more or less modeled after it, so there was precedent in his mind for a designation of some type.

It was Shirley who first suggested the name "Seekers" to Robert. She reasoned that we were each seeking to know the Lord better and to find His will for our lives. Robert liked her idea and found a verse in 1 Chronicles 16:11 that fit the name nicely, a text that perfectly summed up the purpose of our group: "Seek the Lord and His strength, seek His face continually." He soon presented the name and thematic verse for our consideration, and both were enthusiastically adopted. Henceforth, we would be known as "the Seekers."

Robert also proposed that each member pledge to abide by certain spiritual requirements that would give the group its special identity and keep it true to its original purpose of growing in discipleship. Again we agreed wholeheartedly with our pastor and waited for him to lay out the content of the organization's guiding principles. Instead, he wanted the group's founding members to formulate its standards, so over the course of two or three sessions we spelled out the terms of a Seekers covenant, aided enormously by Robert's gentle leadership and wise counsel.

Robert took our deliberations and produced a professionally printed contract in the form of a once-folded, three-by-five inch card that delineated the commitments of each group member. The blood red, four-sided card—a little thicker than the standard business variety—was intended to be signed by each disciple who joined the Seekers. The front of the card pictured a large red cross boldly outlined in black, with the name "The Seekers" printed above. Below the cross were the words from 1 Chronicles 16:11. On the card's back was written the plan of salvation in five sequential steps, with a verse of scripture accompanying each. Our church's name, address, and phone number were at the bottom.

The front of the Seekers covenant card.

The card opened on the inside to reveal the stipulations for becoming a member of the Seekers. Here is the exact wording:

"MY PERSONAL COVENANT"

As a member of "The Seekers" and recognizing that I belong to the Lord and out of gratitude to Him for all that He has done for me, I covenant, with His help, to strive to make the following things a vital part of my Christian life and daily living:
I will carry my Bible to school with me each day as a witness to my own heart and a strength for my own life and pray at the same time that it will be a witness for my Lord.
I will do my very best to attend all of the meetings of "The Seekers" unless I am providentially hindered from attending.
I will read the book "In His Steps" by Charles Shelton.
I promise to do my very best to visit and witness in a personal way for Christ each week.
I will do my very best to read my Bible daily and to pray for each member of "The Seekers" daily as well as other people.
I will be faithful in my attendance at the teaching, training, and worship services of my church.
I will seek to live before others that they will respect my religion.
I will seek to know the will of God in every time of decision.

Below the eight items to be pledged was a signature line found at the bottom right corner, with the biblical reference "Philippians 4:13" underneath. Robert solemnly cautioned us to be absolutely sure that we were willing to live up to these commitments before signing our cards. The three who had met together from the beginning signed right away. Gary was more deliberate, but soon he, too, put his signature on the covenant.

The Monday night group now had a name, a formal charter, an experienced leader, and four official members. The Seekers stood poised to expand their outreach and extend their influence for the Lord in Beauregard and beyond.

****

At the beginning of the new school semester in late January, two of the Seekers—Billy and Gary—had transferred from Beauregard High to Macon Academy. Their new educational home was located near Tuskegee, a distance of approximately twenty-five miles, prompting the formation of a carpool with other students in the area. One fellow commuter was a hot-shot jock from Opelika by the name of Jimmy Blanton.

Visually distinguished by jet-black hair and a delightfully goofy smile, Jimmy's appearance sometimes reminded me of a young Jerry Lewis. And like many of Lewis' early film characters, Jimmy was the kind of guy who was virtually impossible to dislike. Girls found his natural good looks, sports star status, and warm and fuzzy teddy bear persona irresistible. Male friends admired his athletic skills, folksy manner, and willingness to "shoot the breeze" with just about anyone.

Jimmy, known for his cheerful disposition and amiable smile.

Jimmy was currently a senior at Macon, having enrolled a year and a half earlier, not to avoid racial integration, but in an effort to raise his grade point average. With basketball his specialty, Jimmy set his sights squarely upon a college scholarship, but wanted better scores on his transcript to enhance his chances of receiving one. Ed and Joyce Blanton felt that the smaller classes and more individualized instruction of a private school would help their youngest child toward achieving his dream.

As a junior Jimmy was good enough on the court to captain the state all-star team, prompting several collegiate schools to send letters of interest. Hopes of competing on the next level were suddenly dashed, however, by a severe neck injury suffered during football practice prior to his senior year. Jimmy's round ball skills declined, colleges shied away, and no firm offers were forthcoming. Coaching basketball, rather than playing it, appeared to lie more in his future.

Jimmy was barely acquainted with his two newest schoolmates and traveling companions. Near the outset of their "rideshare" arrangement, Jimmy sat in his car and waited for Gary to arrive. When Gary pulled up and exited his vehicle, Jimmy immediately noticed a Bible on top of his books, but said nothing about it. They drove over to Billy's house, and Billy also climbed aboard with the Holy Scriptures perched aloft his stack of texts. Jimmy could not contain his curiosity any longer.

"Yawl forgive me, but would yawl mind telling me why yawl are taking yawl's Bible to school?" Jimmy loved the word "yawl," and possessed the Southern brogue to make it charmingly authentic. "Am I missing something, yawl?" he chuckled.

Gary and Billy laughed and explained that they were part of a new youth group at Providence and that one of the requirements was to carry their Bibles with them to school each day. Then they shared a little about their commitment to the Lord and invited him to come to church with them sometime.

Jimmy and his family were members of First Baptist, Opelika, but he had attended sporadically in recent years. A few months earlier a football buddy, Mike Rotten, had cornered him in the locker room and related how he met Jesus over the summer. That started Jimmy to thinking about his own relationship with the Lord, and now two new friends were sharing their spiritual testimony. He began to feel that he was missing something important in his life.

Over the course of the next several weeks, Gary and Billy continued their Christian witness to Jimmy.

Through their friendship he began attending Providence where he met Brother Robert and other members of the Seekers. He also came to a Monday night meeting and observed the unconditional commitment to Christ we shared. During the church's spring revival—Reverend John Rigby served as evangelist as he had two years previously when Billy became a Christian—Jimmy decided to transfer his church membership to Providence, even while harboring significant doubts about his soul's salvation.

On the same Sunday morning that Jimmy joined Providence, another young man stood with him at the altar. Tommy Hilyer was a sophomore attending Jimmy's old school, Opelika High. Slender in build and average in height, he sported a face full of freckles and a head adorned with puffy, afro-style hair. Tommy stood out in any crowd of teenagers as the least homogenous of the bunch. His appearance might be compared to a young Harpo Marx, with the flair and creativity to rival Groucho's older brother. In all probability, Tommy was the most multi-talented young person in Beauregard.

Tommy, debonair and multi-talented.

He arrived in the area by way of Huntsville and Birmingham, his father Horace and mother Blanche in the construction business. Through the years they experienced both boom and bust, with the latter their current economic situation. Hard times drove Horace to drink heavily, temporarily splitting apart the family of six, though recently he had stopped and they had reunited, settling in Opelika and looking for a fresh start. Monetary woes continued unabated, however, and they moved to Beauregard in late 1970 chasing cheaper quarters.

Part of Horace and Blanche's strategy to bring healing to their family was to attend church together, something they had rarely done. Shortly after arriving in Beauregard, they set out one Sunday morning to find a place of worship and happened upon Providence. Entering its doors for the first time was traumatic for Tommy. Wearing flashy bell bottom pants and a wild afro hairdo, the hip big city boy looked decidedly out of place among the rural church's young country bumpkins, none of whom he knew. He felt that every teenage eye in the building was sizing him up and putting him down. Following the service's final "Amen," he determined never again to set foot inside Providence.

A great deal of anger had built up in Tommy's fifteen year old soul, most of it directed toward his dad. In his mind it was Horace who was responsible for the constant chaos that surrounded his life. Tommy blamed him for the family's dire financial predicament, for moving them around through the years, and for bringing them now to a little ramshackle house in the backwoods community of Beauregard. The son wanted no part of his father's efforts to repair the damage of the past by insisting they go to church. Nonetheless, Tommy did return to Providence, albeit kicking and screaming, and even began attending our youth Sunday School class.

On a Monday night in late winter, following the Seekers meeting, Brother Robert asked Billy and me if we would accompany him to Tommy's house. We didn't know much about Tommy, but agreed that it would be a good opportunity to get to know him better and to witness for Christ. Upon arriving at the residence, we first noticed the house's unfinished features. There were no inside doors and little in the way of paint or trim. The landlord had agreed to rent the house at a reduced rate upon the condition that the Hilyers complete its interior construction.

As we sat down with Tommy's parents, we learned that Robert had been in their home before. After some small talk, our pastor mentioned that Billy and I were hoping to see their oldest son, and soon Tommy reluctantly joined us. Before we left, Robert took one of the newly printed Seekers cards and handed it to Tommy. He asked Billy to share a little about the Seekers, and then briefly went through the plan of salvation on the back of the card. After encouraging Tommy to continue attending Sunday School and other church activities, he asked me to end our visit with prayer.

This was the first time anyone had personally talked with Tommy about receiving Christ into his life, and it made a lasting impression. Blessed with natural intellectual acumen and curiosity, Tommy subsequently studied the card thoughtfully and considered seriously what was shared, deciding to reflect more deeply about spiritual things. He believed in God, but the image in his mind had been that of an angry, anti-authoritarian, pro-teenager sort of deity, not the God of the Bible. He believed in Jesus, but as a distant historical figure of the past, not as a living person with whom to have a relationship.

In the weeks ahead Tommy continued to attend Providence and undergo spiritual self-evaluation. "Am I a Christian or not?" was the pressing question for which he sought a definitive answer. The answer came during the early spring revival led by John Rigby. Horace insisted the family attend, and on the first two nights of the meetings, Tommy came to the conclusion that his belief in God was inadequate. He had not received Jesus Christ into his heart and could not call himself a Christian. Nevertheless, he resisted the invitation to salvation at the end of each service, holding tightly to the back of the pew in front of him.

On the revival's third night, Tommy came to church in a sour mood. He and his father had engaged in an animated confrontation beforehand. Tommy declared his intention to stay home and study for a biology test. Dad declared otherwise. In truth, biology was easy for Tommy and he wanted to attend the revival, but he was feeling particularly resentful toward his dad that evening and had no desire to sit with him in church. When Horace was adamant that everyone in the family must go, Tommy grew furious, taking his biology book along as a defiant symbol of antipathy. Stepping into the car, he loudly announced that he would probably fail the test the next day, and it would be entirely the fault of his father.

During the service Tommy sat on the same pew as his family, but as far away from dad as possible. With biology book in hand, he pretended to be studying, but his thoughts were actually far from science. While half-listening to the evangelist's sermon, he mostly reflected again upon the witness of Brother Robert, the testimony of the Seekers, the spiritual needs of his own soul, and the ugly relationship with his father. It was abundantly clear that he must invite Jesus into his life to become a Christian, and the urgency intensified as the revival service progressed toward conclusion.

The struggle within his soul was fiercest when the invitation hymn was sung. He felt that he was spiritually lost, without Christ, and bound for an eternity in Hell if he died that moment. Yet he understood that a decision for Christ would require treating his father differently, to forgive and seek forgiveness, and to forge a new relationship with someone he loathed more than loved. For many people, stepping out and taking the hand of Jesus is an easy thing to do. For Tommy, it meant a major transformation in the dynamics of his young life.

The divine tug on his heart proved too strong. Tommy found himself letting go of the resentment toward his dad, letting go of the pew ahead of him, and walking toward Brother Robert, who stood at the front of the sanctuary. There he prayed for Christ to enter his life, and became the newest believer in our youth group. Billy and I and others greeted him with a smile and a hug, as did his father and family. There were many miles to travel before father and son came to have the love and respect each desired, but reconciliation began that evening at Providence's altar.

As revival services concluded the following Sunday morning, Tommy again went down the center aisle to the front of the sanctuary, this time to publicly profess his new faith, and to request baptism and church membership. There he glad-handed Jimmy, and together they joined Providence on April 4, 1971. Soon they also joined the Seekers and helped direct the group's attention toward leading revival and missionary efforts of their very own.

****

Jimmy and Tommy were not the only new members of the Seekers that spring season. Other young people were personally invited to attend the meetings and sign the Seekers covenant. Robert's intention was for us to grow slowly but surely, while preserving the integrity of the group and maintaining its focus upon discipleship.

Following the spring revival, more and more youth expressed interest. Several young ladies began to come regularly, among them Judy Patterson—our fifth official member—Sharon Mayberry, Bonnie Parker, and my sister Vicki. The group was never meant to be an exclusive club, but a means of fostering commitment to Christ in the church and community.

The location and format of the meetings necessarily changed as the group expanded. Our sessions moved from Robert's small office to the church library, and from there to the sanctuary where we sat facing one another while reclining on the floor between pulpit and pew. Robert began our time together with several familiar praise choruses—"God is so Good," "He is Lord," "He's Everything to Me," and "Pass it On" were popular in our era—before leading us in Bible study and sentence prayer. At some point we were encouraged to share how the Lord was working in our lives and at our schools. A brief ceremony of signing the personal covenant was incorporated whenever someone decided to join. Our sessions concluded with the love circle commitment time.

One of Robert's signature events grew out of the Monday Seekers meetings, something he dubbed a "Witnessing Party." The idea came to him after hearing that a group of Auburn University students were promoting a beer party. This bothered Robert to such a degree that he told Shirley, "If they can have a party that's all about drinking beer, why can't we have one that's all about sharing Christ?"

The premise was simple. Young people love parties, so why not bring them together with food, music, and games for the purpose of testifying for Jesus? Robert enlisted Providence families to host these Friday or Saturday night gatherings in their homes, and tried to make sure the experience was fun. Word-of-mouth invitations were issued to church youth and teenage friends in the various schools. In the midst of the party, the music was halted and Robert asked everyone to sit around and give testimonies about what Jesus had done in their lives. Usually a couple of the Seekers took the lead. After sharing for a while, the food, music, and laughter started up again.

Robert's reasoning was crystal clear. Teenagers want to be together and have a good time. They love to converse, sharing their ideas and experiences. They also need the Lord in their lives to provide forgiveness, wisdom, and direction. In an era before cyber social media, Witnessing Parties served as supervised spiritual chat rooms, with stereos, Cokes, and pizza thrown in. They were an effort to keep Christian youth strong in the faith, as well as an opportunity to reach out to young people who were not involved in church.

Witnessing Parties were a big hit among the teen crowd in Beauregard. Before long, youth from other area churches joined in, giving us the chance to connect with Christian young people in the larger Auburn / Opelika community. The weekend socials also created wider interest in the Seekers movement, causing more and more youth to come and check out our weekly sessions. By the time Camp Ada beckoned in early June, thirty to forty young people were attending the Seekers meetings.

****

The eighth and final article of the Seekers covenant, "I will seek to know the will of God in every time of decision," rose to special prominence within our group in the late spring of 1971. It had been modeled after a similar commitment in the book *In His Steps,* and was intended to be our version of WWJD. Like the characters in Charles Shelton's famous novel, we resolved to take no decisive action without guidance from the Lord. For teenagers nearing the end of their high school days, perhaps the most significant decision we faced was the choice of a career.

Brother Robert was keenly aware of the issue's importance, and was careful to provide proper pastoral counsel. Robert believed there is a divine plan for each of our lives, something for which we are specifically gifted, and that the Lord reveals it to those who diligently seek Him. Our lives can never be as fulfilling and fruitful as the Lord intends, Robert taught, unless we find and submit to God's vocational will. He stressed that the Lord does not call every Christian to preach or to be a missionary, but that we should simply be open and obedient to His leadership.

It's not too much to say that discovering God's calling became an obsession for many of us. "What are we supposed to do for the rest of our earthly lives?" we asked. Or more correctly put, "What is *God* calling us to do?" As we pondered, explored, prayed, and sought divine direction, the final covenant promise made to the Lord when joining the Seekers turned out to be the most revolutionary of all.

For me, figuring out God's will in the matter of occupation did not come easily. During my junior year of high school, the career path I envisioned was pretty simple. Sports dominated my interests, and while not a particularly gifted athlete, my mind was as sharp as anyone's when it came to knowing the various professional and college teams, their players, and the vast array of statistics they produced. Surely God would use this ability, I reasoned, to bring Him glory as a sportscaster or sportswriter. But the Lord did not give me peace concerning this decision, and I continued to wrestle with it well into my senior year.

The member of the Seekers most immediately impacted by the issue of vocation and call was Jimmy, the only one in our inner circle about to graduate. His plans were to enroll at nearby Alexander City Community College and pursue a coaching career. When Jimmy began attending Providence and the Seekers, however, he started having second thoughts, unsure if this was the route God was leading.

There was, in fact, a more basic and important issue Jimmy felt compelled to address—doubts persisted about his salvation. As he listened to the Seekers share testimonies in our Monday meetings, at Witnessing Parties, and during Providence's worship services, he came to the realization that he had no testimony to share. There was not a time when he could recall encountering Christ in repentance and faith. He was baptized as a young child, but now questioned its validity. He had joined First Baptist and Providence, but the uncertainty lingered: had he joined Jesus?

On Sunday, May 9 Jimmy found himself walking the Providence church aisle again, little more than a month after becoming a member. It was the eve of the Auburn / Opelika Area Crusade for Christ, and evangelist Bill Sauer was in the Providence pulpit. Many churches like ours had spent months preparing for the county-wide spiritual emphasis, and the Seekers were assisting by publicizing it in the schools and agreeing to serve as counselors each night of the event.

At the conclusion of Sauer's sermon, Jimmy could not turn off an inner voice directing him to respond to the invitation. Brother Robert met him at the front of the sanctuary and inquired about the reason for his coming. Jimmy said that he didn't exactly know; he simply felt God's leadership and wanted to be obedient. Sensing his spiritual insecurity, Robert asked if he were sure of his salvation, to which Jimmy replied in the affirmative, despite his many doubts.

Upon returning home Jimmy fell on his knees in prayer and heard the Lord admonishing him to total honesty and transparency. Beside his bed the eighteen year old poured out his heart to God, confessing that he didn't really know whether he was saved or not. He had joined the church and been baptized, but drifted away for many years before recently returning. He didn't know what all this meant in terms of salvation, but he was certain that if he wasn't a Christian already, he wanted to be one now. At that moment, Jimmy decided to ask Christ to come into his life for sure.

In the midst of self-surrender, Jimmy believed he heard the inquiring voice of God's Spirit from deep within his soul. Was he willing to relinquish the attachments that were of highest importance to him— parents, siblings, friends, vehicle, money—in order to serve the Lord? As in the Gospels, when Jesus asked if His followers loved Him more than family, and on another occasion, if the rich young ruler were devoted more to God or to his wealth, the Lord began to assess the genuineness and strength of Jimmy's freshly-rendered commitment. Jimmy responded by stating that he was willing to lose everything, if necessary, for the sake of Christ.

Then, with immense anguish, he heard the Lord asking for the forbidden—his most cherished possession: "Jimmy, are you willing to give up your basketball?"

The teenager initially shook his head from side to side, replying with a barely audible "No." For most of his life, basketball had consumed his thoughts; it had always been his daily focus and the key to realizing his future dreams.

With unmistakable clarity, the Lord's rejoinder fell like a lead weight upon Jimmy's spiritual ears: "If I don't have your basketball, then I don't have your heart."

The words stung like a taser gun, and Jimmy's resistance was instantly broken. He immediately prayed with renewed fervor, "Okay God, take my basketball, take everything, it's all yours. I'm all yours!" That Sunday night Jimmy fully surrendered his heart to the Lord, and never doubted his salvation again.

As was the case with the Apostle Paul, it didn't take long following his conversion for Jimmy to discover what the Lord wanted him to do with his life. Scripture indicates that Paul met Christ on the Damascus road, and three or four days later began to hear the call to missionary work. Three days after Jimmy's salvation experience, God commissioned him to preach the gospel.

The call came during the Bill Sauer crusade at Duck Sanford Park in Auburn. Jimmy met several of us there and was excited to tell about the spiritual commitment he had made the previous evening. We rejoiced with him while waiting for the opening night's service to begin. The evangelist's assistant came by to make sure we had enough counseling materials to share with youth who made decisions. Noticing Jimmy sitting with us, he mentioned the need for additional counselors and asked if he could lead others to faith in Christ. The answer he received back was vintage Jimmy: "I can't, but Jesus can through me."

Jimmy took the literature, scanned it, and found inside the plan of salvation and a written prayer for accepting Christ. Billy, who had been through the training sessions for counselors, gave him a few tips on how to use the material. During the invitation time, Jimmy had the opportunity to share Christ with a young person who answered the altar call of the evangelist. On Tuesday night he led another inquirer to faith in the Lord, and Wednesday a fellow student from Macon Academy came down, whom Jimmy also helped to become a Christian.

Following the Wednesday night service, the Lord spoke to Jimmy about his future. After sharing Christ with people for three consecutive nights, God told him with utmost clarity, "This is what you will be doing for the rest of your life." On Sunday morning, May 16, Jimmy walked the center aisle at Providence for the third time in six weeks. On this occasion, he gave his heart to the gospel ministry.

Joining Jimmy at the altar once again was Tommy. The Lord had been dealing with him as well concerning call and ministry. One word kept reverberating through Tommy's mind each night of the crusade and especially during the time of decision—"missions." He had never talked to foreign missionaries nor been influenced in the past toward mission work. Yet the call he felt was very specific—the call of missions to distant lands, to go far away and share the gospel of Christ with those who have never heard.

Tommy's personality perfectly suited his sense of call. He's the kind of person who looks down from an airplane with dismay that there are so many people and places he will never get to know. Inherently adventuresome and gregarious, wanting to travel and see new faces, the opportunity to do so in the name of Christ and for the purpose of introducing Him to others was a natural extension of his God-given identity. Standing beside Jimmy, Tommy announced to the congregation his surrender to missionary service.

Billy, too, arrived at Providence's altar the third Sunday morning in May. While serving as a counselor at the crusade, he had come under conviction about submitting his life more fully to God's will. Following the crusade's final service, he, Gary, Tommy, and Brother Robert were at the church sharing and praying together. Later Billy went upstairs to a small Sunday School room to pray alone. There he gave his basketball and football aspirations to the Lord and unconditionally surrendered to follow whatever path God had chosen for him. Having made a deeper commitment, he walked the church aisle two days later to voice his decision publicly.

In point of fact, Billy was already sensing God's call to the ministry. Unlike Jimmy and Tommy, however, he struggled at length with the issue, increasingly feeling the Lord's summons to preach, but reluctant to let go of long-held ambitions and perceptions of inadequacy. Over the course of the next month, Billy spent a lot of time in prayer and in private conversation with Robert, who believed God's ministerial call was upon the young man. "God will show you what He wants you to do if you keep seeking Him," was the pastor's oft-repeated advice to Frank and Frances' eldest son.

The theme of Providence's annual youth camp in June was "Living in the Spirit," and it was here that Billy clearly perceived the Spirit leading him to be a pastor. Among other leadership responsibilities, he spoke at the week's worship services, feeling a tremendous peace while in the pulpit. He returned home from Camp Ada knowing the Lord's will, but hesitant to answer the call. Robert came back to Beauregard with Billy heavy upon his heart, earnestly praying that God would have His way.

A week after camp Robert was unsettled about what to preach on the next to last Sunday of June. What could he say to help Billy—and others like him—step out on faith and follow the Lord's beck and call? Normally he didn't preach with a particular person in mind, but this proved the exception. He rummaged through old sermons to see if any stood out as one God could especially use at this pivotal moment. He finally settled on a message entitled simply, "Follow Me," and as he prayed over it, his thoughts returned time and again to Billy and his struggle. Robert then did something atypical before stepping into the pulpit. Across the top of the sermon he wrote the words, "Preach this for Billy."

As Robert preached that Sunday morning, in the pews sat Billy, listening intently and hearing the echo of his pastor's message resonate throughout his soul: "Follow Me! Follow Me!" When Robert extended the invitation at the sermon's conclusion, Billy knew what he must do. Turning to Tommy, he entreated his new friend, "Pray for me, please, because I'm really struggling. I know what I need to do, but I'm scared to do it." Tommy prayed for Billy. Robert prayed for Billy. Many of the Seekers were praying for him that day. And before the last stanza of the hymn was sung, Billy stepped out, telling Robert and Providence that God was calling him to preach the gospel.

During the same spring season, God was also dealing with a fourth member of the Seekers about the call to ministry. Beginning with the April revival at Providence, and continuing through the Bill Sauer crusade in May and Camp Ada in June, Gary increasingly sensed the Lord leading him to make a commitment to preach. But as was the case with Billy, he didn't want to do it.

He had no desire to be a preacher. Like Jimmy and Billy, he wanted to be an athlete. Wouldn't it be enough, he pleaded, to play sports for a living and give his Christian testimony? Or couldn't he coach and influence kids for Christ? In his mind, with the notable exception of Brother Robert, preachers were stereo-typed as sanctimonious do-gooders—men who wore stiff suits, hollered behind the pulpit, and buried the dead. That definitely was not Gary.

Yet as he sat in the congregation at the John Rigby revival, he felt profoundly convicted that God wanted him to be a preacher. His mind drifted back to the time his mom dedicated him to the Lord when he survived the peanut incident as a baby. And to when he was twelve and promised the Lord that he would do anything—even be a missionary—if his mom lived through her crisis with ulcers. Now, on the threshold of age seventeen, though the Lord was not necessarily calling him to mission work in Africa, he was quite sure God wanted him to minister the gospel somewhere.

At first Gary denied it. He went forward during the Providence revival, telling Brother Robert that he thought God was calling him to be a recreational minister. Robert may well have never heard of that call, but he told Gary he would pray with him about it anyway. Pastor Schoonhoven at Liberty also asked if the Lord was calling him to preach. Gary's voice said "No," even as his heart responded with confirmation. The more he balked, the louder God's call sounded: "I want you to preach my Word, Gary."

At Camp Ada the divine voice became deafening. This was his third youth retreat under Robert, and on Wednesday morning he was scheduled to deliver the message during morning worship. The words he planned to share concerned total commitment to the Lord. Before the service Gary went away by himself, bent down on his knees, and prayed, "Lord, I can't ask others to do what

I'm not willing to do myself. If you want me to preach, I'll do it. If you'll just make it clear that this is what you really want me to do with my life, I'll do it." He then got up and proceeded to share the message God had put upon his heart.

That evening around the campfire service, Gary found sufficient clarity concerning God's will. The spiritual pressure that had been building inside his heart swelled to the breaking point. He felt the time had come to make a decision, and he chose to move in the direction he believed God was leading. In the warm glow of the beach bonfire, Gary announced to the group that he was answering God's call to be a lifelong preacher of the gospel.

Later that night Gary walked out onto one of the sandbars of Santa Rosa Sound and asked the Lord to give him a way of capturing the moment—some heavenly signal that would forever denote the reality of his call to preach. He looked up into the star-laden sky and observed the biggest, brightest full moon he had ever seen, as if it were smiling back at him from across the water. To his soul, this was the Lord's reply. Like the rainbow in Genesis, every glimpse of a radiant full moon serves as Gary's divine reminder of the personal covenant he made with God on June 9, 1971, the day of his surrender to the Christian ministry.

One by one, Jimmy, Tommy, Billy, and Gary publicly answered the call to vocational ministry, all within about a month of each other. The quartet's individual commitments to spend their lives in the service of Christ provided the springboard for a collective new ministry involving the Seekers, a ministry that soon took

the group to numerous churches and communities to share
the gospel.

****

The most exciting part of our messianic age
occurred during my senior year of high school and the
two summers surrounding it. The Seekers blossomed into
full bloom with anywhere from thirty to a hundred youth
attending the Monday meetings, many signing the
covenant to seek the Lord and His will for their lives.
Numerous young people in the Auburn / Opelika area
committed themselves to Christ through our witness, and
God continued to call individuals into full-time Christian
ministry. Spiritual electricity pervaded our group,
charging us with fervor for the Lord and sparking us to
share Him with others.

Following the rousing Camp Ada experience of
1971, the Lord gave Robert an ambitious vision for
reaching other communities for Christ through the
Seekers. Like the biblical church at Antioch that sent
Paul and Barnabas to evangelize the Roman world,
Robert felt impressed to send us out from Providence to
share our faith with neighboring churches and towns.
Soon a revival ministry was born.

The Lord had already called enough preachers to
serve as evangelists for the undertaking. It was not
Robert's intention that his young charges learn to
sermonize by sitting in a classroom or reading from a
textbook. He wanted us to gain immediate firsthand
experience in the laboratory of the church. Therefore

Jimmy, Gary, Billy, Tommy, and I—months before I answered the call—were promptly ushered to the front of congregations small and large, with Bible in hand and a message on our hearts. We may not have known the methodologies of biblical hermeneutics or the intricacies of systematic theology, but we knew what God had done for us, and in Robert's mind that was good enough to preach the gospel.

Gary, Billy, Jimmy, me, and Tommy,
all lined up and ready to preach.

We were also blessed with a large Providence youth choir available to provide music for the revival services. Complementing them was a new female ensemble from Opelika known as "the Messengers." Consisting of five young ladies who loved the Lord and sang for His glory, the Messengers had formed the previous December at approximately the same time as the Seekers. It was as if the Lord had led both groups to begin in order to link up for ministry later on. Sisters Kathy and Debra Gore, along with good friends Debbie McCollum, Ann Parish, and Carol Spivey, sang at the first

Seekers revival, and the quintet accompanied us to numerous churches thereafter sharing the Word through song. Their signature selection, "He Touched Me," repeatedly inspired reflection about the wonder and joy of God's salvation.

The Messengers quintet sang at many of the early Seekers revivals.

In addition to preachers and singers, plenty of young people were available to share their testimonies, offer moral and prayer support, and help out with logistics. With all this in mind, Robert set up a series of youth revivals at various churches in Alabama and adjoining states. Over the course of the next fourteen months, the Seekers would conduct exactly twenty-five revivals, with many more in the years to follow.

Most were weekend engagements. We swooped into town—often on the Old Blue Goose—late on a Friday afternoon, spent the next fifty hours there, and hoped to have the whole community converted and committed to the Lord by the time we left on Sunday night. Some of us remained the entire weekend, residing in the homes of church members. The choir and others joined as much as possible, usually the first two nights of the weekend and during the day on Saturday.

Four worship services comprised the weekend's feature attraction, but other events were also scheduled for the purpose of fostering spiritual renewal. A social after the Friday night service allowed us to meet and greet the youth of the church. On Saturdays we went out into the community to publicize the revival and invite folks to attend. Sometimes a Saturday or Sunday luncheon was incorporated into the itinerary. A highlight of our short stay was the Witnessing Party that followed the Saturday evening service. On Sunday mornings we often taught Sunday School to the youth and adult classes. Special times of prayer for the revival were also included throughout the weekend.

Among the Seekers, those serving as evangelists were the spiritual leaders of the revivals. Although we were known collectively as "the preacherboys," none of us had any experience delivering a formal sermon. Putting together a gospel message from scratch, therefore, presented quite a challenge. Our sermons were supposed to be the focal point of each revival service, yet we hardly had a clue regarding how to craft them. As with everything else that had to do with ministry, we looked to Brother Robert for guidance.

Our pastor recognized how daunting the task appeared to greenhorn teenagers, and decided to take us down to his favorite Christian book store, the Alabama Bible Society in downtown Montgomery, for help. There we were shown numerous volumes filled with sermon starters, biblical outlines, and pulpit manuscripts. We also found several books of sermon illustrations available for purchase.

"So this is how preachers come up with all their sermons!" I recall thinking to myself, with no small measure of relief. A major issue, as I pondered the call to preach, was how a person of relatively few words could generate all the things a preacher has to say during a thirty minute monologue.

Brother Robert also offered his example of how to deliver a sermon. We noticed that he didn't preach extemporaneously, but typed out his messages in manuscript form, taking them into the pulpit along with his Bible. Yet in the act of preaching, he was careful to maintain eye contact with the congregation while sneaking peaks at his notes.

To do this well, Robert told us he rehearsed his sermons before delivering them, and encouraged us to do the same. "Fellows, go find a wall somewhere and practice preaching to it. And try to look at a picture or a particular object on it as much as possible," he counseled. We took his advice, preaching to the walls before ascending the pulpit to preach to people. Remembering some of our early sermons, no doubt the hearing-deprived walls got the better end of that deal.

Our first three revivals were held in July, part of a three weekend religious blitz sponsored by the Seekers and a new organization in the area, the Lee County Youth for Christ. The latter group formed in response to the recent Bill Sauer Crusade as a means of fostering Christian growth and ministry among teenagers in our county. Jimmy served as its first president, and many of the Seekers made up its leadership team and membership.

Appropriately enough, Providence was selected to host the initial Seekers revival that took place July 9-11, with Jimmy, Gary, and Billy preaching and the Messengers providing special music. Tommy and I shared our testimonies, the Providence youth choir sang at each service, and young people from across the county attended the weekend rally, as well as the next two held at Northside and Liberty churches, respectively.

As the preacherboys alternated serving as evangelists at these and other revivals, it quickly became apparent that each of us had our own distinctive style of delivering God's Word. It was amazing to see how the Lord took individual personalities, gifts, and mannerisms and molded us into unique heralds of the gospel.

Jimmy, the eldest in our little band, was perhaps the most enthusiastic about preaching. So eager to preach was Jimmy that he sometimes protested—in good-natured fashion—when left off the preaching roster. "Now if any of yawl get to feeling bad and need me to preach instead, yawl be sure and let me know. I've got a real good sermon all ready to go," was the way he politely voiced his objection.

Sometimes Jimmy went ahead and preached anyway, though not at the revival. On more than one occasion those rooming with him were awakened from sound slumber by the long-after-midnight sounds of Jimmy quoting scripture and sermonizing in his sleep. Afterward we told him that that's when he did his best preaching! "But what's the big idea," we needled, "of keeping us awake all night with your sermons while putting everybody at church to sleep with them?"

A favorite message Jimmy shared in the revivals became known as his "Fried Chicken Sermon." It had the double effect of saving souls and whetting appetites at the same time. When Jimmy was growing up along U.S. 280 in Opelika, the Pines Restaurant was located just below his house. He often ate there, and the manager, Mrs. Porter, treated him like family. She'd see Jimmy enter and automatically know what he wanted—a heaping plate full of fried chicken, with potatoes and a biscuit thrown in.

One day Mrs. Porter brought out his usual order. As Jimmy eagerly reached down to pick up the chicken and take his first bite, it was so hot that his fingers were instantly burned. He let out a howl loud enough to startle neighboring diners. Later he managed to find a spiritual lesson in the painful experience.

"Even though that fried chicken was hot enough to hurt me," preached Jimmy, "I wouldn't let go because it looked and smelled so good, and I wanted it so bad. That's the way sin is, yawl! It'll look good and taste good, but then it'll burn you! And all it'll leave you with is a plate full of bones, some burned fingers, and a scorched tongue."

We all nodded in agreement and voiced our "Amen!" with souls hungry for God and mouths watering for some of Mrs. Porter's yummy fried chicken.

Jimmy loved to sing almost as much as he loved to preach and eat. The problem was, like Barney Fife and Lucy Ricardo, Jimmy's ability to carry a tune left a lot to be desired. This hit home once when he was preaching at a revival service and his father Ed—a big bear of a man, who possessed a pleasant singing voice and regularly used it for the Lord—was present. As the service concluded after his sermon, Jimmy decided spontaneously to sing along with the Messengers, who were providing a few encore numbers to their earlier performance.

When they finished singing, Big Ed came up to Jimmy and gave his biological offspring some fatherly advice. "Son," he counseled, "I think you'd better stick to preaching, because take it from me—you ain't much of a singer. In fact, you sing like you're in prison—always behind a few bars and can't find the key!" Jimmy wisely followed his father's guidance, but has long looked forward to someday singing in the heavenly choir—where he expects to croon right alongside his old man.

Gary's homiletical style was no less earnest than Jimmy's. He, too, preached with conviction and passion, although his pulpit career commenced rather shakily. As Gary prepared to deliver his first formal sermon, he was scared to death. Dressed in suit and tie with Bible in hand, knees knocking and voice cracking, his debut at Providence's July youth revival lasted all of twelve minutes.

Self-doubt troubled his young soul prior to a second scheduled sermon at Opelika's Northside Baptist Church. As he sat upon the platform before the Sunday morning service, Gary stared out at the packed congregation and observed several rows of young people sitting in the back, giggling and laughing and cutting up. In his insecurity he wondered if they were snickering at him. After all, who did he think he was parading around like a preacher? He was no better than any of them, so why should they bother to listen to his message?

As Gary's mind raced with uncertainty, he silently began to pray. "Lord, I need your help now. If I'm up here on my own, then show me. But if you are in this, please let me know. Confirm it to me somehow."

With no full moon to encourage him, he decided to take his Bible and thumb through it, seeking a timely word from the Lord. His eyes landed upon Jeremiah 1:4: "Before I formed you in the womb, I knew you and called you." It was exactly the validation he needed. Reassured of God's will for his life, Gary proceeded to deliver the sermon that morning, and never again doubted the call of God to preach the gospel.

Unlike Jimmy, Gary never quite looked the part of a preacher. A handsomely rugged, backwoods kind of guy, strong and tough and hardworking, he appeared largely out of place in coat and tie. He made up for it with a deep, forceful voice that resonated well in the pulpit, lending a ring of authority to what he had to say. He was aided by a natural gift for leadership, combined with a heart full of compassion for people.

Gary was probably the most cerebral of the preacherboys, his sermons usually thoughtful and creative with a tendency toward boldness. It wasn't long before he acquired the reputation of being something of a maverick in the pulpit. During our fourth Seekers revival, at First Baptist Church of Wetumpka, Gary was tapped to preach at the opening night's service. There were not a lot of folks in attendance, and the spirit of worship was decidedly unenthusiastic. Despite this, Gary preached fervently on the topic of the Second Coming of Christ. It felt like he was talking to a pile of rocks.

At the end of the sermon, he gave the invitation but saw no one respond. He decided he'd seen enough. As the invitation hymn continued, midway through the third or fourth verse, Gary suddenly hollered out, "Stop! Stop the music!"

It's a wonder the song leader and pianist didn't drop their hymnals. They and the congregation let out a collective gasp. What was this brash, inexperienced teenage preacher doing?

"Let's just stop the invitation right now!" shouted Gary. Once there was silence, he looked around at the audience and continued. "That's how it's going to be, folks, when Jesus comes back—just as unexpected, just as sudden. You'll be sitting there like a knot on a log and suddenly He'll return. And when Christ comes, it'll all be over! Just like this invitation is over!" With that Gary promptly walked off the platform and out of the sanctuary, leaving everyone stunned at the abrupt conclusion to the service.

He didn't stay gone long, however. In a few seconds Gary arrived back in the pulpit, looked out at the pews, and declared, "I was wrong, people. The invitation to come to Christ is never over until Jesus returns. You've still got time to commit yourself to Him tonight." We started singing again, and individuals slowly began to trickle down the church aisles. The attitude of indifference that had hung over the service gradually dissipated. There was movement toward the Lord that night and throughout the remainder of the revival.

The Lord would use Gary's occasionally unconventional tactics to challenge lukewarm congregations. More than anything, he simply sought to elevate their spiritual temperatures. The authenticity of his walk with God and consistently convivial manner also enabled his sermons to be received by his Seekers colleagues as inspirational calls to greater Christian service.

Billy likewise developed a characteristic preaching personality. Fast, furious, and effusive might sum up his early pulpit style. From the moment Billy opened up the Bible before a congregation, his preaching motor ran wide open, seldom slowing down.

His first sermon, entitled "The Abrahamic Faith," typified what became his trademark fast-paced delivery. In the audience sat Joe White, our agriculture teacher and FFA sponsor at Beauregard, a man much beloved by his students and a long-time pillar of Providence church. After listening to Billy's initial full-throttle oration, he came up to his former pupil and attempted to pay him a compliment—sort of.

"That was a pretty good message, son," intoned Mr. White, "what I could understand of it."

Compounding our old teacher's difficulty in processing the excess of words was Billy's tendency to stutter when he became overly excited. Since Billy loved sharing about the Lord, stammering occurred not infrequently during his sermons, adding to their verbosity and the amount of time it took to deliver them. A nervous habit of punctuating the conclusion of sentences with the catchphrase "and everything" extended their length even more.

Billy was what we called a "marathon preacher." His sermons were of the cat's tail variety—"fur to the end." If he preached less than an hour, we figured we'd gotten out of church early. It wasn't that he intentionally meant to be long-winded; if that were the case, we would have been greatly annoyed. Rather, Billy found so much in the Bible to talk about that he genuinely couldn't help himself.

A loquacious pattern also held true whenever he testified or engaged in prayer. No one wanted to preach when Billy was on the docket to give his testimony. He could easily go on for half an hour, and inevitably took the opportunity to get in some preaching of his own. By the time one of us stood up to deliver the main sermon, the audience was ready to sing the closing hymn and go home.

Sometimes Billy's penchant for lengthy prayers made us late for the revival services. Our custom was for the preacherboys to pray together in the pastor's office a few minutes prior to entering the sanctuary. We always wanted Billy to pray first so the rest of us could peak at our watches and know how much time was left to pray. If it was Billy's turn to preach, he especially liked to pray long, and there might not be enough time for the rest of us to voice our petitions. That was alright; we knew and admired how much Billy loved the Lord. We were happy to let him do most of the praying.

At one revival, however, some of us were kneeling and waiting for Billy to finish his prayer when suddenly he began to scratch his legs, then his thighs and buttocks. He finally concluded his petitions with a hasty "Amen," and informed us that he thought there were ants in his pants! Sure enough, we looked closely and the little critters were crawling all around where Billy had been kneeling.

He quickly removed his trousers and swatted the ants away as best he could, before re-dressing and hurrying into the sanctuary and up to the platform. During the service he continued to scratch away as inconspicuously as possible, and to our great delight, preached one of his shortest sermons ever. From that day forward, whenever Billy waxed too long for our comfort level, we threatened to fill his britches with itches of the vermin variety.

Billy was usually the sharpest dresser among the preacherboys. The tan blazer, dark pants, and red silk tie he liked to wear in the pulpit richly complimented his handsome blonde appearance. The preaching jacket he preferred was made of wool fabric and accented with blue and brown stripes, a gift from an anonymous benefactor. He had unexpectedly received a call from Duke's clothing store in downtown Opelika inviting him to pick out a free coat. The light colored, thirty-nine inch long soon became Billy's favorite, not least because it could be readily mixed and matched with several pairs of pants—blue, brown, or even black.

Some of us vainly attempted to keep up with Billy's pulpit apparel. Not to be outdone, on my eighteenth birthday I asked my parents for a new preaching outfit. They obliged and mama took me down to J. C. Penny's at Midway Plaza, allowing me to choose from among their extensive collection of trendy coats and pants. To her horror I chose a hot pink polyester suit that nearly glowed in the dark. To compliment it, I insisted on purchasing matching pink and white tie, wide-brimmed white belt, pink socks, and white Pat Boone style shoes—the kind of accessories all the rage in the sickly seventies.

Today, of course, I share my mother's dismay at the pungent pink attire I loved to sport at many of our revivals. It accomplished its purpose, causing me to stand out and making me feel special—not exactly Christ-like marks of humility and service. I'm mollified somewhat by the kookiness of fashion in general during that iconoclastic decade, and by the knowledge that I wasn't unaccompanied in the wild wardrobe I wore.

I still possess the gaudy pink suit, hidden away deep within the recesses of a remote home closet. Though it's now a struggle to fit into, on occasion I don the formerly avant-garde jacket when teaching ministerial classes. For my students, it allows them to see that their typically straight-laced Bible professor was once young and zany and spiritually immature. For me, however, the funny pink garb stirs up fond, if embarrassing, memories of our messianic age.

****

Tommy and I rounded out the quintet of young men who served as primary evangelists for the early Seekers revivals. We accepted the role reluctantly. Unlike Jimmy, Gary, and Billy, neither of us had answered the call to preach. Tommy felt led to do mission work, and much preferred sharing his testimony or doing one-on-one witnessing. I wasn't yet sure what the Lord wanted for my life, but initially felt more comfortable leading the Witnessing Parties or working behind the scenes.

It was a struggle for us to come up with sermons for the services. When Tommy found a book of homilies by Charles Haddon Spurgeon, the famous nineteenth century London preacher, he started committing some of them to memory. Having no experience preaching and comparatively little biblical knowledge, and feeling overwhelmed by the challenge of delivering a formal sermon, Tommy began using Spurgeon's messages in the pulpit.

This perturbed Jimmy, who worked hard at crafting his sermons. There weren't many incidents of friction among the preacherboys, but Tommy's verbatim use of Spurgeon proved an exception, causing Jimmy to voice a complaint to Brother Robert. To Jimmy's surprise, Robert took up for Tommy, defending his pulpit practice.

"Jimmy," explained our pastor, "if Spurgeon hadn't wanted his sermons to be preached by others, he wouldn't have published them in a book. He wrote them to be preached, and whether it's him or Tommy or someone else is not really important. What's important is that God's Word is shared, and that people hear it and are blessed by it." Robert's answer pacified Jimmy, who promptly began using some of Spurgeon in his own sermons.

The first sermon I delivered was during our third Seekers revival on July 25, 1971 at Liberty Baptist Church. I guess it's fitting that the church of my childhood should host my inaugural pulpit experience. The white-frame building with its cozy sanctuary was comfortably familiar. Many of the congregants were the same as in years past, including my grandmother and Gary's parents. Happily, the old outhouse I abhorred as a boy had given way to more modern facilities.

The Lord's house where I first heard the gospel from Reverend Land now offered the opportunity to stand where he stood and share what he shared. I don't recall being excessively nervous on that Sunday evening. I preached a message on the Ten Commandments, going over each in turn. I still have the faded manuscript, typed out decades earlier on a manual typewriter in black and red colored ink. No doubt I borrowed many of its points and illustrations from a book or two on the topic, though none of it reads like Spurgeon.

There was nothing I recall that was especially noteworthy about the sermon or the worship service. Some said I mixed up the seventh commandment, declaring, "Thou shalt not *admit* adultery," but I'm fairly sure they were just giving me the business. I do remember feeling an unexpected sense of ease and delight while preaching, resulting in more openness to God's call in that direction.

Early August found us in Wetumpka, a small town of about five thousand located fifteen miles north of Montgomery. Shelton Harden, our former minister of music at Providence, now held the same position at Wetumpka's First Baptist Church, and invited us to lead their youth in revival. We nearly missed the first service—the Old Blue Goose expiring in route, a broken fan belt waylaying us on the side of the road. Fortunately, Wetumpka was close enough to find substitute transportation and make it there on time.

When we arrived, the church felt like an iceberg, with little enthusiasm for revival among youth or adults. Fairly or unfairly, several churches we visited seemed that way, perhaps because we were so used to the highly charged spiritual atmosphere of Providence and the Seekers meetings. It was here that Gary scolded the audience for their unresponsiveness after his sermon, at one point marching off the platform in frustration before returning to the pulpit.

The next afternoon we were lounging around our host's home, talking among ourselves and waiting to be served a meal before heading to church for the Saturday evening service. Noticing some periodicals stacked neatly on a bookshelf, Gary picked up a few and began looking for one that interested him. Suddenly he let out an audible gasp. In his possession was an issue of Playboy magazine! He held it up for the rest of us to see, with the sardonic comment that it might partially explain the church's lackluster spiritual condition. In shock, we all agreed—while trying not to stare too eagerly at the scantily clad woman on the cover.

Gary must have gazed upon the Playboy bunny a little too long, for later that night he felt a bit more flirtatious than usual. He was staying with a family who had an attractive and engaging teenage daughter. She came to the bedroom that Gary and Jimmy shared and innocently asked if there was anything more they needed before going to sleep. Gary playfully responded there was, that the Bible says we should all "greet one another with a holy kiss," and she had neglected her Christian duty. Taking the hint, she promptly came over and planted a wet one upon his cheek, before turning around and heading out the door!

Gary was probably the most amorous among the preacherboys, though in late adolescence we were all on the lookout for love. The prep stars among us had no problem keeping steady girlfriends. Jimmy and Billy were dating Macon Academy coeds; Gary's sweetheart was Joe and Jo White's daughter, Carol, also a member of the Seekers. Tommy and I were mostly left to dream about attracting such angelic beauties, and to pray that God would look down from heaven with sympathy upon our lonely plights.

I felt the Lord had answered my prayers and sent the girl of my dreams when I hit it off with a young Dixie darling named Pam Whitley. Pam was a year younger, and the prettiest girl my eyes had ever seen. Trim and well-built, she possessed long shimmering brown hair, eyes that sparkled, and a smile that made my heart flutter. If love is to be measured by physical attraction, it was love at the first sight of Pam. We met during the second Seekers revival at Northside where she attended with her grandparents, with whom she also lived. Her perky personality and love for Jesus made Pam stand out among her church's youth, and soon she began attending the Seekers meetings.

Over the course of the following year, we got to know each other and began dating. I was in heaven with Pam by my side and was sure it would be that way forever. We dated on into my freshman year at Mobile College, and I returned home to Beauregard as often as possible in order to be with her. The four hour drive each way was well worth it to look into her vibrant eyes, hear her soft voice, and taste her moist lips.

On Friday, February 9, 1973, I left Mobile under the strangest wintry weather conditions anyone could ever recall in Alabama. Heavy snow was falling, and the forecast was for much more. Mama advised me on the phone not to make the trip, that it would be too dangerous traveling in the hazardous road conditions, especially for someone with zero experience driving in them. Snow, of course, is a rarity in central and southern Alabama. I probably hadn't seen more than three or four inches my entire life, and could not fathom a snowfall keeping me from embracing my one true love.

I took off heading north up Interstate 65 on my journey home to see Pam. The green Chevrolet Nova I was driving hadn't made it past Atmore's exit when the snow accumulation, falling temperatures, and icy surroundings caused me to think twice about my decision. The highway was a slushy mess, with a single lane of traffic crawling along at no more than thirty miles per hour. Snowflakes fell profusely upon my windshield, making vision difficult. Cars and trucks were slipping and sliding all over the place, many of them ending up in the median or ditch. I briefly entertained the notion of turning back toward Mobile, but quickly scuttled the thought. I wanted to see Pam!

The four hour trip took almost twelve, and by God's grace I somehow chugged into Opelika a little before midnight. The snow was still coming down. The total accumulation, I later learned, reached fourteen inches in the region, a new record by far. It had been a tedious, tortuous, scary marathon in my little Nova. I must have glimpsed a hundred stalled or wrecked vehicles along the way. Now, finally, I was heading down Highway 37 and into Beauregard, only a few minutes from home. It was too late to visit Pam that Friday night, but I'd see her the next day, and she'd know how very much I loved her.

Life has a way of laughing at you, and I guess it's best to laugh along with it. Only three hundred yards from my parent's house, I lost control of the Chevy and landed squarely in a ditch near the driveway of my old place of worship, Pierce Chapel United Methodist Church. Maybe the joke was on me, sort of a divine spanking for foolishly making such a dangerous trek. But I also saw the loving hand of the Lord at work. Instead of being stranded in the freezing cold in the middle of nowhere during the "Blizzard of '73," I was able to get out of my car and walk the short distance home, where my worried parents welcomed me at the front door.

The next morning we managed to maneuver my car out of the ditch, and Saturday afternoon I carefully drove over to Pam's house, hoping not to add to the total of 327 traffic accidents reported in the east Alabama area over that historic weekend. While there, her grandfather suddenly experienced severe chest pains. Pam and I frantically helped him into my Nova, raced through the icy streets of Opelika, across the slippery Second Avenue Bridge, and on to the Lee County Hospital. There he received the medical attention needed to survive the onset of a heart attack. Maybe, I concluded, God wanted me to come home after all.

Pam must not have been too impressed with my wintertime gallantry. A few weeks later there arrived devastating news: she wanted to date other guys. She tried to let me down easy, but it absolutely ripped out my heart. It took a long while to get over the first girl I ever truly loved. I dated others in college, but none matched the intensity of devotion I always felt for Pam.

It's amazing, looking back, that there was never a hint of scandal among the preacherboys or the early members of the Seekers. Almost all of us were in our mid-to-late teens, and the hormones were definitely raging. Perhaps there were shenanigans going on behind the scenes, but I was never aware of it. There were no pregnancies, no sexual rumors, no lurid conversations, no instances of moral impropriety that I or others in my field of friends can recall.

This was truly remarkable in such a large group of teenagers, especially given the amount of time we spent together and the number of overnight trips we took. The different era in which we lived may serve as partial explanation. The decade of the seventies, while relatively relaxed in its sexual mores', did not provide the widespread and easily accessible exposure to pornography and sex that media do today.

Still, I think there are more obvious reasons for the integrity maintained among the Seekers during those early years. The close relationship we shared with the Lord through prayer and Bible study directed our attitudes and actions away from promiscuity. And the deep respect we felt for one another and for Brother Robert served as powerful motivations to keep our hormones in check.

Robert made it a point to talk to us—sometimes in the Seekers meetings, more often in smaller group settings or individually—about the vital importance of preserving our purity. Too often, he cautioned, Christian young people and adults allow the devil to gain a foothold in this area of their lives and are led down the path of ruin. Sexual sin did not disqualify us from salvation, he taught, but stained our character and cheapened our witness, and would surely bring disrepute upon the Seekers.

Pam and I heeded his counsel, as did the other young couples in our close-knit circle of the committed. As with Jesus and the earliest disciples, chastity was a cardinal virtue of our messianic age.

****

Society Hill, near Tuskegee, beckoned next, the Baptist church hosting us for the fifth Seekers revival August 13-15. Their pastor, George Husky, was a good friend of Robert's. Two things stand out about our weekend in this little community. Here we began what became a regular feature in all of our revivals, the Witnessing Party, and at Society Hill we first became aware of receiving remuneration for our services.

Witnessing Parties had been part of the Seekers outreach ministry for a few months now, but with revivals taking up so many weekends, several weeks had passed since the last one. Robert hit upon the idea of making the event part of our revival, scheduling it following the second night's service on Saturday. We decided to hold it outside, weather permitting, recreating as much as possible the campfire effect at Ada.

Sitting in chairs in circular fashion under the stars, we sang songs and shared testimonies around a small blaze of limbs and leaves. We also placed a small wooden cross in the background and set it afire so it could be seen in the darkness. At the conclusion of the Party, an invitation was given for individuals to come to the old rugged cross.

We were obviously naïve to the implications of planting a burning cross on an Alabama church lawn in 1971. Its association with the Ku Klux Klan as a terrorist tactic and symbol of racism and hatred were well known across the South. Living on the outskirts of Tuskegee, with one of the heaviest concentrations of African-Americans in the U. S., Reverend Husky was exceedingly disturbed by the social faux pas and voiced his concerns following the Witnessing Party. Needless to say, it was

the first and last time we pulled that stunt. In future
meetings we illumined the wooden beams with railroad
flares, and rejoiced over and over again as young people
came to Jesus by the light of the cross.

It was also at Society Hill that we discovered the
purpose for the monetary offerings taken during the
revival services. Collections were received at the
previous four revivals, but we assumed they were for the
host churches or for the revivals' expenses. Now we
learned that Society Hill's offerings were intended
expressly for the preacherboys and were being sent to
Providence on our behalf.

Some of us talked it over and decided we
shouldn't accept these gifts. We were not preaching for
money and felt that taking honorariums might denigrate
the spiritual experience. We also recognized that a host
of Seekers were involved in the revivals, and to single out
the preacherboys for compensation would be a huge
mistake.

Brother Robert sat us down and recommended that
we accept the donations. It was God's way of taking care
of His servants and the church's way of expressing its
gratitude, he explained. Robert suggested, however, that
instead of taking the money and splitting it among
ourselves, we set it aside and use it for a worthwhile
Seekers ministry project. His idea won unanimous
support, and the revival offerings went into a ministry
fund maintained for the Seekers at Providence.

As we continued leading revivals, the Seekers
account steadily increased in value. Someone—probably
Robert—came up with the idea of sending Tommy on an
international mission trip. We thought it would be an
excellent use of the money; Tommy was loved and

respected by us all, the only one of the preacherboys called to foreign missions. Such a trip would give him a taste of his life's calling, put the Lord's money toward evangelism and missions, and enable Tommy to share his global experience in future revivals.

Soon it was announced at each revival that all offerings would go toward Tommy's upcoming missionary journey. It wasn't long before enough funds accumulated to make arrangements for the excursion, and on July 18, 1972 Tommy left for a month-long sojourn in Africa. The trip was an incredible personal adventure for Christ as he spent time primarily ministering in the countries of Uganda and Kenya, while residing with agricultural missionary Paul Eaton.

Going with his missionary host into the African bush, he found mud and grass hut villages, children wearing nothing but beads around their waste, and goats and chickens running free. He also found a hunger for the gospel. Tommy learned enough of the Swahili language to witness to many of the natives he encountered.

Walking along the lengthy Nile, visiting tribes such as the Sigulas of Lake Victoria, going into various communities and schools, Tommy shared Christ through personal word and Christian film, seeing several come to faith in the Lord during his short stay. He returned to us bleary-eyed and exhausted, but with renewed enthusiasm about God's call upon his life.

A decade later, Tommy's early taste of overseas life evolved into a full-course meal with his appointment as a Southern Baptist missionary to Spain. From his base in Western Europe, he often returned on mission for the Lord to the Dark Continent, a faraway land that first

captivated him as a sixteen year old member of the
Seekers.

****

As school started back in late summer, Robert
decided to limit the number of Seekers revivals to no
more than two a month. Throughout the fall season, as
we held services at churches such as Union Grove, where
Preacher Weekly had been pastor, and First Baptist in
Hurtsboro, Robert's former congregation, the Lord
increasingly dealt with my heart about the call to ministry.
The more I preached, the more comfortable I felt behind
the pulpit. The more time I spent with Jimmy, Gary, and
Billy, the more I believed their calling should be my own.

Though clearly sensing a divine summons to
preach the gospel, doubt plagued my thoughts through the
autumn months. Was I simply trying to keep up with the
Joneses—or in my case, the preacherboys? Was the
impression on my heart genuinely from the Lord, or was
it more of an emotional decision based upon friendships
and peer acceptance?

Looking for an answer, I took my time in making
a commitment to the ministry. I prayed, talked with
Robert and the other preacherboys, and earnestly sought
the Lord's will through His Word. I also needed time to
relinquish the goal in life I had set for myself—to be a
sports broadcaster or journalist, a dream I was most
reluctant to give up.

During a Christmastime revival at Summerville
Baptist in Phenix City, I found I could no longer postpone

a decision. The weight of the Spirit was too heavy, the voice of the Lord unmistakable. The vocation of a Christian minister—and specifically, preaching and teaching the Bible to God's people—was what I was meant to do. During the Witnessing Party on Saturday night, December 11, I publicly announced my intention to follow God's will for my life.

A large measure of peace entered my heart on that occasion, combined awkwardly with a sizeable dose of fear and trepidation. The latter emotions were calmed significantly by the joy and affirmation expressed by my Seekers family. The other preacherboys extended hugs and high fives, declaring they believed all along that God wanted me to be one of them permanently. Brother Robert, with the trademark twinkle in his eye and a warm toothy grin, clasped my hand in his and audibly praised the Lord for my decision.

The early months of 1972 brought the greatest spiritual movements of our revivals. January found us at the First Baptist Church of Tuskegee, where nearly forty decisions were recorded during the three day weekend— eighteen of them professions of faith in Christ. Heaven came down two weeks later, February 11-13, when we were in the Florida panhandle city of Crestview. More than seventy-five decisions for the Lord were registered at Southside Baptist, almost half for salvation.

By common consent, the Sunday morning service in Crestview was the most glorious time of worship we experienced in any of the revivals. The youth choir sang, the Messengers inspired us with music, Gary gave his testimony, and Eddie McCutcheon, another young man considering the call to preach, shared a powerful gospel message. The invitation lasted nearly as long as the rest of the service, with close to fifty individuals walking the aisle and publicly committing their lives to Christ.

Following the spiritual highs of January and February, we floated on cloud nine down to Enterprise, Alabama the first weekend of March. George Palmer, Robert's lifelong friend and fellow Bible Lover's Club member, was pastor of the Mount Pleasant congregation there. Some revivals stand out because of the spiritual harvests we witnessed or the funny incidents that took place. Others come readily to mind due to the personal stories of the individuals we met.

In the audience at Mount Pleasant were Charles and Nan Barnes, a couple whose teenage son had been killed in a traffic accident a year or so earlier. The initial night of the revival was the first time they had been back to church since his death. At the close of the service, Billy asked the congregation to link hands and sing the chorus, "God is So Good." The Lord did a work in the Barnes' hearts, and afterward Charles told Billy their story, mentioning that since the tragedy they had not been able to worship or believe the Lord was good until that evening.

A few months later the preacherboys were heading down to the south Alabama city of Geneva for a revival at Devco Baptist Church, where our former minister of music, John Jordan, was serving. We stopped in Montgomery to get gas and discovered we didn't have much money in our collective wallets. We were joking that we would probably have to pray our way back home from the revival when suddenly we heard someone shout and attempt to get our attention from the Holiday Inn across the street.

Looking closer, we realized it was Charles and Nan. They came over excitedly, extending handshakes and hugs all around. They were especially glad to see Billy, with whom they had stayed in touch. Before departing, Nan told Billy she had something for him, and promptly reached into her purse and handed him a birthday card. She had been meaning to mail it, she said, but now Billy could save her the postage. After thanking her, Billy opened it up and found $25 in cash. Immediately turning toward us with a broad smile on his face and waving the bills in his hand, Billy winked and declared, "Gas money, boys!" The Lord indeed provides for His servants, we duly reminded each other.

On the second weekend of May, a "Reunion Revival" was held at Providence. Youth from the eighteen churches who had hosted Seekers revivals over the previous ten months were invited to come for a series of worship services and fellowship. "Youth who Care…Youth who Share…Youth who Dare" was the theme selected for a celebration of singing, testimonies, and preaching. Providence housed and fed more than two hundred visitors who asked the Lord to revive them again so they might do His will in their churches and communities over the upcoming summer months.

The summer of '72 found us conducting revivals at such churches as Farmville in Auburn and Cloverdale in Dothan before ending at Liberty Baptist in Bullock County during the final week of August. The church was situated near a railroad that ran close by its sanctuary windows. At each evening's service the Wabash Cannonball came rolling down the tracks at approximately 7:15. The building shook, the windows rattled, the floor moved, and the worship service came to an abrupt halt. We had to wait for the Chattanooga Choo Choo to whistle on by before resuming our songs and sermons.

Here I am, preaching an early sermon.

Following the "train revival," some of us left home to further prepare for the ministry to which we'd been called. Jimmy and Gary headed off to Clarke College, a small Baptist school in Mississippi. I chose to stay in Alabama to attend Mobile College, another Baptist educational institution. Billy and Tommy remained in Beauregard to finish high school and lead more Seekers revivals, which Jimmy, Gary, and I often joined.

It had been a great ride in little more than a year: twenty-five revivals, hundreds of decisions for the Lord, a multitude of good times, and a rich assortment of ministerial experiences that would pay valuable dividends.

Probably my favorite part was the closeness and camaraderie, the love and appreciation we shared for one another as Seekers of the Lord. Visiting all those churches, riding aboard the Old Blue Goose, witnessing about our faith, leading others in worship, and continuing to grow together in the Lord enabled us to forge an emotional and spiritual bond that has remained true through the passing years, even in absentia.

As with everyone, I suppose, there have been seasons in my life when the burdens have grown unusually heavy, times when my heart has inexplicably grown cold. Especially then, memories of Seekers meetings past have mercifully flooded my soul, strengthening my faith and renewing my spirit.

The young men and women who first comprised the Seekers were ignorant about a lot of things—things that have gained greater clarity in the light of advancing years. Yet there is no doubt that we understood and practiced the most basic component of New Testament Christianity: we loved the Lord and one another, and possessed an intense desire to share the joy of these relationships with the world around us.

It is this extraordinary combination of blissful innocence, loving devotion, and spiritual enthusiasm that I cherish the most about our messianic age.

Chapter 5
"Fawzy"

The most interesting character among the Beauregard preacherboys was a young man who came lately into our fellowship. Already twenty-six when we first met in 1972, he also came from afar. His name was Fawzy Shorrosh, and Nazareth, Israel was his hometown. His native land alone put him closer to Jesus than the rest of us, in our provincial way of thinking. Upon coming to know him, however, we learned that much more than geography linked him to our Lord.

His first name sounded peculiar, but in a pleasing sort of way. Often people mistakenly called him Fonzy, after the popular 1970's TV star on Happy Days, with whom he shared a passing resemblance. He quickly set them straight, slowly and deliberately pronouncing his name. "Fow-zee," he corrected, stressing the primary syllable that rhymes with "wow." After meeting Fawzy and hearing his story, "wow" was the reaction of many who made his acquaintance.

What made Fawzy so intriguing were the extraordinary adventures he experienced before coming to Beauregard, like a modern version of the Apostle Paul appearing before our very eyes. We were mesmerized by his accounts of growing up as an Israeli citizen, joining the communist political party, being captured in war-torn Gaza, suffering for two years as a prisoner of war, and finding himself trapped in an enemy nation. What most enthralled us, however, was his dramatic conversion to Christ during the 1967 Six Day War between Israel and the Arab nations of Egypt, Jordan, and Syria.

Standing 5'4" with slender build, Fawzy was a bundle of energy and charisma in a small package. He flashed a quick and easy smile that especially stood out because of his dark shade of skin and coal-colored hair, hand-me-downs from the Sabra Jewish heritage of his Galilean roots. He possessed a thick, yet charming accent that sometimes butchered the English language in a style frequently humorous. Fawzy's initial naiveté regarding American speech and customs led to many amusing incidents, not a few concerning the basic necessities of food and communication.

Fawzy's many adventures and misadventures produced a rich testimony for Christ.

Only a couple of weeks after arriving in the U.S., for example, Fawzy went with Gary to get a bite to eat. He possessed little money, and friends like Gary occasionally took him along for a meal on their dime. They stopped at a fast food hangout near their college campus in Newton, Mississippi, a modest establishment known as Dog-N-Suds, where you could order through the window and eat outside. Fawzy knew little English, only a few simple words he was taught by missionaries in Jordan, along with several he had picked up since landing in America.

As they strode to the front window of the restaurant, Gary asked, "Fawzy, what do you want to eat tonight? There's what they have," pointing to a large menu board on display beside the window.

Fawzy fumbled for words as he gazed at the unfamiliar menu, finally shrugging his shoulders and responding, "I don't know, Brother Gary." "Brother" was Fawzy's customary way of referring to male fellow believers.

Realizing his mistake, Gary tried to help out his new friend. "How about a hot dog?" he suggested. "Do you like hot dogs, Fawzy? That's probably the best thing they have here."

Fawzy was incredulous. He wasn't acquainted with much of the American vernacular, but he did understand "dog," and it shocked him.

Looking with horror at Gary, he adamantly replied in broken English, "NO DOGS! I poor, brother, but I eat NO DOGS!"

He also didn't eat cats. Not long afterward a female employee at the college asked Fawzy, who was a trained electrician, if he could repair a fluorescent light in her kitchen. He came over and fixed it in no time. She was happy with his work and invited him to stay and have a home-cooked meal. He declined, as the custom of his country dictated. She insisted, and finally he agreed, sure he was in for a succulent feast.

"Now Fawzy, I understand you haven't been in the South very long," said the grateful woman, "so for supper tonight we're gonna eat something we're famous for around here."

Fawzy's mouth began to water in anticipation of what might be on the menu. "Thank you, ma'am," he said, while wondering what fine treat was in store.

The woman continued: "I'm gonna fry us some CATFISH and HUSH PUPPIES. There'll be plenty for both of us!"

Fawzy could barely conceal his disgust. "What kind of place is this," he wondered to himself, "that eats cats and dogs?"

Not all American cuisine turned Fawzy's stomach. The first time he encountered ice cream was a hallelujah moment. After dining in a Laurel, Mississippi restaurant, he was given the soft-serve treat for dessert, and loved it! Like an enthusiastic little kid, he eagerly anticipated each delicious spoonful, lapping up the last tasty drippings of ice cream soup.

He went on about it so much that the waitress brought out a different flavor for him to try—chocolate. When she returned to inquire how he liked it, he told her that he preferred the white kind, wanting to know its name. She laughed at his innocence and informed him it was vanilla. Fawzy had no difficulty pronouncing "ice cream" or "chocolate," but could not easily voice the word "vanilla" since there is no "v" sound in Hebrew. The best he could do was something like "anorilla."

A week or so later he found extra spending money in his pocket and decided to visit a local eatery near campus. He went there and ordered.

"Some ice cream, please."

"What kind do you want," requested the attendant behind the counter.

"Anorilla," said Fawzy, confidently.

She said, "What kind?"

"Anorilla?" said Fawzy, less confidently.

"I'm sorry, what kind was that?" the server asked in a higher pitched tone.

"Chocolate," said Fawzy, with considerable disappointment.

"Oh, chocolate, chocolate," she repeated, as she proceeded to dip him a scoop.

"V" was not the only letter in the English alphabet that gave Fawzy a problem. His native language doesn't have the letter "p" either. In Hebrew it corresponds to our letter "b." The adjustment from "b" to "p" was not an easy one for Fawzy. With an English tutor's assistance, he practiced distinguishing the two sounds with exercises like putting baby powder on the palm of his hand, holding it up to his mouth, and pronouncing the two letters. The sound that blew the powder away from him was the "p."

Failing to say "p" occasionally landed Fawzy in trouble. Such was the case on an early public speaking engagement. He had mastered enough English to share his Christian testimony and was invited to fill the pulpit one Sunday at a local Baptist church. During the course of his address, he unconsciously reverted back to the more natural pronunciation of "p" words with the "b" sound.

This happened most conspicuously when he repeatedly thanked the "bastor" of the church for the opportunity to speak. Some in the congregation thought he was saying the word "bastard," upsetting a few, but giving most a hearty chuckle at their pastor's expense.

Another embarrassing moment occurred when he went with Billy to a church near Hattiesburg, where Billy was preaching a revival. At the pastor's home Fawzy was sitting at the dinner table with others, answering their questions and exchanging chitchat. In the course of conversation, he placed one elbow on the table while resting the other arm in his lap. A large dog sat between him and the pastor. The pastor's wife sat directly across from Fawzy, and Billy was sitting to Fawzy's left.

The pastor's wife suddenly began laughing at one story he shared that she found particularly amusing.

"Fawzy, you're pulling my leg!" she cackled, using a vivid American expression.

Fawzy immediately brought his hidden arm up to the table and stared at her with dismay, the smile on his face replaced with alarm.

"No ma'am, it must be the dog!" he quickly responded.

In the Middle East, a man accused of such behavior toward a married woman risked a severe beating or even death. Fawzy nervously looked over at her husband, actually fearful that he might be attacked. The woman started to laugh again and tried to clear up the misunderstanding, but before she could finish Fawzy once again loudly proclaimed his innocence.

"Ma'am, I not touch your leg!" he insisted. "It was the dog!"

They could all see that Fawzy was plainly disturbed, and he became more agitated as the lady of the house tried to clarify what she meant. She and Fawzy were talking over each other from across the table when finally the pastor asked both to stop.

"Would everybody just calm down for a minute?" he asked, his voice rising above theirs. Fawzy wanted to flee the table then and there, but Billy assured him he should stay.

"Now Fawzy," the pastor said, "my wife didn't really mean that you were pulling her leg. It's just a figure of speech we use over here. She didn't mean anything by it."

Fawzy nodded thoughtfully, as if he understood, before responding with the last word.

"Okay, sir. But it was not me. It was the DOG!"

Despite these rough beginnings, Fawzy soon began to enjoy American cuisine and to assimilate American culture. He also learned to speak the English language quite well, and in the process found expanded opportunities to share his faith. Many of these initially came under the evangelistic banner of the Seekers.

Within a month of immigrating to the States, Fawzy became fast friends with Gary and Jimmy, the Beauregard preacherboys who happened to be attending the same Baptist college. They brought him to Providence and introduced him to Brother Robert, who soon took the Israeli citizen under his wing. Fawzy began accompanying us on our revivals, sharing the remarkable story of his conversion to Christ and journey to America. That epic saga is a fascinating part of our messianic age.

****

While Beauregard is the figurative Galilee of my spiritual experience, Fawzy has no need to resort to metaphors. He spent his childhood and teenage years in the land of Jesus—literal Galilee, a scenic terrain filled with high hills, lush valleys, and a beautiful lake of the same name. Although he never met the Lord there, the gospel seed was firmly planted at a young age by a faithful mother and dedicated Baptist missionaries. It eventually sprouted in enemy territory, where soon it grew into the lovely flower of a dynamic Christian life.

Fawzy was born in the Galilean city of Haifa on March 17, 1946 during an epochal period in the long, idiosyncratic history of the Jewish people. Declarations of independence were already in the air, and two years later Israel became a sovereign nation for the first time since the biblical era. Not since 63 B.C., when General Pompey conquered the Jews for the Roman Republic, had Israel functioned as an autonomous state. For more than two millennia the Promised Land was ruled by various national entities, the most recent of whom were the British.

Shortly after Fawzy's birth, the Shorroshes moved to Nazareth, father and mother settling there with their five children. Five more mouths to feed were added to the family in ensuing years. An eleventh child, born a year or so ahead of Fawzy, suffered a fatal fall before reaching toddlerhood. Curiously, he too was called Fawzy, with Fawzy number two assuming his deceased older brother's name.

Fawzy's father, Tawfic, worked at a nearby rock quarry as a stonecutter. His mother, Farouse, labored at home caring for her children and extended family members, while also doing needlecraft she sold to

Nazareth's tourists. Husband and wife could not have been more different.

Tawfic cut a distinguished figure, with salt and pepper hair, dark beard, olive skin, and wiry body hard-muscled from long days in the quarry. His handsome appearance was frequently overshadowed by an intense anger, fueled by the family's dire economic straits and his ongoing health issues. Kidney problems often incapacitated him and later brought disablement, robbing him of work and compounding the family's money woes. Surly in attitude and prone to violent temper, he hated his lot, and tended to make home life miserable for Fawzy and his siblings.

By contrast Farouse, a strong, slightly heavy woman of dark-eyed beauty and rich facial expression, consistently presented a friendly and gregarious disposition, full of love and encouragement. Regardless of the family's finances, she maintained a happy and hopeful outlook on life. Her attitude largely stemmed from the devout Christian faith she practiced at Nazareth's Baptist church, a small congregation led by Dwight Baker, an American missionary assigned to the area. Farouse usually walked the two miles there and back each Sunday and Wednesday to attend its services.

Commitment to Christ had defined her life since coming to know the Lord while working as a clerk in Egypt, and now provided the motivation to pass along her spiritual perspective to Fawzy and the rest of the children, as well as to her husband. In leading her family down the path of the straight and narrow, Farouse sought to maintain certain standards of Christian conduct in her household. One of these concerned the cinema. For many earnest Christians like Farouse, going to the movies in the 1950's was strictly taboo. Her children, of course, didn't see it that way and were dying to visit the theater, but their mother strictly forbade it.

On one occasion the family visited relatives in Haifa for Farouse's birthday. The children took their mother to a restaurant to celebrate, and later conspired to coax her toward the city's movie theater. When they arrived at the entertainment complex, she demanded they depart immediately. As luck would have it, Reverend Baker and his wife happened to be attending the movie and assured Farouse that the film was perfectly harmless. Fawzy and his siblings stayed to watch Tarzan rescue Jane, much to the delight of Cheetah the chimpanzee, not to mention the Shorrosh boys and girls.

Such indulgences were few and far between. For the first ten years of his life, Fawzy's family lived in a small sixteen by eighteen foot room in his great grandmother's house. There they ate, slept, bathed, played, and generally occupied time. The house contained no heating, making it a challenge to stay warm in winter. There was also no electricity or running water. The neighborhood cistern, which supplied most of their water needs, was located several houses down the dusty dirt road, as was the mud-frame outhouse they and other families in the community utilized.

Food and clothing consisted of bare essentials. Peas and pita bread comprised the staples of their limited diet, both cooked on a mud-brick fireplace in the back yard before being brought into the house. The family gathered around the pot of peas, stewed it into gruel, and scooped it up with the pita bread—also known as Bible bread. Whatever dry bread remained they collected into a basket and served for breakfast the next morning. Often it was dipped in hot tea to soften, giving it a mushy consistency that was more edible.

Another of the family's basic foods was lentil soup—the so-called meat of the poor—which provided the protein necessary for nutrition. It could be prepared in a variety of ways, enabling a slightly different taste each meal. Cheese was a special treat their father sometimes brought home. Now and then they transformed it into lebani, a mixture of cream cheese and olive oil stored in a clay jar. Lebani was spread onto pita bread and eaten during the late afternoon supper.

One outfit of clothing, usually a hand-me-down of some sort, sufficed year round or as long as it fit. It was worn throughout the day and night, removed only to bathe and launder. Most of the children's clothing was received through the generosity of churches in the United States and supplied by the Baptist missionaries in Nazareth.

When Fawzy's great grandmother died and her home's ownership transferred, the Shorrosh family moved to equally cramped quarters on the other side of town. A third move occurred during Fawzy's early teen years, this time to a house containing three tiny rooms. It was located near a nunnery along the road leading to the Sea of Galilee, which lay about fifteen miles to the east. To Fawzy, the last home he knew in Nazareth seemed luxurious.

The Shorrosh's poverty was not uncommon. The post World War II city was populated by approximately thirty thousand people of diverse economic levels and religious sympathies. Row upon row of square-shaped, flat-roofed, one-to-three room houses lined its dirt streets, typical domiciles constructed of stones and sun-dried mud. Sprinkled in among them were bigger and fancier dwellings, occupied by the landlords and merchants of the city.

Nazareth encompassed several ethnic groups, a pot pouri of nationalities, religions, and cultures, giving the community a decidedly cosmopolitan flavor. Among them were Jews of various stripes. The Sabra Jews, to whom Fawzy's paternal family belonged, were the dark-skinned natives of the land, sometimes called Palestinian Jews, who had resided in Nazareth the longest. After Israel became a nation, thousands of lighter-skinned Europeans, otherwise known as Ashkenasic Jews, migrated into the city from Russia, Romania, Hungary, Poland, Germany, and elsewhere.

The majority Arab population was divided into two major groups, identified chiefly by religious affiliation: Palestinian Arab Muslims and Palestinian Arab Christians. Arabs had resided in Nazareth for centuries, and as a result most Jewish residents, including Fawzy, conversed in Arabic and Hebrew. There were various other Muslim and Christian inhabitants as well, notable among them a number of Coptic Christians.

Fawzy especially encountered the multicultural character of his hometown when attending school. Until the fourth grade he went to one of the city's two public primary schools, whose composition was majority Muslim. A private school administered by Baptist missionaries offered better educational opportunities, particularly for the Christian community of Nazareth, and Farouse earnestly desired to send her children there. The tuition was impossible to pay, so initially all she could do was make it a matter of prayer. Her prayers were wondrously answered when the school decided to waive its tuition, allowing some of the Shorrosh children to attend, including Fawzy. There he studied for free from the age of eight until thirteen. The Christian atmosphere and biblical teaching would later bear sweet tasting fruit in Fawzy's life.

School was something he simultaneously enjoyed and hated. On the one hand, he possessed an insatiable appetite for learning, eagerly absorbing any new knowledge presented by teachers and textbooks. School also provided a temporary escape from the abject poverty of his home life. On the other hand, Fawzy constantly encountered ridicule from classmates regarding his ragged clothes, unkempt appearance, and perpetual lack of money for basic school supplies and food items. The humiliation was extremely upsetting, frequently driving him to tears. It also drove him away from God.

Penury that doesn't go away promotes contemplation of its cause and cure. The latter is imagination's first flight, and so it was with Fawzy. From earliest days his mother had steadfastly taught that God would take care of them, that one day the Lord would bring about better things for Fawzy and the family. "Keep trusting in the Lord and the future will be bright," she repeatedly encouraged. It was easy for Fawzy to accept her hopeful philosophy during his younger years, and with little boy fantasies he envisioned God as the magical panacea for all of their economic problems.

But after several years of little improvement, he began to doubt his mother's promises. He also began to doubt her God, and then openly to blame and reject Him. What kind of God would allow their destitute conditions to exist and continue unabated, he reasoned? What sort of God would keep them in poverty if—as his mother insisted—He really loved them? As Fawzy grew older and began to think for himself, the Christian God made little practical sense from his overtly materialistic perspective.

What made better sense were the religious and political views of his father. An avowed atheist and active member of the Communist Club of Nazareth, Tawfic blamed the government most of all for their impoverished conditions. The only hope he saw for better days was a change toward the socialist state model of Marx and Engels, where the goal is wealth equally distributed among the masses. Communist doctrine also promoted the belief that God is merely a mythical construct, and religion of any kind a coping mechanism of the ignorant and oppressed.

His father's alternative vision of the world was further impressed upon young Fawzy when at age twelve he met Kahlid, an active member of Nazareth's Communist Youth Club. The seventeen year old took an avid interest in Fawzy, enthralling the preteen with stories of trips to faraway places. Kahlid began taking Fawzy to meetings of the club, where he came to better understand the doctrines espoused by his father. There he felt the acceptance he never found at school, and enjoyed the friendship, games, food, and discussions of the group. He even started participating in the club's political activities, including demonstrations against Nazareth's current political regime, and acts of petty vandalism toward the city's mosques and churches.

When Fawzy became a teenager, Tawfic forced him to quit school and seek employment. Most children look forward to their thirteenth birthday, but Fawzy dreaded the milestone, because he feared his father's mandate. He begged for the opportunity to continue at the Baptist school; although he no longer believed in their God or religious teachings, he knew they were providing a good education and recognized its value for his future. He also wasn't ready to go to work. Tawfic was insistent, however, that Fawzy do as his siblings before him and help support the family.

He didn't actively seek a job at first. He hoped that by waiting, his father would relent and allow him to return to school. Rather than purposefully attempting to find work, Fawzy spent his first teenage months engaging in Communist Youth Club meetings and activities. There he found plenty of literature to read and study, albeit from the communist perspective on things. There he also found like-minded individuals who were curious about the world and committed to changing it for the better.

Fawzy's stalling tactics did not dissuade his father; Tawfic was adamant about his son joining the work force. After several weeks of delaying the inevitable, Fawzy was hired by the Heroot Electrical Company, the subcontractor for a huge government apartment complex going up outside of Nazareth. The apartments were being constructed for the ever-swelling tide of Jewish immigrants coming to Israel in the late 1950's.

Fawzy hoped to learn the electrician's trade, but was offered an entry-level position pouring concrete, a labor-intensive task made more taxing by the seven mile walk to and from the job site. As rough as it was for a thirteen year old, he stuck with it, faithfully handing over his paycheck each week to Tawfic to help with the family's finances.

After a few months on the job, Fawzy asked his supervisor about learning the trade he desired, and was thrilled to be moved into the role of an electrical apprentice. He learned the skill easily and capably, and soon was trusted to do small wiring jobs throughout the housing project.

During this time he also advanced in his commitment to the Communist Club, officially becoming a member of the organization, carefully learning the party doctrines, and taking on leadership responsibilities. He increasingly felt comfortable arguing the communist cause and helping with public demonstrations on behalf of their political agenda. Outward action served as a channel for the inner hurt, frustration, and hatred developed over the course of his childhood. Hostility toward God, parents, and authority figures boiled over in the communist crusade he adopted, believing it was the answer to his and the world's ills. Ironically, Fawzy became more and more like his father even as he hated what his father had become.

The rage in his heart reached a crescendo pitch when a supervisor at work, aware of Fawzy's communist party activities, falsely accused him of painting an enormous swastika on one of the buildings at the construction site. The police were called and Fawzy arrested. Although quickly released for lack of evidence, the experience further fueled the distrust and bitterness he felt for those in power. The sullen attitude toward his bosses intensified, and the promotion of communism among his co-workers escalated. The result was the loss of his first job and a heightened resentment toward those in charge, the perceived purveyors of social injustice.

For the next two years Fawzy found little steady work. Although he obtained another job almost immediately at a competing electrical firm, he was fired within a week when his association with the communist party became known. After two firings in the space of a month, Fawzy concluded he was being blacklisted in Nazareth, and freelancing small electrical jobs was the best he could do. The closest he came to a regular paycheck was when Rasheed, a friend at the Communist Youth Club, hired him to help out at his electronics store. Through Rasheed, Fawzy learned the basics of radio and television repair, a growing business in Israel at the time.

Rasheed's wages were meager, so at age sixteen Fawzy searched for better paying electrical work outside of Nazareth, finding employment in Haifa near the Mediterranean coast. He commuted the ninety minute round trip by bus, leaving at five-thirty in the morning and returning around six at night. The schedule was grueling but worth it as he finally began to accumulate savings. He kept half the salary for himself, putting most of it toward the goal of opening an electronics shop of his own.

That dream was dashed a few years later when older brother Nabeh decided to get married. Marriage was an expensive proposition in Israeli culture, and Nabeh had no money. He and Fawzy were always close, only two years apart, and Nabeh had helped Fawzy in the past during difficult times. Nabeh asked his brother to let him borrow the money for dowry and nuptials. Although Fawzy knew it was unlikely he would ever be repaid, he didn't want to stand in the way of Nabeh's happiness, and permitted him to have most of the funds in his savings. The wedding was an elaborate and festive affair, but Fawzy did not enjoy it. Three years worth of hard-earned money was gone, his ambition shattered.

Fawzy was not enjoying life at age nineteen. Depression was with him constantly. He began to drink heavily and to generally avoid people. He hated his plight, and could perceive no quick end to the poverty, injustice, and despair around him. The only light in the darkness was the Communist Club, so he committed more of himself to the party, and was rewarded with an appointment as an official delegate at the organization's upcoming youth conference in Moscow, which he subsequently attended.

Through it all Farouse never ceased praying for Fawzy or witnessing to him. Sometimes her encouragements were met with verbal insults or mock laughter. She was not deterred. For almost twenty years she had been faithful in sharing Jesus with her son, and she was not about to stop when he needed God the most. Even though in the short-term this meant a strained relationship, she believed that his eternal happiness was far more important.

The path to finding that happiness was paved with more misery and despair, with heavy doses of heartache and suffering mixed in. For Fawzy, the Apostles Paul and Barnabas were not exaggerating when they declared, "It is through many trials that we must enter the Kingdom of God."

****

Less than a year after Nabeh married, Fawzy himself fell in love. Romance brought a temporary reprieve to the melancholy that resided deep within his soul, before ultimately and wretchedly exacerbating it. Apparently it was necessary to experience the depths of despair before ascending to the true source of happiness.

Her name was Dawlit Mwas, two years his younger and Nabeh's new sister-in-law. Fawzy had first noticed her at his father's vegetable stand. The disabled Tawfic set up the stand in the front room of the Shorrosh home as a means of earning extra income, and Fawzy assisted Dawlit on one occasion when she stopped to purchase a few tomatoes. She was beautiful to his eyes, with dark hair hidden under a colorful headband and scarf, lovely olive tone skin, and impeccable pearly white teeth. A delicately tapered waste perfectly complemented the slender figure she presented.

He saw her again at Nabeh's wedding, where they were introduced. Their paths crossed once more a few weeks later, a chance encounter while Fawzy was visiting his brother. He took advantage of the opportunity to get better acquainted, and afterward abruptly declared he wanted to marry her! He liked how she looked, the way she talked, the fact that their families were already connected. He and she were just the right age for marriage, he reasoned. Maybe matrimony was what he needed to finally experience happiness in life.

In Middle Eastern culture interaction between unmarried parties was strictly limited by social decorum. When a man decided he wanted to marry, he announced his intention by going to the prospective bride's father or male guardian to begin negotiations and receive permission or refusal. If the woman and her family found the suitor and his offer acceptable, a contract of sorts was drawn up and they became engaged. In Fawzy's case, Dawlit agreed to marry him, and although he had little to offer except his family's good name, her father gave his blessing to the union. Fawzy and Dawlit were to be married!

The anticipation of marriage and promise of love began to bring Fawzy out of the despondency he felt. Though long hours of work in Haifa still filled most of his days, now he was making money to save for a new life with Dawlit. Family members noticed a spring in his step and a smile on his face long lacking. He especially enjoyed getting to know Dawlit, although it was always under the strict supervision of her parents or siblings. His love for her steadily grew, even to the point of sending secret love letters—unusual for Israeli culture. Fawzy believed that he had found the one woman with whom he wanted to spend the rest of his life.

Over the course of their engagement, however, he began to wonder if Dawlit felt the same way. She had begun to cry when they were together. He asked repeatedly for the cause of her unhappiness, but she would not or could not tell him. The obvious questions popped into his mind: Had she found she didn't love him? Was she having second thoughts about their marriage? She answered "no" to each inquiry. What was it, then, that made her so sad? Fawzy could not get an answer, nor was he able to figure it out.

Dawlit's puzzling behavior was extremely disturbing. Sensing that the only girl he ever loved was slipping away, and not knowing the reason, Fawzy resorted to clandestine means to discover the truth. He asked his friend Rasheed, owner of the electronics shop, for a listening device to plant in the Mwas' home. He put it in a big box radio that he repaired for Dawlit's father. What he found both eased his mind and traumatized him.

The "bug" divulged that Dawlit indeed wanted to
marry him, just as she maintained, and that he was not the
source of her unhappiness. But it also revealed the
stunning news that Dawlit was infertile. This was the
source of her tears, though not the only one. The family
was hopeful that surgery could reverse her condition, and
plans were afoot to undergo an operation.

Even more shocking, the surveillance disclosed
that Fawzy was actually "plan B," the alternative choice
of Dawlit's parents in case things didn't go well with the
medical procedure. If Dawlit's surgery should be
successful, they planned to break the engagement and
enter into a marriage contract with another man named
Elijah. Dawlit would marry Fawzy only in the event she
remained infertile! He now understood why her grief was
unspeakable.

Fawzy, of course, was outraged by the Mwas'
deceit, distressed that his wedding was in jeopardy, and
crushed at the news that Dawlit could remain barren. He
loved children and had always dreamed of raising little
ones of his own. Facing the future without kids had never
occurred to him. The disclosure that the woman he had
chosen to be the mother of his children might be unable to
give birth was devastating. Yet he loved her, and still
wanted to marry her.

Not long after, Dawlit underwent successful
surgery, with Fawzy at her side for much of the
hospitalization. He bought flowers and brought them to
her room, a rare sight for an unmarried man in Israeli
society. Their love strengthened, as did their desire to be
married. Hope began to renew in Fawzy's heart that
perhaps things would work out after all. Then suddenly,
tersely, all hope was destroyed. During Dawlit's

convalescence at home, her parents took steps to officially break the engagement. There would be no marriage to Dawlit.

There was nothing Fawzy could do about the situation. Dawlit was forbidden to see him, and she would not oppose her family's wishes. For the next few months he missed a lot of work, drank himself silly, and wallowed in self-pity. Utter darkness enveloped his soul.

Depression of an unfathomable order prompted suicide attempts on two occasions following the breakup. The first occurred at the conclusion of an especially gloomy day, when Fawzy determined he didn't want to wake up the next morning. Before going to sleep, he took what he thought were enough pills to end his life, but he succeeded only in making himself violently ill. Through the course of several vicious episodes of nausea and vomiting, his mother stayed with him, nursing him back to health after a few long days.

The other incident took place at a job site outside Haifa. Fawzy decided he would leap from the high rise where he worked to almost certain death below. He went inside the building to find pen and paper to leave a suicide note behind. When finished, he walked to the edge of an upper floor and without looking down jumped—right into a huge pile of sand! Trucks had unloaded a shipment of sand in the exact location underneath the opening from which he leaped.

As Fawzy recovered from the deliberate fall, he could not help but wonder if his mother was right— maybe there was a Higher Power who loved him and was watching over him. He would be compelled to contemplate the possibility more earnestly in the days and weeks to come.

****

In the spring of 1967, as he turned twenty-one years old, Fawzy decided to make a dramatic change in his life. There was so much misery associated with Nazareth that he felt it was time to move elsewhere, to remove himself from the constant oversight of parents and siblings, and to make a fresh start in another town where the painful memories of Dawlit could fade more easily. He also wanted the opportunity to find a good steady job without worry of communist ties hindering the process. As he shortly found out, the decision to leave Nazareth would bring enormous ramifications.

But where should he go? He thought of lands far away, of departing the country once and for all. He learned through Rasheed that plenty of jobs for electricians were available in Canada. After making inquiries, however, he found that only those conversant in English or French were wanted. He finally focused on places closer to home, including the ancient and fabled city of Jerusalem, located sixty miles due south.

Fawzy had never been to the most famous of all biblical habitations. In the late 1960's, it was on the verge of becoming a teeming metropolis populated by an ever-increasing mass of Jewish immigrants, with the building and development that inevitably accompany such growth. This is what made Jerusalem so attractive to job seekers like Fawzy, despite the dangers inherent in working there.

Soldiers and barricades were everywhere. Since 1948 Jews and Muslims had engaged in an intense border dispute concerning the Old City section, that part of Jerusalem containing the Holy Land's most sacred sites. The city was divided, with Israel ruling West Jerusalem, and Jordan controlling the Old City and East Jerusalem. Soon they would clash in a violent and definitive way.

In April—just as the rumblings of war were heard—Fawzy purchased a one-way bus ticket to Jerusalem, deciding it was his best bet for making a new start. After arriving, he was sorely disappointed. While staying in a cheap downtown hotel, he spent several weeks looking for work as an electrician, managing to find temporary laborer positions, but nothing long-term.

Growing impatient and short of cash, but unwilling to return home, Fawzy decided impetuously to head forty miles further south to Beersheba. One of the largest cities in the country, Beersheba was renowned for Abraham's pact with Abimelech that allowed him use of a well to water his animals. It was now known as the capital of the Negev, the gateway to the arid and inhospitable desert of southernmost Israel.

On June 5, only days after Fawzy arrived in Beersheba, Israel launched a surprise attack against Egypt, whose Sinai and Gaza borders were as few as twenty-five miles in the distance. The so-called Six Day War had begun. Fawzy saw Israeli tanks rolling into the area to commence a preemptive strike upon Egyptian forces stationed at the boundary of the two countries. Looking toward the sky, he spotted fighter jets winging their way en route to Egyptian territory.

Israel's military would amaze the world with a quick, three-pronged triumph over its Arab neighbors. It

took only four days to defeat Egypt and gain possession
of the huge Sinai Peninsula to the south, as well as the
tiny coastal property on the Mediterranean known as the
Gaza Strip. In three days they forced Jordan to concede
the Old City and East Jerusalem, along with the large
West Bank mass of land bordering the Jordan River. By
the end of six days, on June 11, it had also triumphed over
Syria, taking the region east and north of the Sea of
Galilee called the Golan Heights. No one could have
predicted the war would be so brief and the Israelis so
victorious.

On the first day of the conflict, chaos reigned in
Beersheba. People were in panic mode, worrying that
they would soon be part of a combat zone. Fawzy was
forced to make a critical decision: should he remain in the
city or flee elsewhere? Since he didn't know anyone
there, he thought it best to leave immediately and head to
safer areas in the north. With buses no longer running, he
was compelled to hire a ride out of town. He found
someone going to Tel Aviv, located on the country's
central west coast, and eagerly climbed on board.

The main highway north of Beersheba was
blocked by incoming military vehicles, so his transport
proceeded west in the direction of the Mediterranean,
intending to turn north toward Tel Aviv at the earliest
opportunity. That opportunity never came. All roads
leading north were closed by the Israeli military, and soon
Fawzy and his fellow passengers found themselves
nearing Gaza—enemy territory embroiled in conflict.
Within a few miles of the border they finally gave up,
deciding to reverse course and head back to Beersheba,
but were spotted by Egyptian soldiers who gave chase.
Fearing that he might be captured, Fawzy abandoned the

vehicle and fled as fast as he could into the surrounding semi-desert.

He ran furiously for maybe half an hour before stopping to rest. He was grateful not to be pursued, and continued on foot for some time, encountering no one but losing track of his whereabouts. Not long before dusk, he began to scour about for a safe place to spend the night. Suddenly he saw planes and helicopters in the twilight and quickly took cover. The sounds of warfare erupted: rifle fire, artillery shells, and bomb explosions all around. He had wandered into a battlefield!

He decided to go back the way he came, racing through the dimly lit wilderness as quickly as possible. Finding a small cave-like dwelling along the way, he determined to hole up there, too exhausted and afraid to travel further. With beads of perspiration cascading down his face, hunger pains growing in his belly, and a mouth parched with thirst, he collapsed into a dark crevice, content to remain there for awhile. The blasts continued for several minutes, then abated, and Fawzy settled into his abode for the night.

He awoke the next morning having slept reasonably well and feeling fairly rested. He carefully inspected the area around the cave, finding no suggestion of life or death nearby. Explosions were heard in the distance, but the fighting had moved away from him. Hunger and thirst were now his biggest enemies.

Fawzy decided to move in the direction opposite the battlefield noise, and soon it was out of earshot. He attempted to travel toward the north, though a priority now was to locate water and food. Throughout the day of walking and searching, he saw no one and discovered no physical refreshment. The barren landscape provided nary a drop of water or ounce of edible sustenance.

While warfare and bodily needs dominated his attention, Fawzy was also unexpectedly consumed with thoughts about his mother. It surprised him how much he missed Farouse and wanted to feel the strength of her love and encouragement. He had treated her shabbily in recent years, with hardly a kind word and repeated ridicule of her religious faith. Yet she was always there for him, constant in her devotion and a bulwark of support, particularly during times of adversity.

He imagined that she was praying for him, asking her God to take care of her son—wherever he was. She had always done this, of course, but now, as he was in immediate danger and lost in unfamiliar territory, her prayers enabled the only bit of comfort he could discern. The assurance of his mother interceding for his safety gave Fawzy a curious sense of inner strength and hope, and turned his mind toward contemplation of the reality of her God. Memories of the faithful Christian witness she bore came flooding back upon him, as did the testimonies of the Baptist missionaries at school and church, and the many scriptures he memorized as a child.

As he ambled around deep within the western part of the Negev, one of his mother's favorite Bible stories came easily to mind. The wilderness wanderings of the ancient Israelites mirrored his own predicament. After a lengthy period of rebellion and idolatry, God brought the Hebrews to the land of promise despite their stubbornness and hardness of heart. Farouse had often applied the story to him. If God could deliver the recalcitrant people of Moses' day, He could certainly redeem her Fawzy!

All alone with his thoughts, Fawzy had the time and motivation to seriously reflect upon his philosophical worldview and religious beliefs. Was the Bible really true, as his mother and the missionaries asserted so steadfastly? Were he, his father, and the communists wrong? Had the Lord delivered him from sure death only weeks earlier? Would He rescue him again in the wilderness? Fawzy found no physical food or water in the sparse desert surroundings, but it was here that he began to ponder their spiritual counterparts.

As the sun was going down, he hiked further along the harsh plain, comprised of few trees or shrubs but lots of sand and rocks. He spotted a sycamore tree and decided to sit and rest beneath it, with thoughts of his predicament, of mama, and of her God echoing deep within the nooks and crannies of his soul. Fitful sleep gradually descended upon him.

The third day of Fawzy's wilderness wanderings began with ravishing hunger pains and excruciating thirst. In the spotty vegetation, he scouted about for anything edible, finally coming upon some busbas plants, bitter in taste but nourishing to the body. He gagged as he swallowed them, made doubly difficult by his severely parched mouth and throat. A little further along, accompanied now by gunfire in the distance, he let out a shriek of delight as he stumbled upon a small pool of water. Though it looked unclean, he knelt down without hesitation and eagerly lapped it up like a wild animal.

After drinking his fill, he unexpectedly heard footsteps rapidly approaching from behind and a loud voice speaking in a stern tone.

"Who are you, young man?

Fawzy turned to see several men, at least five, dressed in non-Israeli military uniforms, each carrying rifles, with one pointed directly at him!

"Get on your feet and raise your hands and identify yourself!" their leader barked.

Fawzy did as commanded, replying, "I am Fawzy Shorrosh."

"Let me see your identification," the military man continued. Fawzy showed him his ID, indicating Israeli citizenship in Nazareth.

"What are you doing in Gaza, Shorrosh?" the man demanded.

"Gaza? Have I wandered into Gaza?" he thought, incredulously.

"I'm lost," Fawzy finally answered. "I didn't know I was in Gaza. I was trying to make it to Tel Aviv when my car gave out of gas," he partly lied, "and then I got lost out here in the desert. I was looking for some water."

The soldiers were about to take Fawzy into custody when the sights and sounds of warfare abruptly interrupted. Fawzy and the men quickly scattered. A tank clambered in their direction and a helicopter flew in above them, riddling the area with gunfire. In the hail of ammunition, they attempted to find safety. Suddenly Fawzy was knocked to the ground by a violent explosion and lost consciousness.

When he came to, there was only silence all around. As he groggily began to recall what had just happened, he first checked himself to see if there were any wounds; he was uninjured. Surveying the area, he noticed no signs of the attackers. Calling out to see if anyone would respond, no one did. He looked around for the soldiers who were interrogating him, and what he found shocked him. They were all dead! Their corpses lay on the ground at various spots among the desert rocks. The sight of their mutilated bodies, with blood gurgling from open mouths, shook him with nausea and great fear.

He began a hasty retreat from the gory scene, not knowing if the perpetrators planned to return. Before fleeing, he had the presence of mind to ruffle through the pockets of one of the dead, where he found the identification document he was seeking. On it was the name Ali Othman Aaid, a Palestinian from Gaza. Thinking it might come in handy, especially now that he was in enemy terrain, he stuffed it into his pants and scampered away.

As Fawzy sprinted through the countryside, the enormity of what had transpired gradually weighed upon him. At a shady spot he stopped to rest and to collect his thoughts, still shaking from the near death experience. Questions began to inundate his mind. Why was he the only one spared in the ambush? Why were the soldiers attacked at precisely the moment of his arrest? Was there indeed a God watching over him? Could it be that the Lord really cared for him and had a plan for his life, as his mother had long insisted?

Tears began to stream from his eyes as he was suddenly overcome with emotion. For the first time since childhood, Fawzy found himself falling to his knees and praying to a God he now believed must exist. At first it felt uncomfortable, and he could only stammer a few halting words. Then he remembered the prayer language of his mother, and the words began to flow more clearly and fervently. Uttering a series of affirmations of belief in God, he repeatedly thanked the Lord for saving him once more from the vagaries of death. Then, as best he knew how, he asked Jesus to save his soul, to take over his heart, and to give him the everlasting life promised in John 3:16.

Fawzy's Damascus Road experience took place amid the dusty land and Mediterranean breezes of the Gaza Strip. Like Paul the Apostle, he said "yes" to Jesus and the scales of spiritual blindness fell from his eyes. For the first time, he experienced the joy of a personal relationship with the Lord. The Christ he once cursed, now he loved and worshiped. In Him, Fawzy commenced finding the contentment that his restless soul had long sought, the peace that surpasses human understanding. The hatred, bitterness, despair, and hopelessness that had ruled his life for so many years started to melt away. Salvation, in the form of God's forgiveness and amazing grace, was profoundly changing who he was.

Much as the Ethiopian eunuch of Acts, Fawzy came to know Christ on a crusty patch of Gaza soil and then went on his way rejoicing. "Thank you, Jesus!" he could not stop shouting again and again, an exclamation that was to become his signature expression of praise and gratitude. Exactly where on earth he was going, he had no idea. It was enough to know that he was ultimately bound for heaven, and that his earthly sojourn was in the powerful, loving hands of the God he now believed in.

****

Although physically filthy and exceedingly weary, Fawzy felt rejuvenated as he continued his wilderness odyssey. The distinct sensation of being a new person, what the New Testament calls a "new creation," imbued his consciousness. He was now a Christian believer, a fact that radically changed his perspective on things. No longer did he feel alone in a foreign land during time of war—the Lord was with him, guarding and guiding as part of the divine plan for his life.

Meandering along, he soon found himself among hundreds of fruit trees. Much of that part of Gaza was planted in citrus, mainly oranges and lemons growing abundantly in the semi-tropical climate. Following his conversion, he spent a night or two in these fields, the citrus groves providing an excellent place to hide. Every few hours he heard the unmistakable sounds of warfare as gunfire, mortars, bombs, and grenades punctuated the air. Overhead, he saw jets and helicopters zooming past. Fearing for his safety, and uncertain how the war was going, he decided to stay out of harm's way for the time being.

When hostilities appeared to abate, Fawzy decided to venture forth from the orchards. He was hungry, and longed for a bath and a clean set of clothes in the worst way. From a hired hand working among the orange trees he learned that Israel had taken Gaza from Egyptian control and instituted martial law in the Strip. The city of Gaza lay only a few miles down the road, and Fawzy decided to go there to seek a way out of the territory.

As he walked toward the city, he saw Israeli troops everywhere and people hurrying about in all directions. By chance he spotted someone he knew, an acquaintance named Izat, who told him that everyone was in a rush to get off the streets before curfew set in. Izat invited Fawzy to go home with him. "Thank you, Jesus!"

Fawzy whispered to himself. The offer of hospitality was gratefully received, and he hurried along with his friend. Izat's family owned citrus groves near the spot Fawzy had been hiding.

Upon arrival, Izat's parents greeted Fawzy warily. They allowed him to clean up and offered a meal, but made it known they were not comfortable lodging an Israeli overnight. There was an old family tomb amid the orange trees, however, and Fawzy was welcome to sleep there if he liked. With no other options available and the curfew in force, Fawzy accepted their suggestion. Izat promised to bring food in the morning.

Fawzy slept in the tomb for four nights, until Izat mentioned that the Israelis were offering to take Palestinians to a refugee camp in Jordan. Fawzy's ears perked up.

"My grandmother and uncles live in Jordan," he said, with excitement evident in his voice. "I'm sure they would welcome me there."

Years earlier, prior to Israel becoming a nation, many of Fawzy's maternal family members had migrated to Jordan. Among the first were three of his mother's brothers, Simaan, Alexander, and Kustanty, all of whom settled in Amman. Not long afterward his grandmother, Um Simaan, joined her sons. She was a devout Christian and staunch Baptist, like his mother. Immediately after Fawzy's birth, his oldest brother Foad followed them there as well, although he recently had relocated to Lebanon. Fawzy knew his brother only as a baby, and had never met his Jordanian relatives. The border to Israel was closed in 1948, and the two countries had been officially at war ever since.

Why Fawzy would choose to go to an enemy nation rather than seek a return to Israel seems puzzling upon first consideration and perhaps foolish in hindsight. The immediate concern of getting out of war-torn Gaza surely played a role, as did the lingering pain of losing Dawlit and attendant desire to move far away. The problem of finding a satisfying job in Israel no doubt entered into his thinking, along with the possibility that relatives could help him land employment in Jordan. Youthful impulsivity or naïveté cannot be discounted. Added to these factors may have been a sense that God was leading him there.

The journey from Gaza to Jordan was not an easy one. As Izat mentioned, Israeli military trucks were transporting any properly credentialed citizen of Gaza who wished to leave. Jordan was already the home of hundreds of thousands of Palestinian refugees, and with the unfavorable outcome of the Six Day War, the numbers were sure to increase. Of course Fawzy was Israeli, so he would have to go under an assumed identity.

Having made his decision to depart, he approached an Israeli transport vehicle and asked to board.

"Where's your ID?" barked the driver.

Fawzy nervously fumbled around in his pants pocket.

"I need to see your ID!" shouted the driver, with obvious impatience.

Fawzy withdrew the document he had taken from the dead soldier, the card with the name Ali Othman Aaid. His listed age and size were about the same as Fawzy's. There was no picture. He handed it through the window, not knowing if they would accept the identification. The

Israeli studied it, looked back at Fawzy, and then returned the ID.

"Okay, Aaid, get in the back," the driver motioned.

He headed toward the rear of the covered vehicle and climbed in. Already on board were approximately twenty-five others jammed like pringles in a can, women and children sitting on benches on three sides, men hunkered down in the middle. Some conversed in Arabic, but Fawzy kept quiet lest his Galilean accent betray his origin, preferring to ascertain as much information as possible from their conversations. The best he could understand, they were headed toward the Jordanian border by way of the former West Bank city of Jericho, now occupied by the Israeli army. The ride was long and stressful. The physical discomfort, body odors, bad diapers, and mental stress combined to make the trip arduous.

After an agonizingly slow four hour trek through the rugged countryside of southern Israel and along the western shore of the Dead Sea, the truck came to the temporary refugee camp set up near Jericho. There he and the other passengers were processed and asked if they wanted to enter Jordan. His Gaza identification was confiscated, and he and others were taken to a nearby border crossing and escorted along a narrow footbridge that crossed the Jordan River.

A Jordanian military truck was waiting as he made it across the tributary. When he touched Jordanian soil for the first time and was herded into the foreign vehicle, Fawzy could not help but wonder if he had made the right decision. There was no turning back now. He prayed for the Lord's watch-care as he entered the ancient land of the Ammonites and Moabites.

****

Fawzy stepped into the waiting Jordanian military vehicle and headed to a refugee camp somewhere within the sprawling, sun-baked wilderness that lay before them. His objective was to proceed at the earliest opportunity to Amman and his relatives who lived there. After traveling for more than an hour into the interior of the desolate land, the truck lurched to a stop. High hills surrounded them as the passengers were allowed time for a bathroom break. Men were directed to go into the desert on one side of the truck, women and children on the other, with soldiers escorting both groups.

Fawzy followed their instructions, but kept moving deeper into the rocky expanse, as if searching for a secluded spot. He was momentarily tempted to flee and head toward Amman, but thought better of it. He didn't know where he was or how far away the city might be. Instead, he seized the opportunity to destroy his Israeli identification, lest it cause problems within Jordan. He was now without credentials of any kind.

Afterward, the truck continued on its journey. Just before nightfall, he began to see the lights of the refugee camp shining ever more brightly in the distance. As they drove closer to the compound, its sheer size was stunning. There were thousands of refugees lingering about and hundreds of tents arranged in no discernible pattern. He was taken to the camp's headquarters, processed, and assigned to the Gaza section where he would reside in an all-purpose tent set aside for male exiles.

Fawzy thanked God for his safe arrival and headed to his temporary quarters. There he found approximately fifteen other men, but said little in order to remain as inconspicuous as possible. He was given a satisfying meal and took a bath for the first time in several days. The sleeping mat felt very comfortable compared to the hard ground of Gaza. Once again he thanked the good Lord, this time for some of life's simple pleasures.

The next day Fawzy approached a mediator at the camp about traveling to Amman to join his relatives. He was told that such a trip was impossible at the moment. The government had not yet decided how to deal with the mass of new refugees from the war, or when to issue papers authorizing their travel within the country. He would have to wait like everyone else until the Jordanian government made its decisions. Fawzy decided to keep a low profile, be patient, and pray for God's will to be done.

After a few weeks, however, he lost patience. Although his basic needs were being met, he felt extremely uncomfortable and out of place at the camp. He appeared to be the only Christian among its thousands of refugees, and it was becoming increasingly difficult for him as a non-Muslim. He tried to remain out of sight during the Muslim calls to prayer and at other public religious rituals, but his absence was noticed and questioned.

The only friend he made was a man named Fadel, an Egyptian teacher who had also been trapped by the war in Gaza. Along with his two wives and eighteen children, he had come to the camp to await return to his country. Sensing Fawzy's awkwardness and discouragement,

Fadel suggested that perhaps his new friend could accompany his family to Amman on their trip back to Egypt. Fawzy seized upon the invitation as an opportunity to finally reach his intended destination. Their plan was for Fawzy to blend in unnoticed among Fadel's children until they arrived at the airport, at which time he would separate and contact his relatives. When news came that transportation was ready, they put their plan into action.

Everything went smoothly as Fawzy slipped onto the bus for the slow two hour trip to the Jordanian capital. He grew nervous at a couple of checkpoints along the way as guards peered in and boarded, but they left him alone. Just outside of Amman, the bus lurched to a stop at another highway terminal. Gazing out the window, Fawzy's stomach churned as he saw Jordanian soldiers inspecting vehicles more thoroughly than before. He grew jittery as two came on board, counted the number of passengers present, looked at their paperwork, and immediately realized there was a stowaway on the bus. As they began to question Fadel about the discrepancy, Fawzy decided he couldn't let his new friend get into trouble. He stood up and admitted that he was the extra person unaccounted for. Quickly he was ushered off the bus, taken to a dimly lit office, and interrogated.

"Who are you and where are you from?" the soldier in charge gruffly asked.

"I am Fawzy Shorrosh from Nazareth, Israel," was his response. He resolved to speak only the truth about himself, whatever the consequences. Using the alias of Ali Othman Aaid would likely mean a return trip to the refugee camp or deportation from the country. Besides, the deception of taking on a Muslim identity had made him uncomfortable as a Christian.

The questioner looked momentarily stunned by Fawzy's answer, then laughed and said something to his fellow soldier. Turning back to Fawzy he continued:

"You can't be serious, my friend. No one in Jordan would admit to being from Israel. Now tell us the truth."

Fawzy assured him that what he had said was so. The man's tone of voice changed markedly.

"So, you're from Israel, huh? Then why did you come to Jordan?"

"I have three uncles and a grandmother in Amman, and I've come to visit them," Fawzy replied. "I am an electrician, and I hope they can help me find work here."

The man shook his head dubiously while looking steely-eyed at Fawzy. "I don't believe you, Shorrosh. Do you want to know what I think? I think you are a spy sent here by the Israelis!"

Instantly Fawzy knew the situation was far more ominous than anticipated. He said a silent prayer as he vehemently denied the accusation. His heart pounded precipitously when he saw the chief interrogator open his desk drawer and pull out a whip in an obvious attempt to intimidate and threaten. With whip in hand and voice rising, the man was a study in sound and fury.

"You're lying, Shorrosh. You are an Israeli spy!" he shouted angrily as he brandished the whip, striking it once across the desk. "You Israelis will stop at nothing to infiltrate our country!"

"No sir, I am not a spy," Fawzy kept repeating. "As I have told you before, I am an electrician, and I am in your country to work and to visit family.

Not hearing what he wanted and frustrated by Fawzy's continued disavowal of covert activities, the army officer decided that violence might evoke a confession. He took the whip and without warning lashed Fawzy with a vicious blow across the shoulder, sending intense pain cascading down both arms and through the rest of his body, a jolt that hurt so badly it drove him to his knees, his face contorted and voice shrieking in agony.

"Admit it, Shorrosh! You are a Jew spy!"

Each time Fawzy ignored or refuted the charge, the whip cut across his backside. The other soldier in the room decided to join in, pummeling Fawzy now and again with fists to the face and stomach. The questioning went on for what seemed like hours. He was repeatedly badgered and insulted, threatened and punished. The beatings were pitiless, with whip, fists, and rifle butt the instruments of choice. Blood and tears flowed freely from his body—black and blue and throbbing with pain—as he drifted in and out of consciousness.

Finally, he was ushered into an office and processed for further assignment. The official in charge took out a form and ordered Fawzy to answer his questions truthfully or risk execution. The form asked about his identity and purpose for being in Jordan. He told them what he had already stated many times: "My name is Fawzy Shorrosh. I am from Nazareth, Israel. I am an electrician. I entered Jordan to find work and to see my family in Amman."

The Jordanian scowled and turned to the other soldier in the room.

"This is nothing but the same old crap. Send him to the prison in Amman! Register him as a prisoner of war."

Prison! Fawzy's mind raced into panic mode, but the Lord quickly calmed his fears with thoughts of His sovereignty and assurances of His care. As he was led away in chains, he remembered how many of those closest to Jesus—notably Peter, John, James, and Paul—had ended up in prison for various lengths of time. Now he was about to join their illustrious company. For the next two years he would suffer incarceration in Amman.

****

The prison in Amman was stereotypically gray, drab, and unclean. The multi-story concrete penitentiary housed the worst of Jordan's criminal population, including murderers, terrorists, and insurrectionists. The prisoners were sometimes housed in groups of four or more, crowded into small spaces that reeked of body odors and wastes. The stench in the air made eating the bland prison food even more of a challenge.

As the only Christian among the guards and inmates, and as an Israeli citizen, Fawzy expected to receive abuse. He was not wrong. Often he felt like a wounded deer preyed upon by a pack of wolves. Routinely isolated and deprived of food, his mistreatment descended to the level of physical cruelty. The chief guard of his cell block was particularly nasty—pushing, shoving, punching, and kicking him at every opportunity. Fawzy also endured incessant criticism, contempt, and insults. Every kind of taunt and slur came his way, laced with profanities and vulgarities, of course.

Through it all Fawzy found a way to respond with a small witness about what the Lord had done for him, and what He could do for them as well. "I am not an Israeli spy. I am an electrician, and a Christian by the love and grace of God," was the answer he gave their malice, concluding, "God loves you, too, even though you treat me this way." They simply spat in his face or cursed him more. Nevertheless, he persevered in his witness for Jesus, inspired by the memories of his mother, and sustained, no doubt, by her constant prayers on his behalf.

The boldness of Fawzy's faith energized him. He had ridiculed Christianity for many of his twenty-one years, jeering and hissing at believers, mocking even his own flesh and blood, much as the Jordanian guards and inmates were heaping derision upon him. Now in the crucible of the enemy, and as a Christian for only a short time, his trust in the Lord was unwavering. He found unusual strength and strange comfort in sharing the gospel while under intense persecution.

Intermittent interrogations and beatings continued over the course of his confinement. He often looked gruesome, with face swollen, lips puffed, and clothes soaked in perspiration and blood. Whelps and scratches were a common sight upon his bruised and battered torso. Sometimes he was dragged around by his long, black, corkscrew-style hair and thrown against the concrete walls of the holding cell.

He had no idea what his captors would do with him. Since tensions were running high between Jordan and Israel, there was the possibility of execution. Conversely, he had heard of instances where the

Jordanians allowed Israelis to languish in prison for a while before taking them to the border and unceremoniously dumping them back into their country. He couldn't help but wonder and worry about his own fate, even as he entrusted himself fully to the Lord.

One day a British Red Cross representative visited the prison, and Fawzy boldly decided to ask for a Bible. The agent told him to say nothing about the request and he would see what he could do. About two weeks later the man returned and smuggled into the prison a small copy of the scriptures. It was a Gideon New Testament, with the familiar lamp logo on the front cover, translated into the Arabic language.

Reading and meditating upon God's Word became Fawzy's chief source of pleasure during the many lonely hours of detention. The stories about Jesus came to life as he opened up its pages. The accounts of Paul's conversion and subsequent persecutions especially fortified his soul. He took great care to handle the Good Book circumspectly around fellow prisoners and guards, and the authorities never confiscated his spiritual treasure.

Unknown to Fawzy, the Red Cross aid worker did far more on his behalf than bootleg a Bible. The man was a believer and a leader in the Christian community in Amman. He began sharing about Fawzy's plight among the evangelical churches in the country, asking them to pray for his welfare and witness in the prison—and if God willed, his eventual release.

After more than two years in custody, one morning Fawzy received an astonishing gift. On November 14, 1969, as inmates lined up for regular roll call, the warden suddenly appeared and announced that a number of prisoners were to be freed immediately. Every year, on the occasion of King Hussein's birthday, government authorities issued a general amnesty in honor of the Jordanian monarch. Essentially it was a way to alleviate overcrowding in the prison, where more space was needed to detain additional offenders.

Looking at an official document, the warden began reading the names of those to be released "at the good pleasure of His Royal Majesty." Fawzy had no reason to hope his name would be called. He was not Jordanian, and the amnesty was strictly for Jordanian prisoners with good conduct records. Other nationalities were not eligible, particularly POW's. For this reason, as he heard the warden call his name, "SHORROSH, FAWZY," he was completely shocked. It must be some cruel hoax, he thought, another sadistic attempt to harass him for their amusement.

When finally convinced it was true, that he would indeed go free as a modern-day Barabbas, he let out a yell, danced for joy, and looked up to the heavens in gratitude, shouting over and over, "Thank you Jesus! Thank you Jesus!" It was likely a careless mistake on the part of the prison authorities, but also a miracle from the hand of God. Fawzy gave glory to the Lord, who had so marvelously answered his prayers and wondrously intervened on behalf of His servant.

Before being released, the prison authorities gave him one last savage beating to remember them by. Fawzy exited the Amman prison in frail condition, with only the clothes on his back and a Bible in his pocket.

****

Fawzy had hoped the Jordanians would deport him back to Israel—more than two years in prison were enough to make him long for home. Instead he was dumped on the streets of Amman, penniless and barefoot, with tattered clothes, dirty skin, long hair, and scruffy beard. The wounds inflicted from the prison beating were in need of medical attention.

He had no idea where his grandmother or uncles lived in the city. For their sake, it wasn't wise to try to make contact while in prison. As he rested against a dilapidated building, pondering what he should do, a Jeep passed by and then slowed to a stop. He saw an older gentleman whom he did not know get out of the vehicle and walk briskly in his direction.

"Are you alright, son?" the man inquired in accented Arabic.

"No, not really," Fawzy responded, after hesitating a moment.

"I'm sorry. Is there anything I can do for you?" the man asked kindly.

"Well, I don't know," said Fawzy, beginning to weep a little. "I just got out of prison, and they beat me up pretty good." He then showed the stranger some of his wounds.

"My name is Roy Whitman," the man said, introducing himself. "You'd better get that seen about. I'll be glad to take you to some friends of mine who can treat you. What's your name?"

"Thank you very much, sir. I am Fawzy Shorrosh."

A smile immediately spread across Whitman's face as he recognized the name.

"So you're the guy we've been praying for all this time!" he exclaimed.

Once again the Lord demonstrated His providence in Fawzy's life. Roy Whitman was among those in the Amman evangelical community contacted by the Red Cross official who slipped Fawzy a New Testament. A Church of the Brethren missionary in Jordan for more than four decades, Reverend Whitman had seen many answers to his prayers through the years, but perhaps none so dramatically as the person who now stood before him.

He helped Fawzy into his vehicle and drove toward the city of Ajlun, located approximately thirty miles north, and to the Baptist hospital there. As they passed through various checkpoints along the highway, Fawzy crouched down on the floorboard to remain unseen. He had no personal identification in an area of the world obsessed with it. By contrast, Reverend Whitman was well known to the guards, who waved him through without hassle.

At the hospital Fawzy obtained the care and rest his body so desperately needed. He also received spiritual nourishment from the hospital's Christian medical staff, his first sustained fellowship with a group of believers since becoming one. There he remained for two or three weeks before feeling strong enough to attempt a visit with relatives in Amman.

The hospital sent a truck to the capital for supplies every week. Fawzy hitched a ride and succeeded in locating the home of Simaan Cheleel, his mother's brother. To his disappointment and embarrassment, he was not well received. They had never met, and to see an Israeli standing at his front door and claiming to be family was quite a shock. Despite initial hesitation, custom dictated that he offer hospitality, which Fawzy awkwardly accepted.

Simaan earned a good living as a produce distributor, enabling his family to live in an upscale home in one of the better suburban neighborhoods of Amman. He could certainly afford to help his nephew, but was wary of the trouble it might bring during the current downturn in Jordanian-Israeli relations. Fawzy never felt comfortable in his home, and looked to leave as soon as possible.

He learned that his grandmother lived only a few miles away with another uncle, Alexander Cheleel, along with his wife and three children. In marked contrast to the reception he received from Simaan and his household, Alexander's family welcomed him with joy and many tears. He would have preferred to stay with them, but believed it was too much of an imposition. The family was relatively poor with a tiny home, and Uncle Alexander obtained only intermittent carpentry work. A third uncle, Kustanty Cheleel, was also ill-suited to accommodate him.

Fawzy's brother Foad had recently moved from Jordan to Lebanon, believing God had called him to minister in that country. Like his mother and grandmother before him, he was a devout Christian, and currently served as pastor of the Baptist church in Ba'labakk, Lebanon. Upon Fawzy's arrival at Simaan's, Foad was contacted and came to see his sibling right away. The two last visited in Nazareth some twenty years earlier-- Foad had not been legally allowed to return to Israel after departing for Jordan. The two brothers embraced warmly and enjoyed getting to know each other while catching up on family news. Before leaving, Foad gave Fawzy a little money and told him to call should he need more.

Reverend Whitman introduced Fawzy to several believers in Amman's Christian community. One introduction proved invaluable. Adel Zomot was a young Jordanian pastor and the manager of a small Christian book store in Amman. He took a special interest in Fawzy, becoming his personal Bible tutor over the next few months. Adel was well versed in the scriptures and gladly mentored his recently born-again friend. The book store became a gathering place of sorts for fellowship, prayer, and Bible study.

One of Fawzy's most pressing problems was the lack of official identification of any kind. Without a passport he could not legally leave Jordan, and without government papers it was difficult to find steady employment. Not having proper ID also meant that he was always at risk of being picked up by the authorities and put in prison again. This, in fact, happened during his brief stay with Simaan. While venturing out for a stroll through the neighborhood one evening, Jordanian soldiers grabbed him and took him to a compound for detainees outside the city. Fortunately he was able to get word to his uncle, who used his connections to bring about Fawzy's release.

Uncle Simaan was not happy about the incident, and relations between the two steadily deteriorated. He soon let it be known that other living arrangements must be made. Fawzy left his uncle's house with little money, no ID, and no idea about where to go. Other family members were in no position to lend him daily food and shelter. Adel, Reverend Whitman, and other believers helped as much as permitted, but Fawzy's sense of pride caused him to refuse their many offers of more substantial assistance.

For a few days Fawzy found himself sleeping in Amman's doorways and back alleys. Except when he ate with friends or at his grandmother's, his daily diet mostly consisted of cheap falafels—pita bread filled with mashed peas. Many nights he went to sleep to the sounds of hunger pains serenading him from an empty belly.

Under such dire circumstances it was exceedingly difficult to practice good hygiene. What he enjoyed most about staying with Uncle Simaan was not the soft bed roll or the home-cooked meals, but the opportunity to bathe regularly and wash his clothes. Fawzy possessed only one outfit of clothing, making the logistics of cleaning a complicated process, with several hours needed to dry his wet garments.

Steady work was tough to come by. He could get a few hours wages here or there by digging ditches or doing odd jobs, enough to buy falafels and occasionally rent an inexpensive room, but initially he had no luck securing anything long-term. Within three weeks after leaving Uncle Simaan's, however, he heard through a friend that Rumzy Electrical Works, a Palestinian-owned business, was in need of an electrician. An acquaintance knew someone at the company and recommended Fawzy, who was hired despite lacking proper credentials. Now he could afford to sleep and eat more comfortably.

The reason Rumzy was recruiting additional help became apparent on Fawzy's first day of employment. The company had recently landed a subcontracting job on a major government project. Jordan's King Hussein was refurbishing one of the royal palaces for his brother, Prince Hassan, and Rumzy was managing all of the electrical work. Amazingly, Fawzy spent the next two months laboring on the palace's grounds outside of Amman.

Each morning he was driven to the king's lavish estate with other workers, and each afternoon was picked up and taken back to the company's downtown office. Initially the guards at the gate of the royal grounds refused Fawzy entrance because he lacked documentation. But Mr. Rumzy personally vouched for Fawzy, explained his importance to the renovation, and took responsibility for him.

Inside the palace, located at the top of one of the mountains encircling the city, Fawzy helped wire several rooms in preparation for the latest in electronic equipment and decorative furnishings. He fashioned voltage receptacles, hung expensive crystal chandeliers, and set up antique ornamental lamps, always with the keen eyes of a soldier looking on. On one occasion the royal mother, Queen Zein, came to inspect the restoration and engaged Fawzy in conversation, even shaking his hand upon leaving. Fawzy silently chuckled at the irony of it all.

On the way to work one morning, Fawzy was again detained by soldiers, who took him to a place of confinement and promptly shaved his head! He learned that he and others without credentials were picked up to be conscripted into the Jordanian army! Although he didn't have ID, he possessed blueprints of the palace that displayed details of its electrical design. As he stood in line to be processed, he decided to show the blueprints to the authorities, hoping to convince them that he worked for the royal family. If they feared discipline from the king for causing delay, perhaps they would let him go.

He also decided to identify himself by using the name Rihani. Some of Fawzy's maternal ancestors originally came to Galilee from Jordanian soil, and Rihani was an old family surname. When he arrived at the front of the line, the soldier in charge gruffly asked his name.

"Rihani," answered Fawzy.

"Rihani?" repeated the soldier.

"Yes sir, Fawzy Shorrosh Rihani."

"My name is Rihani, too!" declared the soldier excitedly, to Fawzy's utter astonishment. The Jordanian then proceeded to relate the names and addresses of some of his people.

"What Rihanis are you related to?" he finally asked Fawzy.

Fawzy mentioned some of his forebears and then showed him the blueprints. The soldier shook his head in affirmation and called for two men to take Fawzy to the palace. "Thank you, Jesus!" Fawzy exclaimed under his breath, believing the Lord had delivered him yet again. When he later ran into Mr. Rumzy at the palace, his boss let out a huge guffaw upon seeing Fawzy's shorn head, instantly recognizing the reason for his employee's tardiness.

It was a vulnerable time in a foreign land, and Fawzy lived in perpetual fear of being thrown into prison or receiving bodily harm. In the volatile anti-Israeli atmosphere of the city, he knew that he was a ready target, that it would not take much for the wrong soldier to arrest him, find no papers, and shoot without provocation. Life was fragile and killing was cheap in Jordan as the decade of the seventies flung open its door.

Despite anxieties involving personal security, Fawzy continued to grow spiritually, visiting Adel at the book store almost daily and worshipping at his church on Sundays and Wednesdays. He spent a lot of time studying the Bible and in prayer with other believers. Comprehending what the Lord was up to in his life was beyond his grasp. He simply must trust God to reveal His purposes in due time.

****

While working for Rumzy, Fawzy found inspiration from another individual who befriended him. Fawaz Amaesh was pastor of the Baptist church in Ajlun, where the missionary hospital was located. This devout Jordanian Christian came to the bookstore looking for him, and soon they were introduced by Adel. Fawaz took a special interest in Fawzy because they were practically related, with Fawaz's wife the sister-in-law of Fawzy's brother Foad. Foad had asked Fawaz to check on his little brother from time to time when he visited Amman, as he often did.

Fawaz was around forty years of age, a behemoth of a man, with a booming voice, jolly demeanor, and infectious smile that brought instant likeability. He was the most vibrant and ebullient Christian Fawzy had ever met. At their first encounter he took Fawzy to a fancy restaurant in the city and spent time getting acquainted with his younger fellow believer. Fawaz proceeded to introduce him to other Christian friends in the country, as well as to pray with him and offer encouragement to continue growing in Christ despite his many hardships.

During the course of their conversations, Fawaz asked about the one thing Fawzy appeared to need most if he were ever to get out of Jordan.

"Have you had any success in obtaining a passport?"

"None," Fawzy answered. "No one I talk to thinks it's possible."

"It will be difficult," Fawaz agreed. "But all things are possible with God, Fawzy!"

Fawaz explained the different grades of passports granted to the public by the Jordanian government. Class three was reserved for native Jordanians, while class six was for Palestinians who had been in Jordan since the 1948 transformation of Palestine into Israel. Fawzy was ineligible for either. Class eleven, the lowest level, was the category he fit into, the only type of passport given to new arrivals in the country.

"I'll pray for you to get a passport," promised Fawaz. "And I'll ask my church to pray, too!"

One individual introduced to Fawzy was a distant relative. Dawood Rihani owned a business not far from the bookstore, a grocery that specialized in imported foods. Fawaz took Fawzy to Dawood's shop where they were greeted with great enthusiasm and an invitation to dinner. Uncle Dawood, as Fawzy called him, was an amiable man in his late forties, a devout Greek Orthodox Christian with four children and a pleasant wife.

Fawzy immediately felt comfortable in their home, welcomed like a long lost family member. Over the course of the delectable meal, Fawzy explained how he had come to Jordan.

"What kind of help can we be to you, Fawzy?" Dawood asked as they finished, with obvious sincerity.

"I need a passport," responded Fawzy. "I don't have papers of any kind, which, of course, makes it very difficult here. Is there anyone you know who could help me obtain one?"

Dawood thought for a moment and then excused himself to make a phone call. After returning to the table, he told Fawzy that he had spoken to a friend who would drop by a little later. Maybe he could be of help.

When Dawood's friend arrived, Fawzy's heart filled with fear. The tall man was in full uniform with an obviously high rank. He was addressed as General and worked for the government! Fawzy's instinct was to flee, but Dawood quickly put him at ease by calling the man a family friend who was not a threat. Fawzy told the general his story and mentioned his need for a passport to leave the country. The officer stated that a passport would be extremely difficult to get, but he would see what he could do.

After a few days the general reported back to Dawood. A passport was impossible to acquire, he found, but he thought Fawzy could receive a government-issued refugee card that entitled holders to food and shelter benefits. The document could also serve as an official government ID. Fawzy should apply at the office of the Ministry of Refugees, he counseled.

Fawzy was skeptical. He had entered the country under the guise of a Gaza refugee, but was actually an illegal immigrant from Israel. He had confessed his true identity to the Jordanian authorities before his imprisonment, and had no intention of posing as a refugee again.

Nevertheless, at the urging of Dawood he went downtown to the Ministry of Refugees headquarters,

where he found mass chaos. The lines were long, with
pushing and shoving and cursing among scores of
refugees. He stood in line for seven hours before finally
giving up. It was a big waste of time, he figured.

Dawood again contacted the general who told
Fawzy to return to the ministry office and he would
personally oversee his application. The following
morning Fawzy was quickly escorted inside the building,
filled out the necessary paperwork, and to his amazement
was promptly granted a refugee card! He finally
possessed an authorized government ID. As he held it in
hand, he audibly praised the Lord with the familiar,
"Thank you, Jesus!"

Looking closer at the card, he saw his photo and
name, and printed afterward in large block letters,
"NAZARETH #1." The incongruity was astounding.
The government had issued a refugee card to a non-
refugee while identifying him as a resident of a prominent
Israeli town. What's more, it was apparently the first
such card issued for a citizen of Nazareth. Fawzy stood
amazed at God's incredible workings in his life. "Thank
you, Jesus!" he couldn't help but utter again.

Over the course of his time in Amman, political
unrest grew worse and his Nazareth #1 card came in
handy more than once. The Palestinian commandoes and
guerilla fighters, who attacked Israel along the Jordanian
border, became bolder with their presence and political
rallies. The police looked the other way when Palestinian
Liberation Organization operatives paraded down the
capital's streets in full military regalia with rifles held
high, a blatant violation of Jordanian law. Frequent
gunfire was more pronounced as skirmishes broke out

between the PLO's supporters and the more moderate Jordanians who resented the influx of refugees.

The growing disturbances in Amman made it a highly dangerous place, especially for new arrivals. Fawzy began to think about relocating away from the city, and increasingly heard encouragement to leave from family members and friends who feared for his safety. But where would he live and work? Without a passport he couldn't leave the country, and there didn't appear to be anything for him elsewhere in Jordan. He prayed earnestly that God would provide direction once again.

****

In the spring of 1970, Fawzy's prayers were answered. The Baptist hospital in Ajlun was in need of an experienced electrician, and through connections with Fawaz and Reverend Whitman, along with a favorable job interview with Ray Smith, a Louisiana missionary who headed Southern Baptist work in Jordan, Fawzy was offered and accepted the position. He hated to leave Amman and the family members and friends he had met over the past few months, but felt drawn to a more secure job in less volatile surroundings. He also believed he could grow stronger spiritually and minister more effectively in the environment of a missionary hospital.

Ajlun was set in the beautiful north Jordanian mountains, less than an hour by car from Amman and only ten miles from the Israeli border. Dense poverty pervaded the community, with ramshackle, unadorned huts lining its streets and roads—some of the harshest living conditions Fawzy had ever seen. The citizenry was largely uneducated and adhered to strict codes of dress among women, most natives wearing lengthy, loose-fitting garments along with head coverings. Surprisingly, a large Christian population inhabited the area, though evangelicals comprised only a small percentage.

Just outside of town was the Baptist hospital, a relatively spacious complex of buildings and grounds. There was the standard combination of clinic, patient beds, medical offices, and cafeteria, but the compound also consisted of a chapel, staff housing, and a dormitory for faculty and workers at the Baptist school in town. Fawzy was part of the hospital's maintenance crew and responsible for all electrical operations. This included rewiring virtually the entire facility during his first three months on the job.

Trained as an electrician at an early age,
Fawzy often utilized his mechanical skills.

It didn't take long to know he had made the right decision in coming to the hospital. Almost immediately he felt comfortable, enjoying his work among employees and patients. Most of the staff were committed Christians, including the infirmary's director, Dr. John Roper from South Carolina, his colleague, Dr. August Lovegreen from Georgia, and Miss Violet Pope, the head nurse from Alabama, all of whom were serving as medical missionaries to Jordan. They were a close-knit group and welcomed Fawzy as a valuable member of their team. Soon they entrusted him with expanded responsibilities that included helping with selected medical procedures in the x-ray department.

The hospital's overtly Christian mission and spiritual atmosphere furthered Fawzy's personal maturation in the things of Christ. The everyday example of the medical leadership provided a much needed model of Christian living and walking with the Lord that made an indelible impression. Each morning he enjoyed participating in the institution's chapel services, enabling staff members like himself to focus beyond the humanitarian reason for their existence.

On Sunday mornings and Wednesday nights, Fawzy took the hospital van into town to attend the Baptist congregation where Fawaz was pastor. He soon wanted to join, but their membership policy called for a one year waiting period of preparation and instruction. After successfully completing the course of study, he was baptized in 1971 by head missionary Ray Smith.

Sunday afternoons were often spent with Fawaz on evangelistic visits to different homes in the area or to surrounding villages where there were no evangelical churches. Fawzy also found a creative way to engage in evangelistic ministry at the hospital. It didn't take long for word to spread that he knew how to repair electronic equipment—especially transistor radios that were all the rage in Jordan at the time. Medical staff, patients, teachers, and townspeople soon inundated Fawzy with their broken radios.

He decided to make his room into a fix-it shop, and designed two large signs in English to hang in conspicuous spots along the walls. The signs functioned as concise personal testimonies and discussion starters. The wood carvings were inscribed with the sayings, "JESUS IS MY SAVIOR" and "GOD IS LOVE." Since Fawzy understood no English, Dr. Roper's son, David, helped with the English lettering. Most of Fawzy's customers couldn't read English either, but he figured correctly that they would ask him about the signs. When they did, Fawzy translated and took the opportunity to share his faith in Christ.

Another avenue of witness opened up, as well. In the early seventies the hospital took on the aura of a MASH unit as fighting intensified among the Israelis, Palestinian resistance groups, and Jordanian military. An army field hospital located nearby cared for government casualties, but injured Palestinians and civilians caught in the crossfire were usually sent to the Baptist hospital. It was Fawzy's responsibility to help transport incoming wounded from the hospital compound's front gate to the infirmary.

Northern Jordan was a seedbed for Palestinian guerrilla units. Its proximity to Israel's border, rural mountainous terrain, and tolerable climate fomented an estimated twenty separate commando groups that settled in the region. They belonged to various Palestinian political factions, united by their efforts to remove Israel's hegemony over ancient biblical land. Not only did they conduct raids and sponsor terrorist activities against Israel, but also fought the Jordanian army for control of areas in the north. Occasionally the Palestinian camps even battled each other for territorial jurisdiction.

As Fawzy came to know the wounded commandoes, he shared his testimony with many. Nazareth was a common point of interest and natural conversation starter. Few had ever been to "Palestine," as they called it. Fawzy painted a picture for them of the land of his birth, its beauty and strengths, as well as the many topographical features that make it such a unique and coveted space. As they listened, he also told of another Nazarene whom he had come to know as Savior and Lord. Although the militants were almost all of various shades of commitment to Islam, Fawzy managed to plant the gospel seed of Christ among them.

During the five years Fawzy was in Jordan, there was no direct contact with his family in Nazareth. Only circuitously did he hear about them. Indeed, it was from Pastor Fawaz by way of Foad that Fawzy received the grievous news that his father had died. The disturbing revelation was tempered greatly, however, by the additional information that Tawfic had confessed faith in Christ in the weeks prior to his death!

The old man attributed his radical shift from atheism to Christianity, in part, to the long distance testimony of his son Fawzy. Foad managed to get word to their dad about the remarkable conversion of his younger brother. Tawfic reasoned that a God who could bring peace and joy to Fawzy must be real after all.

"Thank you, Jesus," Fawzy repeated softly, even as he wept on Fawaz' shoulder.

Fawzy ached to return home to comfort his mother and siblings, but apparently God wanted him in Jordan. Every possibility for obtaining a passport had been thoroughly pursued—and rebuffed. On several occasions he pled his case to officials in the passport offices of Amman and Irbid, to no avail. Hopes were raised when Uncle Dawood managed to meet with the prime minister of Jordan, Wasfi al-Tal, on Fawzy's behalf, but were quickly dashed when told that the recent Palestinian insurgency had made obtaining a passport out of the question. A short time later after their meeting, al-Tal was assassinated on November 28, 1971 by four gunmen associated with the PLO.

All Fawzy could do was trust the Lord to give direction, and pray to be used for His glory while living in a hostile land.

****

In 1971 Fawzy's cousin, Anis Shorrosh, whom he had never met, visited Ajlun while leading a Christian tour group from the United States. Anis had lived and worked in Ajlun years earlier before immigrating to America. A Middle East pastor for several years, he now led a Christian evangelism ministry headquartered in Mobile, Alabama. After getting acquainted, Fawzy joined Anis in showing the group the sites in and around Ajlun, including the magnificent twelfth century Arab fortress Qalat ar-Rabad, built to ward off medieval crusaders. At a height of 4000 feet, it had long dominated the city, offering sweeping views of the lush Jordan Valley below.

One of the missionaries at the hospital, Dr. August Lovegreen, suggested that Fawzy consider joining Anis in the U.S., perhaps for study purposes. He personally knew the president of a small Baptist college in Mississippi that he believed Fawzy could attend. Fawzy dismissed the idea as implausible. He had no passport or money. He only possessed an eighth grade education and didn't speak English. It was on the other side of the world. The notion was unrealistic, he decided, and gave it no more consideration—for the time being. The thought firmly planted itself in the back of his mind, however.

Over the course of the following year, civil and military strife in Jordan intensified, and the country's political climate steadily deteriorated. Israel retaliated against the Palestinian commandoes by bombing their camps in northern Jordan, heightening tensions between the two nations. In response, Jordan outlawed Palestinian organizations from operating on Jordanian soil. Skirmishes between the guerrilla groups and the government's soldiers escalated as the Jordanian army sought to root out resistance groups from the countryside. The Palestinians, led by Arafat's PLO, defended themselves with remarkable success, eventually gaining the upper hand and taking command of several towns and villages throughout the northern tier of Jordan.

Not only was this a time of bloody conflict, but the Jordanian government began exerting more pressure upon non-citizens like Fawzy. It took steps to limit the number of refugees in the country and boosted its efforts to arrest illegal aliens. His Nazareth #1 card was voided so that once again he possessed no official identification.

The government crackdown developed into a major concern.

Although Fawzy lived and worked within the relative security of the missionary compound, he had mingled openly with many of the Palestinian groups that were now outlawed. He befriended them in order to witness about Christ, but the authorities could easily misinterpret his intentions. He was increasingly afraid the government would arrest him as a Palestinian revolutionary, an illegal immigrant, or—worst nightmare of all—an Israeli POW released by mistake.

Under the circumstances he didn't think it wise to remain in Jordan much longer. The only possible place to go, it seemed, was to his brother's home in Lebanon. Although he couldn't get there legally, a pro-Syrian Palestinian organization offered to sneak him into Syria, from which he could enter Lebanon with Foad's assistance. The group was comprised of volunteers from Iran and Syria who came to Jordan to help the Palestinians in the fight against Israel. Fawzy became well acquainted with them while helping their injured at the hospital.

He needed proper documentation when in Syria, and reluctantly agreed to be photographed and identified as part of their resistance movement. Being Israeli, he certainly was not a Palestinian sympathizer; the ruse was simply his ticket out of Jordan. Four photographs were made, with only one included in the falsified paperwork. The other pictures were kept by the Palestinians, and soon would fall into Jordanian hands.

In the early part of 1972, Fawzy said goodbye to friends and fellow believers in Ajlun, not knowing when or if he would see them again. He then crossed with the commandoes from Jordan into Syria for the brief, uneventful trip to Lebanon. Foad helped obtain a 90 day visitor's permit to travel in his country.

When Fawzy arrived in Ba'labakk, he was warmly greeted by his brother's family. He enjoyed meeting his sister-in-law, Rifka, for the first time, as well as his three nephews and little niece. The children were genuinely excited to see the young uncle whom they had heard so much about, and the family quickly made him feel at home in their presence.

Fawzy spent the first few weeks in Lebanon getting to know his relatives and helping Foad with his ministry at the Baptist church. He also volunteered at an international aid organization known as Operation Mobilization, an agency comprised of young Christians whose purpose was to assist local congregations in the area. They were currently constructing a new church facility in the neighboring town of Riiak, and Fawzy joined them in the effort and in door to door evangelism.

The sojourn in Lebanon gave Fawzy the opportunity to ponder and pray about his future. Now that he was finally out of Jordan, what next? Foad added his voice to those who encouraged him to seriously consider study in the United States. Fawzy had shot down the notion months earlier, but now events and circumstances converged to make the idea much more attractive.

For one thing, he was no longer sure he wanted to remain in the Middle East. Though someday he hoped to return to Israel, it was not likely to be in the near future. Settling in Jordan was out of the question, and Lebanon— the most viable option among the three countries—did not especially appeal to him. The political realities and ongoing hostilities in his home region made the thought of living in a distant land increasingly agreeable.

What most intrigued him about the United States—in his decidedly post-communist mindset—were its democratic ideals, religious freedoms, and Christian history. To experience American culture and to receive an American education were opportunities that few in his position would turn down. With the help of his missionary friends in Jordan and their influential contacts in the U.S., he believed the possibility was within reach—if he could obtain the money and proper documentation.

As he thought and prayed about the next step in his life, he was drawn more and more to the prospect of coming to the United States. Getting there, he knew, would take a special dose of divine intervention, but he firmly believed that if God were in it, nothing could prevent it. The American Embassy in Beirut could let him know exactly what qualifications were necessary. With this purpose in mind, he and Foad made the fifty mile trek over the Lebanese mountains and southwest toward the Mediterranean coast to the country's capital.

At the U. S. Embassy Fawzy received discouraging news. Because he was only a visitor in Lebanon, he must return to Jordan to obtain a passport, as well as other necessary credentials from the Jordanian government. To receive a student visa, he must hold a high school degree and pass an English language examination. In addition, he needed a letter of acceptance from an American college or university. The requirements were formidable; the odds appeared heavily weighted against him.

As the brothers returned to Ba'labakk, a crucial decision loomed. Should he return to Jordan and try again to obtain the passport and other essential documents? Or should he seek permanent residency status in Lebanon?

While he prayed and deliberated, Fawzy was offered employment by a friend of Foad. A new Christian elementary school was being constructed nearby, and an electrician was needed. Fawzy took the temporary job, being paid the handsome sum of $700 for his services, the most money in his pocket since his brother Nabeh's wedding, and enough to pay for an airline ticket to the United States.

He now had the desire and the money to travel to America. A passport and visa would be harder to come by, but he fully believed that if the Lord were in it, He would find a way to provide them. As his visitor's permit was set to expire, Fawzy decided not to close the door of opportunity just yet. He would make one final visit to Jordan before giving up on the idea and settling in Lebanon. The trip back, he knew, could be dangerous and futile, but he felt he must go. He bathed it in prayer, turned it over to the Lord, and prepared for another journey to Jordan.

****

Using his underground connections, Fawzy exited Lebanon and crossed through Syria once more on his way back into Jordan. His friends in Ajlun were delighted to see him again, thrilled to have him back in their midst. Over the course of his three month absence, the region had actually become more politically stable, with government forces retaking most of the key areas of northern Jordan. Still, Fawzy was in the country without legal certification, and faced the persistent possibility of arrest.

With great relief he found that his old job had not yet been filled, so he resumed working at the hospital. The medical staff was exceedingly pleased, not only to have him back as a co-worker, but also to know that he had come around to their way of thinking about going to the United States, renewing their pledge of assistance toward that goal.

It was at this juncture that Fawzy made a new friend, a young woman whom God would use to remove a major obstacle in his path to America. Her name was Siham Rubady, a teacher at the Baptist school in Ajlun, who had recently returned home from university studies in Damascus. In addition to teaching responsibilities, she was also working on an advanced degree in languages and attempting to learn Hebrew. After getting to know Fawzy, she asked if he might tutor her in his native tongue, an assignment he readily accepted. It didn't take Siham long to grasp Hebrew, and soon she would easily pass the university's proficiency examination.

Siham was different from most women Fawzy encountered in Jordan, not only in her devout Christian faith, but also in her unconventional ways and modern outlook on life. After years of study in Damascus, she returned with a more liberated attitude toward provincial customs like traditional dress and male/female interactions. This brought more than a little gossip and scandalous talk her way from the locals. Fawzy liked Siham's independent spirit and non-conformist perspective, and they quickly bonded as good friends.

Siham was a prominent member of a young women's organization in Ajlun that held its national meeting in Amman in the late summer of 1972. The honorary head of the national group was King Hussein's former English wife, Princess Muna. At a social gathering Siham was granted a private audience with the royal lady, who talked with her about her studies, future goals, and hopes for the country. In the course of their conversation, Siham mentioned Fawzy, how he had helped her with Hebrew and wanted to continue his education abroad. Through a series of unfortunate events, he was now stuck in their country, unable to obtain a passport. Was there anything Her Royal Highness could do?

Princess Muna was impressed with Siham, and appeared to take special interest in Fawzy's predicament. He was an Israeli who took time to help a Jordanian citizen and leader of her own favored women's association. In her way of thinking, his act of kindness should be rewarded. She asked Siham for further information, including Fawzy's family name, which Siham remembered as Rihani. Then the princess requested an aide write down the pertinent information about Fawzy, and told Siham that she would be in touch.

At the conclusion of the conference, Siham hurried back to Ajlun and asked Fawzy to come to see her at once. He could tell she was excited, though she wouldn't say why, so he hastily left the hospital, not knowing what to make of the mystery. When he arrived, Siham met him at the front door, holding her hands behind her. She was smiling, with a twinkle in her eye and enthusiasm in her voice. Fawzy couldn't decipher her behavior, but was relieved that apparently nothing was wrong.

Playfully, she alluded to something she held behind her back. "I've got a present for you," she teased. "I bet you can't guess what it is."

"Is it a car?" Fawzy supposed, played along.

"It's better than a car," Siham retorted.

"What could be better than a car?" he asked, half seriously. "A car would be just about the best present I could ever receive."

"This is something better, I promise," she assured him, and brought an envelope around for him to see.

"Do you know what this is?" she continued. He could only shake his head from side to side and shrug in ignorance. "This should finally help you get your passport!" she exclaimed, gleefully waving the envelope in the air. Siham quickly shared about her visit with the princess, and how before leaving Amman she was handed the envelope and instructed to tell Fawzy to take it and a recent photo to a passport office as soon as possible.

Even Siham, however, did not fully understand what she held in her hand. Astonishingly, inside the envelope was a directive from Princess Muna ordering the government's passport offices to issue Fawzy a category three passport, the highest civilian classification possible! With it he could leave Jordan at anytime and travel virtually anywhere in the world!

Fawzy was overwhelmed by the spectacular good news and ecstatic over the prospect of finally receiving his long-desired passport. Yet, as they celebrated together, he couldn't help but register the voice of doubt, lest it all be too good to be true.

"I've been to the passport office so many times," he noted, "and all they ever do is throw me back on the street empty-handed."

"You've tried everything else to get a passport, Fawzy; maybe this is God's way of getting it for you," Siham gently encouraged.

In recent days he had received similar encouragement from Fawaz after unburdening much of his pent-up frustration. "God has it all under control, Fawzy," the good pastor counseled. "He could send you a passport tomorrow!" Now it was tomorrow, and Siham was giving him the dream-like envelope and urging him to take it to the government office.

Fawzy decided to go to Irbid, a city twenty miles north of Ajlun. Previous trips were exercises in futility, but on this occasion things proceeded much differently. When handed the envelope containing royal authorization to approve his application, they extended VIP treatment, and he walked out of the office the same day with an elite passport in his pocket.

Returning to Ajlun, Fawzy went straight to the hospital and then to Fawaz, showing one and all the precious passport, conveying the amazing news that their prayers had been gloriously answered! He also visited again with Siham, and they rejoiced once more over what God had done, pausing for her to explain more thoroughly the extraordinary circumstances that brought about the treasured document. There was no doubt in their minds that the Lord had intervened in order to send Fawzy to America.

****

Acquiring a passport was one of two major obstacles Fawzy faced in receiving a student visa to study in America. The other was obtaining approval for what was called an I-20. An I-20 was essentially a bundle of paperwork required by United States embassies providing evidence that an international student met its qualifications for a visa. Four kinds of evidence were necessary: a letter of good conduct from the country issuing the student's passport; a letter from that country's Ministry of Education validating a student's high school diploma; successful completion of the Test of English Foreign Language (TOEFL); and a letter of acceptance from an American college or university.

Perhaps surprisingly, the letter of good conduct stating that he had no criminal background was the easiest of the four items for Fawzy to obtain. Despite past prison time, POW status, and association with Palestinian commandoes, the level three passport and contacts at the hospital enabled him to get the letter of recommendation with no problem.

The other hurdles proved more of a challenge. With an eighth grade education, he could not receive a high school degree in the traditional manner. The only way to meet this requirement quickly was by utilizing the services of a diploma mill, accompanied by the time-honored practice of Middle Eastern bribery. Unscrupulous as it was, Fawzy felt he had no choice and immediately found a private school in Irbid that awarded the equivalent of a G.E.D. Students in his situation were supposed to attend classes for at least a year; Fawzy went for less than a week. With time of the essence, he induced the head of the school to grant him a diploma for the sum of five dinars. The Ministry of Education in Amman then issued an official letter of endorsement based upon the mock degree.

The English requirement appeared the most daunting. Fawzy knew only a few words of English, not nearly enough to pass TOEFL. Without success on TOEFL, he could not study for a post-secondary degree in America. He discovered, however, that he could still receive a student visa if the declared purpose for coming to the U. S. were to study the English language at a college or university. To this end he enlisted the help of medical missionary August Lovegreen, who contacted his friend Lowery Compere, president of Clarke College in Mississippi. Drs. Lovegreen and Compere wrote letters to the American Embassy in Beirut on Fawzy's behalf, asking that he be allowed to come to the United States for the expressed purpose of studying English at Clarke College. The college also sent an official letter of acceptance. His I-20 was now complete.

Successfully navigating the complexities of international bureaucracy in such a short period of time may have been the most extraordinary aspect of the entire immigration experience. Coordinating documents among five agencies in three countries over the span of six weeks was truly remarkable. Confirmed in his heart was the belief that the Lord indeed wanted him in America.

Less than a month after securing his passport, Fawzy left Jordan for the second and final time. Before departing, a few friends at the hospital threw a small farewell party in his honor. Fawzy had worked there for more than two years and had grown enormously in the Lord under their watch. They hated to see him go, but believed that relocating to the United States was the Lord's will. Dr. Roper, the staff's director, presented him with a monetary gift of $300 toward the anticipated visit to America.

Fawzy also bid farewell to Fawaz and members of Ajlun Baptist Church. The pastor and congregation proved to be a solid rock of support for the young Israeli Christian, faithfully standing with him in prayer during the long ordeal to acquire a passport. He paused, as well, to say goodbye to Adel and Siham, thanking them again for all the help they had provided. These were friends whose love and fellowship he would sorely miss.

Among the few possessions he carried to Lebanon were his passport and the two certification letters from the Jordanian government. He later learned he left Jordan with little time to spare. Mere weeks following his departure, Jordanian soldiers came looking for him at the hospital. Pro-Syrian commandoes he earlier befriended had been captured, and Fawzy's name and picture surfaced among records seized at their camp. He was now a wanted man in Jordan.

Following a number of bus rides, check points, and border crossings, Fawzy finally arrived back at Foad's house. The return to Ba'labakk was filled with rejoicing as he celebrated what great things the Lord had done for him in Jordan. By now it was approaching October. After staying a few days, he made arrangements to leave for the American Embassy in Beirut. Saying bittersweet goodbyes to Foad's family, Fawzy and his brother made the drive once more to the Lebanese capital.

Upon arriving at the embassy, he was greeted at the visa desk by a clerk who was friendly, smiling, and eager to help. Fawzy stated that he was making application for a student visa to study the English language, and presented the necessary paperwork from the Jordanian government. As Fawzy quietly sat before the embassy official studying his documentation, he silently whispered an "open-eye prayer." His prayers became more audible when she left her desk with his credentials in hand to enter an adjacent office.

Several anxious moments later she returned still smiling, giving reason for optimism. As she sat down again at her desk, she told him that an official letter of acceptance from Clarke College had been received, as well as recommendation letters on his behalf from Drs. Compere and Lovegreen. The only requirement remaining was to take the TOEFL exam, which could be scheduled immediately. Fawzy took the test and failed miserably, as he knew he would. It made no difference; he would study English in America.

Later, when he again sat before the clerk's desk, she handed him a folder of papers, and lying there on top was the cherished visa! Tears of joy welled in his eyes as he signed official papers and paid the fee, then politely thanked her and hastily left the building. He was barely out on the street when—unable to restrain his exuberance any longer—he let out several shouts of "Thank you, Jesus!" His prayers had been marvelously answered. In his hand he now held both a passport and visa!

Fawzy quickly booked airfare to New York and Mobile, spending all but the last three dollars of his savings to purchase the expensive tickets. As they approached the Beirut airport, Foad insisted on stopping by a department store to buy a few clothing accessories for Fawzy, along with a small black suitcase to accommodate his things. Inside the airport terminal, the two brothers hugged at length before Fawzy walked through the departure gate and climbed aboard the plane for the long flight ahead. At long last, he was coming to America!

****

When Fawzy landed in Mobile on Tuesday, October 17, it was nearly one o'clock in the morning. He was late arriving because he had missed the outgoing connecting flight from New York. Color television was something he had never seen before, and New York's John F. Kennedy International Airport displayed it everywhere. In 1972, airport TV consisted of small individual units attached to waiting area chairs, all in pay-per-view style. Fawzy didn't realize he was watching on somebody else's dime as he paused to stare at them from behind. At one point he attempted to change the channel on a set, and was promptly baptized into American slang culture, New York City style.

Fawzy lingered over the new technology a little too long, and the flight to Alabama departed without him. As a consequence, there was no one to pick him up at the Mobile Regional Airport when the later plane arrived. Anis was scheduled to meet him, so Fawzy looked for his cousin when he came through the gate, but to no avail. Anis had obviously given up and returned home, not knowing if or when the younger Shorrosh was going to appear.

Since Fawzy spoke limited English, he decided to show a slip of paper printed with Anis' name to the few people milling around the airport lobby, asking as best he could if anyone knew where he lived. After half an hour of getting nowhere, Fawzy didn't know what to do. He must have sounded desperate to a middle-aged father and teenage daughter who entered the lobby from the parking lot. The man told Fawzy to take a seat and he would soon be back to help.

The stranger was true to his word, taking Fawzy to his car and driving him to downtown Mobile, approximately ten miles away. Fawzy sat mesmerized by all the beautiful street lights that lined the roadways entering the large Gulf coast city. When the man suddenly pulled into a police station, Fawzy started fidgeting. He had been detained in prison in one foreign country; he didn't want to repeat the experience in another.

The man succeeded in easing Fawzy's nerves—they were only there to get help, he assured. They went inside the law enforcement headquarters where officers managed to contact Anis, who lived on the other side of Mobile Bay in the suburban community of Spanish Fort. The anonymous Good Samaritan insisted on driving Fawzy the rest of the way, and twenty minutes later Anis met them at the front door in his pajamas.

Fawzy wanted to thank the exceptionally kind American who went "the second mile"—or more accurately, the thirty-second mile—on behalf of a foreigner.

"One minute! One minute!" Fawzy yelled in Hebrew, just before the man drove off.

There were only three dollars in his pocket, so he reached into his suitcase where several dozen ancient coins were stashed, artifacts he thought might be marketable in his new country. Fawzy had personally excavated them from an old Jordanian tomb a year earlier. He grabbed a fistful and thrust them toward the man.

"A gift! A gift!" shouted Fawzy, smiling, motioning the man to take them. After considerable reluctance, finally he did. Showing gratitude with antiquated, but possibly valuable, Middle Eastern currency was about all Fawzy had to offer.

Anis escorted him into the house and to the family's guest bedroom. There would be ample time to visit the next day; now they needed their sleep. It was a fitful and short first night of rest for Fawzy in America. His mind raced seemingly nonstop, full of wonder about his new surroundings. How was he going to do here, so far from home? Had he made the right decision to come? Would he ever fit in with such a different culture? What was the college going to be like?

Although his trust was firmly rooted in the Lord, these kinds of questions bombarded his thinking, nonetheless. And not only were mental gymnastics keeping him awake; his ears kept hearing intermittent and odd noises that he could not figure out.

After only a little sleep, he arose and joined the Shorrosh family in the kitchen. He knew Anis, but not his wife Nell or their four children. They all laughed when Fawzy asked about the strange sounds he had heard through the night, especially when they realized he was talking about the air conditioning unit, something he had never experienced back home. Fawzy spent the rest of the day getting to know the family and making plans to travel to the college the next morning. The fall term was well underway, and he felt he needed to get there without further delay.

Clarke College was located in the small central Mississippi town of Newton, about a three hour drive to the northwest. Anis asked Fawzy whether he preferred car or bus as his mode of transportation. Social custom dictated that Fawzy select the option less onerous to Anis, so he chose to travel by bus. Without rebuttal, his cousin took him to the terminal in Mobile and made arrangements for someone from the college to meet Fawzy when he arrived.

When he boarded the bus, Fawzy noticed what he believed to be two rough-looking characters sitting in the back. They were actually African-Americans with afro-style hair—all the rage in the 1970's. This was the first time he had encountered the fad and wasn't quite sure what to make of it. Taking a seat at the very front, directly behind the driver, made him feel a bit more secure in the company of the unknown. It also helped to guard against missing his stop in Newton, as he had the earlier flight to Mobile.

Fawzy never quite understood the length or itinerary of the trip, thinking the college was in a neighboring town and the ride a brief one. After almost an hour he began to worry that he was on the wrong bus. They had not yet made a stop and were far out of town. Through the windows he saw more and more trees and fewer and fewer buildings. He decided to ask the driver for reassurance, leaned forward, and inquired with thick accent and voice rising, "Newton? Newton?" The bus driver shook his head from side to side and told Fawzy that Newton was much further down the road. Fawzy didn't comprehend a word of it.

For the next two hours, time and again, they went through the same routine. Fawzy was driving the driver crazy. At the initial and ensuing stops, the bus captain leaned back toward him and vigorously exclaimed, "NO Newton! NO Newton!" When the passenger vehicle finally arrived at Fawzy's intended destination, the driver calmly got up from his seat and walked back to Fawzy, put one hand on his shoulder and pointed the other toward the door, bobbed his head up and down and with a broad smile emphatically announced: "NEWTON! NEWTON! NEWTON!" He was happier to see the little town than was Fawzy.

At the Newton bus station, the dean of students met Fawzy and took him on a whirlwind tour of the town and campus before escorting him to the men's dormitory. The city of Newton was located about an hour east of Jackson and populated by approximately three thousand permanent residents. The college conveniently sat in the shadows of the downtown area, which consisted of several shops and eateries frequented by the student body. A two year school owned by the Mississippi Baptist Convention, Clarke enrolled around three hundred students in the fall of 1972. Its relatively small campus included nine or ten main buildings that accommodated classrooms, dormitories, library, student center, cafeteria, and administrative offices. A chapel was nestled near the center of the grounds, serving as the symbolic focal point of college life.

Fawzy spent the first few days settling into dormitory life and attending English language sessions at the library. Although extremely happy to be in the States, he found adjusting to American culture difficult, with the first week at Clarke especially tough. He felt much like a frustrated toddler who cannot communicate his most basic desires. There was no one on campus with whom he could carry on a normal conversation. Most of what was spoken sounded like gibberish to his Hebrew and Arabic ears, and he could never be sure whether he actually understood what was going on around him. To make matters worse, the cafeteria food tasted as bland as Gerber's to his Middle Eastern palate. With no vehicle or money to go anywhere or do anything, he mostly stayed in his dorm room reading his Bible and attempting to learn English.

Sensing that it could be a difficult transition, Nell Shorrosh soon called and invited him for a weekend of Israeli food and conversation, which Fawzy eagerly accepted. After classes on Friday a fellow student, Lonnie Baxter, took him to the depot to catch the bus for Mobile. The bus fare was three dollars, however, and Fawzy was almost a dollar short. Lonnie was leaving for his home in Stateline and suggested that Fawzy could ride with him and then catch the bus from there. Since it was closer to Mobile, the fare would be cheaper and one he could afford.

Arriving in Stateline later that afternoon, Lonnie took Fawzy to the bus station—located at a little store in town—where the clerk issued him a ticket for two dollars. The bus was scheduled to pull in around five o'clock, so Lonnie bid his friend goodbye and Fawzy took a seat in the corner of the store to await his transportation. When the time progressed past five, Fawzy grew concerned and went to the clerk to see if she had any information about the bus.

She stared at him for a moment, and then an utter look of dismay came upon her face. She had completely forgotten about him! The bus had already come and gone! She excused herself and hurried to the back of the store where she and another employee talked excitedly while gesturing toward Fawzy. She returned and tried to explain the situation to him, along with a possible solution. Fawzy did not understand at first, but finally figured out that although he had missed the bus, there was another one coming later that night. It did not make a scheduled stop at the store, however, so he would have to catch it on the main highway outside of town.

Still not grasping everything clearly, but thinking this must be the American way, he allowed them to take him out to U.S. Highway 45. There they left him on the side of the road with his suitcase, instructing him to flag the bus down when he saw it coming in the distance. Dusk soon descended and there was still no sign of the bus. The later it grew, the harder it became to tell what was coming in the distance, and in the twilight he found himself signaling freight trucks and other large vehicles.

He didn't know what to do. Here he was alone at night, stuck in the middle of nowhere in a foreign country, with only a few cents in his pocket. It was also an unusually cold autumnal evening. Fawzy sat on his suitcase between the highway and dense forest, praying and pondering, trying to decide whether to continue to await the bus or to walk back into town and contact Lonnie. A patrol car soon came by, spotted him shivering on top of his luggage, and stopped. The officer shined his flashlight on Fawzy and then slowly exited his vehicle.

"What are you doing out here, son?" he asked, approaching warily.

Fawzy thought he was in trouble. He couldn't understand the thick Southern drawl, and nervously responded, "Sir?"

"Why are you out here on the highway like this?"
the officer repeated. Fawzy could only guess at what he
asked.

"I'm waiting for the bus to Mobile, but no bus has
come," Fawzy answered in a combination of broken
English and Hebrew, attempting to explain his
predicament.

After a few seconds, the Mississippi lawman
seemed to understand and attempted to be helpful. He
talked Fawzy into coming with him to find a warm place
to spend the night. The bus station was now closed, so he
took Fawzy to the town's empty detention facility,
instructing him to stay there until someone came the next
morning. He then left, bolting the door behind him, and
locking Fawzy inside.

Fawzy slept as best he could under the
circumstances; at least the jail was better than freezing to
death alongside the highway. As it grew late into
Saturday morning, however, he wondered if he had been
forgotten once again. Finally, a little before noon,
someone showed up with a key, and he quickly made his
way to the bus station.

He decided it was too late to proceed to Mobile;
he only wanted to return to campus. But when the bus
bound for Newton arrived, they refused to exchange his
unused ticket for the one he now needed.
Understandably, Fawzy became upset and even began to
weep a little. Stuck in a strange, uncooperative place,
both tired and hungry, he had experienced just about
enough of America.

At this emotionally fragile moment, God sent
another Good Samaritan his way. An anonymous
bystander saw what was happening and felt sorry for the

frustrated foreigner. He reached into his pocket, purchased the ticket for Newton, and handed it to Fawzy. With deep gratitude Fawzy took the unexpected gift and hurried to board the bus before it departed. As he walked into his dorm room later that afternoon, little more than twenty-four hours after leaving, he vowed never again to ride an American bus.

The vow was short lived. Only a week or so later, he found himself enduring another typical misadventure. Anis called and told him about a good friend who lived in Columbus, Georgia, an older woman known affectionately as Mama Cochran. She wanted to meet Fawzy. Mama and her husband were major supporters of Anis' evangelistic association, and he felt sure she would also want to assist Fawzy. It would be well worth the trip, Anis promised.

Despite misgivings, he agreed to go. Mama Cochran sent a round trip bus ticket, and Fawzy left Newton on a Friday bound for Columbus, arriving without incident early that evening. Mr. Cochran picked him up at the bus station and straightway took him to meet Mama. When Fawzy walked through the door, he found a large, rotund woman topped with plenteous gray hair and splendidly equipped with an engaging smile and sweet disposition. He also saw that Mama had prepared a table full of fragrant foods for her special guest, all the more pleasing since he was famished. Anis had mentioned what a great cook Mama was, how she knew the way to satisfy Middle Eastern tastes.

"Are you hungry, Fawzy?" Mama asked soon after pleasantries were exchanged.

"No ma'am," Fawzy answered. Of course, this was not true. His stomach was empty and his mouth watering as he surveyed the scrumptious feast spread before him.

"Well, okay, but as you can see there is plenty here if you change your mind," Mama replied, somewhat disappointed.

She and her husband then sat down for supper, cheerfully conversing with Fawzy as he sat at the table not eating a thing. In his mind he kept thinking, "You've got to be kidding me! They're eating all of this food while I'm here starving!"

Later, as they withdrew to the living room, Mr. Cochran could not stop raving about the meal, complimenting Mama on how much he enjoyed her cooking, and teasing Fawzy on what a treat he had missed. "Next time you'll know to come hungry, Fawzy!" he chortled. Fawzy didn't find it amusing.

That night Fawzy was voracious for food. "What am I going to do?" he asked himself. He came up with a plan. After the Cochrans retired for the evening, he would sneak into the kitchen and swipe some leftovers from the refrigerator.

When the hour drew late, he carefully made his way there, trying his best not to make a sound. As quietly as possible, he opened the fridge and peered in. To his disgust, everything was wrapped in foil or plastic! He decided there was no way to open the leftovers without raising the suspicions of the Cochrans, so he returned to his room with little to show for his efforts.

The next day the same thing happened.

"I hope you'll want to eat something this morning, Fawzy," Mama said at the breakfast table.

"No ma'am, but thank you," Fawzy responded, again untruthfully. Once more he sat at the table with an empty plate as they ate their fill.

Lunch was no different, and by now Fawzy was ravenous with hunger. Mercifully, that afternoon Anis called. Fawzy asked if he might talk with his cousin, and in Arabic told him that he was starving to death at Mama Cochran's! Anis immediately started laughing. Irritated, Fawzy declared it no laughing matter and attempted to describe the seriousness of the situation.

"I know, I know," Anis finally responded. "That's what's so funny! The same thing happened to me when I first came to this country!"

What had happened was a clash of cultures. In Israeli society it's polite to initially decline any offer of hospitality from someone else. You always allow the host to insist upon their generosity as a means of discerning their sincerity.

Anis told Fawzy to give the telephone back to Mama. He then explained the misunderstanding and requested that she insist upon feeding Fawzy, which she was more than happy to do. Over the course of the remainder of his visit, Mama stuffed Fawzy's belly with so much food that he was utterly miserable on the long ride back to Mississippi. His stomach felt as though it had been on a five hour roller coaster by the time the bus finally arrived in Newton.

Mama was indeed a very good cook, exactly as Anis described. He was also right about her altruistic spirit. Mama became an extremely generous patron of financial support for Fawzy, regularly sending money to help with food, housing, and books. Although he worked many hours on the college's maintenance crew and was generally frugal with money, there never seemed to be enough to make ends meet. Sometimes he had no idea how to pay a particular bill. The college's fiscal affairs officer, Kelton Valentine, was always after him, it seemed, to settle an outstanding debt. Often an unsolicited check arrived in the mail from Mama Cochran—just in the nick of time.

Mama's munificence was extraordinary. When, for example, Fawzy began receiving invitations from churches to share his testimony, transportation was a problem. Mama Cochran promptly solved it by buying him a car—a blue Chevrolet Vega, the first vehicle he ever owned. She also pitched in a gas card, having the bill sent directly to her each month. Then she bought him suits, shirts, ties, and shoes so that he might be properly dressed when testifying for the Lord. Mama was a godsend, an answer to prayers on Fawzy's behalf. For her part, the gifts served as spiritual investments in the work of God's kingdom on earth.

The Lord sent Fawzy another good friend as he transitioned to a new culture in the fall of 1972. Gary Dennis was a freshman at Clarke that year. The Beauregard preacherboy reserved a special place in his heart for outsiders, easily befriending them and quickly gaining their trust. When he saw a slightly older international student having a tough time fitting in to campus life, he sought to intervene, and Fawzy welcomed Gary's company. His new friend helped with English, sat alongside him in the cafeteria, and introduced him to fellow students.

Within a month of Fawzy's arrival, Gary invited him to Beauregard for the weekend. It was then that Fawzy met Brother Robert, a brief introduction where he shared bits and pieces of his life story. Robert was smitten with the devout Israeli Christian and hoped to use him in future Seekers revivals. Fawzy's testimony, he believed, would add a powerful witness about the life-changing effects of a personal relationship with Jesus Christ.

*Robert gladly took Fawzy under his
ministerial wing, forging a special friendship.*

****

At Clarke Fawzy continued to improve in English proficiency, enabling him to pass the TOEFL examination and take courses that counted toward the bachelor's degree. Developing his communication skills made college life much more enjoyable. He joined the Baptist Student Union where he made many new friends, often going with them on missionary projects. While participating in BSU ministry, he also began sharing his testimony in public.

As his comfort level increased, Fawzy acquired the reputation of being something of a lady's man, with young women finding his charming accent, amusing gaffes, and fascinating life story irresistible. Debbie, a coed from Illinois, was enthralled with Fawzy, and they soon became fast friends. She owned a car and often took Fawzy on shopping excursions and to restaurants. One Saturday Fawzy called to ask if she were doing anything special.

"Yes," she said, "I'm going to a shower. Would you like to come with me?"

Fawzy was still learning English, and the only shower he knew anything about was the kind in the bathroom. Debbie's invitation sounded unseemly.

"Debbie!" he uttered, with astonishment. "No!"

"Yeah, really Fawzy, it'll be alright. I believe you'll like it if you come."

"DEBBIE!" he responded again, with higher pitched voice.

"Listen, I know what you mean, Fawzy," she said. "You think you'd be out of place there, but you can just sit on the side and watch. I think it'll be okay."

By this time Fawzy was outraged and distressed, with tears welling in his eyes. The girl he thought was the sweetest Christian on campus was talking shamefully to him. He hung up the phone and went straight to Gary.

"I can't believe Debbie! You Americans are crazy!" he fumed, explaining the situation.

Gary assured his friend there must be some misunderstanding, and immediately called Debbie to find out what was going on. He laughed as they spoke, and then attempted to clear up the miscommunication.

"Fawzy, I guess we Americans are kind of crazy," explained Gary. "We're crazy in language. We have more than one kind of shower over here. There is the shower we take in the bathroom. But there is also something called a baby shower, where gifts are brought to a woman who is about to have a baby. Debbie's going to that kind of shower, a baby shower. She didn't want you to watch her taking a shower in the bathroom."

Needless to say, Fawzy expressed relief in learning that Debbie was not being scandalous, but decided against accompanying her to the baby shower anyway—just in case Gary was wrong about the crazy American language.

Over the Christmas holidays Fawzy returned to Beauregard, where for the first time he attended a Seekers meeting. Gary had told him a lot about the group, how God moved powerfully among the youth of Providence, bringing hundreds to salvation and calling many into the ministry. Fawzy enjoyed sitting on the floor of the sanctuary with a large number of us, singing, sharing, and praying, as the Seekers had done virtually every Monday night for more than two years.

During the course of his visit, there was occasion to get better acquainted with Robert and to meet the other preacherboys. One evening we gathered around the pastor's desk and knelt to pray, as we often did when we were together. Brother Robert, Jimmy, Gary, Billy, Tommy, and I were joined by Fawzy as we directed our petitions to God. Fawzy's name was frequently called, each of us asking God to bless our new brother in Christ whose faith and testimony were so inspiring. We gladly adopted him into our little band of disciples; it was as though he had been with us all along.

Our messianic age merged with Fawzy's as the year 1972 drew to a close. God reached across continents and cultures to bring us together—Beauregard and Nazareth, American and Israeli, Gentile and Jew—united then and forever by Christ at Memory Rock.

Chapter 6
"God is So Good"

There is probably no lovelier portrait of Christian community than in the opening chapters of the book of Acts. According to Saint Luke, the earliest believers spent lots of time together—breaking bread, engaging in prayer, worshipping God, and sharing all things in common. There was much in the way of good will among them, and day by day the Lord added to their number as more and more people responded positively to the gospel through their witness.

I've often thought the Seekers must have received a heavenly taste of what the nascent church experienced. The level of our spiritual excitement and growth didn't approach the Pentecost disciples, of course, but the same dynamic was surely at work.

Like the first Christians, we thoroughly enjoyed one another's company. Whether breaking bread, breaking camp, or breaking Robert's rules of order, there was a filial closeness, an innocent intimacy where each felt welcome and sensed his or her own spiritual worth. The common bond of Christ's lordship and love united us with a joy and purpose not of this world.

As with the original disciples, we, too, spent an inordinate amount of time in prayer. Lengthy, spontaneous prayer meetings were a common occurrence, arising at various venues of church, school, vehicle, and home. Not only was prayer an integral part of our worship, but of many social occasions as well. Whether gathering to attend ballgames or revivals, asking for God's protection and blessing was normal and expected.

Praying together with frequency and fervor provided motivation to live for the Lord and empowered us to share Christ wherever we went. As a result, God's Spirit repeatedly anointed our witness in marvelous ways. Through personal evangelism, Sunday church, Monday Seekers meetings, and weekend youth revivals, hundreds came to know the Lord, thousands recommitted their lives to Him, and not a few answered the call to minister the gospel full-time. The Lord added to His own day by day.

The names and faces of those impacted by the testimony of the Seekers are mostly a blur to me now. I'm left to wonder: What happened to them? Did they follow through with their commitments? Did they grow stronger in their Christian faith? Did they go out to witness and win others? Are they still living for the Lord these many years later? As with the multitude in Acts who gladly received the gospel at Pentecost and beyond, only the light of eternity will provide the answers.

When our little group met to break bread, pray, or witness, there was perhaps nothing we enjoyed more than blending our voices in praise to God. "I've Got Peace Like a River," "He is Lord," "He Keeps Me Singing," and "He's Everything to Me" were only a few of the "psalms, hymns, and spiritual songs" in vogue during our era and frequently sung as an expression of worship.

The signature song of the Seekers, however, was a traditional spiritual entitled "God is So Good." The tune was Robert's personal favorite, one he taught us early on to sing with reverence and feeling. It's a simple little chorus that thrice repeats its title—each time in a higher pitch—before concluding in a lower tone with the appreciative line, "He's so good to me."

"God is So Good" was sung at virtually every Monday meeting and at the close of numerous revival services. We enjoyed making up our own words to the music, substituting lines like "He loves me so" or "He's coming soon" for the refrain. The lyrics could go on for quite a while as we waxed creative in proclaiming our praise to the Lord.

The song has continued melodiously now for several decades within the hearts of the Seekers who first surrounded Brother Robert. Its truth has remained steadfast in good times and bad, through glad occasions and sad occurrences. Though often interrupted by bumps in the road and heckled by hiccups along the way, the musical sound of the Lord's goodness and mercy has followed us all the days of our lives.

As the decade of the 1970's wound down, the Seekers gradually ceased to meet on Monday nights and to function as an organization. The original core group scattered here, there, and yonder, and a new crop of Providence youth preferred to blaze its own spiritual trail. Robert, characteristically, adapted with the times, repackaging his tried and true formula of Bible study, prayer time, spiritual songs, and personal witnessing into a discipleship program that appealed to young people of a different era.

For committed Christians—in whatever generation they find themselves or by whatever name they are called—seeking the Lord and leading others to know Him never go out of style. The spiritual fashion statement made by the very first disciples remains trendy for true believers of every messianic age.

****

In late December of 1972, Robert watched as six young men left an impromptu prayer meeting held around his office desk at Providence church. Jimmy, Gary, Fawzy, and I soon headed back to college following the Christmas break, while Billy and Tommy remained in Beauregard to continue their senior year of high school. We would gather again periodically over the coming months to lead Seekers revivals at First Baptist in Bessemer, Girard Baptist in Phenix City, First Baptist in Ocean Springs, and a host of other churches.

Over the course of the next few years, Robert's ministry at Providence reached maximum spiritual strength. Sunday attendance continued to grow, offerings multiplied, facilities were enlarged, and—most importantly in Robert's eyes—numerous individuals came to know Christ. The spotty data for those years can't tell the whole story, but they do paint a remarkable portrait of the Lord at work through a faithful pastor.

Robert, behind Providence's pulpit--a comforting sight for his parishioners.

Perhaps the single greatest month statistically in the church's history arrived in the spring of 1973 as a harbinger of good things to come. During the four Sundays in April, Providence averaged 329 in Sunday School and 159 for the evening's Church Training classes, with offerings of $1597.00 per week. A record 47 new members joined the church.

Numbers can be cold, calculating, and impersonal. But for Robert, numbers especially represented people, individuals who were learning about the Bible, dedicating their lives to Christ, finding their place of service in God's kingdom, and growing toward maturity in the Lord. For this reason his pastor's columns often focused on numbers. "Just a few years ago we were trying to reach 150 for Sunday School," he wrote in the fall of 1974.

> *We have seen that number double and for the first three Sundays during November we have averaged 318 per Sunday. I see the great possibility of this 300 being doubled in the next couple of years. I believe God will do anything our faith will claim for His glory* (Providence Bulletin, November 24, 1974).

Sunday School attendance would not double, as he hoped, but it did rise 31% from an average of 252 in 1974 to 330 two years later. Robert's tireless promotion and constant encouragement by written and spoken word paid handsome dividends. The church topped 400 in Sunday School on occasion, with 465 on February 15, 1976 the all-time high attendance for the organization.

Robert loved to set statistical goals for his congregation. The church, no less than the individual, should "press on toward the mark of the high calling of God in Christ Jesus" he believed. The fact that these goals were seldom met did not discourage him in the least. Prodding his flock toward bigger and better things for the Lord was what mattered in his eyes.

> *November 17 we are praying for and looking forward to the greatest day in Sunday School and Church Training attendance this church has ever experienced. This can only be realized as every person becomes concerned about reaching absentees and prospects. We have set a goal of 350 in Sunday School and 200 in Church Training* (Providence Bulletin, October 27, 1974).

As was almost always the case when he set goals, the numbers came up a little short at 341 and 154, respectively. Robert proclaimed victory anyway.

> *I thank God for a wonderful day in His church last Sunday. I sensed a real note of victory last Sunday when it was announced that we had 341 precious souls present for Sunday School* (Providence Bulletin, November 24, 1974).

The numbers that were most important to Robert were the ones that indicated baptisms. Baptisms represented individuals who had come to know Christ, whose eternal destinies had been forever changed. It was his commitment to evangelism and missions that lay behind his emphasis on baptismal numbers.

*Souls! Souls! Souls! To save lost souls was the
constant passion of Jesus. He saw people lost
from their way, lost from God, lost from their
highest possibilities in life, lost for time and
eternity. One who loves the Lord Jesus in
sincerity cannot fail to love lost souls* (Providence
Bulletin, January 21, 1979).

The year Robert arrived, only seven baptisms were
recorded. In eight of his fifteen years of ministry at
Providence, the church approached or exceeded fifty
baptisms, with a high water mark of sixty-seven in 1972.
Several factors no doubt contributed to the significant
increase. Robert's consistent example of one-on-one
witnessing, coupled with periodic training sessions on the
practice of personal evangelism, likely were major
reasons for the church's success in local missions. Added
to these were his emphasis on outreach through the
Sunday School, persistent prayers on behalf of the lost,
and a willingness to schedule two or three evangelistic
revivals every year.

Throughout his ministerial career, Robert was a
tireless worker when it came to saving souls and reaching
the unchurched. He never wavered in his fervor for
winning the lost to Christ and filling up God's house on
Sundays.

*I am praying that individuals will become
burdened for other individuals, that families will
become burdened for other families and that
churches will support other churches as we pray
for revival. If our local church would take*

*seriously the command of God to go out into the
"highways and hedges" to invite the people to
church this building could not hold the multitude
of people that would be present on Sunday
morning and night* (Providence Bulletin, February
17, 1980).

Other statistics stand out during Robert's tenure at
Providence. Overall church membership grew from 336
in 1968 to 1109 in 1983. Receipts that totaled $21,663
for the church year ending in 1968 rose to a high of
$182,317 in 1980. Perhaps most tellingly, gifts to foreign
missions that stood at $37 in the year before Robert
arrived, peaked at $6,428 after he had been there for a
decade.

With the congregation rapidly growing, Robert
and the church's leadership saw the need for more space
to accommodate the influx of new attendees. In June of
1973 the church voted to proceed with plans to construct a
combination social hall and children's building, and
$200,000 was borrowed to finance the new project. On
June 2 of the following year, the two story brick structure
was formally dedicated—just in time for the start of
Vacation Bible School the next day.

Six months after the dedication, Robert described
how the new facility was serving the Lord's purpose at
Providence.

*What a thrilling experience it was to walk through
the Children's Building last Sunday morning and
to see it completely filled with boys and girls
studying God's Word under the leadership of a
dedicated group of teachers. I praise the Lord*

every day for a church with the vision to build a building like this that we might meet the needs of boys and girls. Last Sunday morning we had 168 children and workers in our Pre-school and Children's Departments (Providence Bulletin, November 17, 1974).

Building buildings, like everything else Robert did as pastor, was not for beauty or show, nor for comfort or legacy. It was for the purpose of reaching people for Jesus Christ.

****

While Robert's ministry flourished at Providence, his "boys" were away receiving an education. Jimmy, Gary, and Fawzy initially enrolled together at Mississippi's Clarke College, with Billy and Tommy arriving there a year later. I was the lone member of the group to start down a different path, opting to prepare for ministry at the Baptist college in Mobile. I was extremely pleased, however, when all my pals eventually ended up with me in Alabama's Azalea City.

*Tommy, Billy, and I formed an
evangelistic team while in college.*

Jimmy's journey to Clarke and then Mobile came by way of Alexander City Community College. Saved and called to preach as a high school senior, coaching basketball was replaced by ministry on Jimmy's career radar screen. As much as he enjoyed preaching in the Seekers revivals and doing volunteer ministry, he was eager to find a salaried job in the Lord's line of work.

While serving on a search committee to hire a Minister of Evangelism for Providence, Jimmy boldly asked Robert and committee members about the possibility of filling the newly created position temporarily until a suitable candidate was found. He was planning to transfer to Clarke in a few months anyway, and could use the ministry experience and extra money to pay for school. The committee and church accepted his proposal, and Jimmy became the second full-time minister at Providence, serving with Robert from April to August of 1972.

At Alexander City Jimmy didn't acquire much in the way of education, matriculating less than a year, but he did find something far more valuable. Anita Liveoak was a pretty and popular coed when Jimmy first laid eyes on her, serving as Homecoming queen for the college. Jimmy felt impressed that the Lord had chosen the striking young woman from nearby Millbrook to be his life partner. Anita had a long line of suitors, however, and Jimmy initially had trouble making headway. He was persistent, Anita finally found time for him, and after a year or so of courtship they married in November of 1973.

Before the wedding Jimmy completed a year at Clarke and served a stint as a summer missionary in Montana. Over the course of three months in Big Sky Country, he served five different congregations through supply preaching, backyard Bible studies, Vacation Bible Schools, and repairing church facilities. The Montana experience yielded valuable ministry lessons not easily attained through reading textbooks or attending lectures. The need to accept people outside of one's cultural milieu, and the mandate to advance God's kingdom through every means available, were two that made a lasting impression upon Jimmy.

After Montana he made his way to Mobile College, bringing his new bride three months later. Like so many young married couples, they lived from hand to mouth, with the major expenses of rent and tuition leaving precious little for the other necessities of life. To help make ends meet, Jimmy worked as a sales associate at the local Western Auto Store in Saraland, and soon took his first pastorate, a small Baptist congregation in Dickinson, Alabama.

Upon graduation in 1975 with a degree in religious studies, Jimmy served his first full-time churches, shepherding Shiloh Baptist, located between Beauregard and Phenix City, and then moving to Hebron Baptist near Plains, Georgia during Jimmy Carter's presidency. By now two precious daughters, Angela and Ashley, had come his way.

About the time Carter left office, Jimmy felt the Lord leading to Georgetown, Georgia, on the banks of the Chattahoochee River, where he settled in to lead its namesake Baptist church. There he and the family remained for a decade, with Jimmy taking the opportunity to earn the Master of Divinity degree from New Orleans Baptist Theological Seminary.

Gary enrolled at Mobile College in the fall of 1974, joining Jimmy and me in lower Alabama— "redneck LA" as folks like to call it. In two years at Clarke, Gary sparkled in academics and spiritual leadership. He continued to participate in a number of Seekers revivals while also engaging in student ministry on the college campus. During summers he served as youth minister at a couple of Alabama Baptist churches, Concord near Beauregard and Cloverdale in Dothan.

With his arrival in Mobile, Gary embarked upon a nomadic existence that included ten moves in ten years, giving Cain a run for his money. Wanderlust began when he heard Alaska calling, or more specifically the voice of Darby Moore, a native of "the last frontier" and her state's representative in the 1974 Miss America pageant. She and Gary met at Clarke and fell in love, deciding to marry the year following her reign.

Much like a yo-yo, Alaska held Gary on a string as he returned on four separate occasions to live and labor. Once he went to serve as youth director at Anchorage's Muldoon Road Baptist Church. Another time it was to eliminate medical debt by working on the oil pipeline. On other occasions he combined extended family visits with itinerant evangelism and church planting ministries. Like a boomerang, to change the metaphor, he also kept returning to the Deep South—as associate pastor of Central Baptist in Phenix City, and as pastor of Center Baptist in Lafayette, Alabama and of Ebenezer Baptist in Hammond, Louisiana.

Through the years of packing up and settling down between Northwest and Southeast, two splendid children came along, Nathan and Hannah, both born in the land of Dixie. Two degrees were earned as well, a Bachelor of Arts from Auburn University and Master of Divinity from New Orleans Seminary.

Billy was a third member of our little company to ultimately make his way from Clarke to Mobile. In Newton he met a talented, attractive sophomore from Clara, Mississippi named Melita Shoemaker. Melita's most distinguishing physical attribute was elegantly thick red hair that cascaded long past her shoulders. The "Ariel look" stood out in any crowd, but what set Melita apart to Billy was her spiritual and moral character. It didn't take long for the preacherboy from Beauregard to fall "redhead over heels" in love.

After completing his freshman year, Billy decided to transfer with Melita to Mobile College. It was here they became engaged, and then married in March of 1975. Two months later, Billy took a summer position as interim pastor of Philadelphia Baptist Church, an established congregation only a few miles from Beauregard. The newlyweds intended to return to Mobile for the fall semester, but never made it back. Things went so well at Philadelphia—nearly forty professions of faith!—that the church asked them to postpone their studies and stay awhile longer. Billy and Melita accepted the offer and remained for several more months.

With the interim at Philadelphia complete, Oswitchee Baptist, a rural congregation in neighboring Russell County, issued Billy a call. He was only twenty years old but felt the Lord's leadership to be their full-time pastor. He served Oswitchee for the next two and a half years, enjoying an excellent ministry experience. It became for him a laboratory of learning on how to shepherd a church, something he would profit from for decades to come.

Eventually Billy felt the need to complete his formal education, so he resigned Oswitchee and moved to Texas to attend Criswell College. He wanted to focus on studying the Bible, and Criswell was a college founded expressly for that purpose by W. A. Criswell, a giant in Southern Baptist life and pastor of the denomination's largest church, Dallas' First Baptist. While at Criswell, Billy served his second pastorate at First Baptist Church of Pattonville, in northeast Texas.

Following graduation in 1980, seminary beckoned. Billy and Melita visited New Orleans and believed the Lord was leading there. At about the same time, Big Creek Baptist in Waynesboro, Mississippi invited Billy to be their pastor. Waynesboro was approximately 180 miles from New Orleans, but Billy managed the commute, combining the church with graduate studies. He served Big Creek for five years while earning a Master of Divinity degree from the seminary. By this time his family had expanded to include a cherished girl and boy, Melody and Jonathan.

Like Billy, Tommy transferred to Mobile College after only a year at Clarke. He came with missions in his blood, the month-long trip to Africa having validated his calling. Tommy knew the Lord wanted him to be a missionary, though the precise nature of the work remained unclear.

Upon graduation in 1977 with a degree in biology, Tommy remained in the city to seek the Lord's direction. He decided to take a job at the Mobile Center for the Deaf as assistant director. Tommy had learned to sign while in high school, falling in love with ministry to the hearing-impaired. A related opportunity also opened up when one of Mobile's prominent churches, Spring Hill Baptist, called him to be their Minister to the Deaf.

While on staff at Spring Hill, Tommy felt the need to attend seminary to further prepare for life as a missionary, even though there was still little clarity regarding the specifics of mission work. Like Jimmy, Gary, and Billy, he decided to do graduate study at New Orleans, commuting from Mobile to earn the Master of Religious Education degree.

Tommy had always wanted to backpack through Europe, and availed himself of the opportunity in the summer of 1980 as a kind of reward for completing seminary. He also thought it was a good way to seek the Lord's guidance concerning the next step in his life. While wandering around the continent, he visited Spanish missionaries Reggie and Karen Quimby, whom he had met at Spring Hill. They were serving in the province of Valencia on the east coast of Spain, residing about twenty miles from the Mediterranean Sea in the small town of Xativa.

He found the Quimby's in a bind. The personal tutor for their three young boys had suddenly decided to remain in the U. S. There was no one else available and qualified to provide the English instruction their sons needed. Tommy's arrival was viewed as a godsend, and they asked if he would consider taking the job. With no firm plans for the future, he agreed to stay temporarily until they could find a more permanent replacement.

After leasing an apartment, he settled into a routine of tutoring the children in the mornings, learning Spanish in the afternoons, and serving the Quimby's mission church as youth director in the evenings and on weekends. Tommy soon fell in love with the Spanish people and culture, choosing to remain through that entire school year, and then for a second. Gradually he began to sense the Lord's leadership to engage in full-time mission work in Spain.

In 1982 Tommy returned to the States to fulfill the requirements for missionary appointment. He lacked a year of church staff experience necessary for the assignment, so he took a temporary position as Minister to Youth and Singles at Thirty-Eighth Street Baptist Church in Hattiesburg, Mississippi. Neither did he possess the requisite divinity degree, so he commuted to the seminary in New Orleans to add biblical and theological courses to his master's transcript.

With all requirements complete, Tommy successfully applied to the Southern Baptist Foreign Mission Board, and in 1983 was commissioned to Seville, Spain on an open-ended appointment. His specific responsibility was to work with an indigenous Baptist church in the city for the purpose of developing an outreach ministry to students at the University of Seville. Tommy believed he had found what God meant for him to do as a missionary of the gospel, and he continued to minister in Seville for the next nine years.

Jimmy, Gary, Billy, Tommy, and I all found our way to Mobile College at various points in our baccalaureate careers. One more member of Robert's preacherboys would join us there as well.

****

Fawzy also transferred from Clarke to Mobile College in the fall of 1974, obtaining a Bachelor of Science degree four semesters later. This was quite an accomplishment for an Israeli citizen with an eighth grade education who knew little English before arriving in America three and a half years earlier.

In Mobile the occasional misadventures of Fawzy continued. His senior year, for example, a frightening mishap occurred on a science expedition. Fawzy needed one hour of credit to fulfill degree requirements and decided to take an ornithology class taught by Dr. Elizabeth French. The course called for a flora and fauna field experience that included a canoe trip down the nearby Tombigbee River. After Fawzy enrolled and learned of the outing, he immediately voiced reservation—he had never learned to swim and was terrified of water. Talking it over with the instructor, he was assured that he would be perfectly safe wearing a life jacket; he could even ride in her canoe.

Fawzy didn't understand what a canoe was and thought of it more in terms of a large pleasure boat. When the class arrived at the launch site and he saw the small, relatively flimsy vessel in which he was set to ride, he promptly balked. Again Dr. French assured him of his safety in her canoe. She was quite experienced at maneuvering the river's currents, she explained, so he had no reason to fear; she would take care of him. Despite misgivings, Fawzy agreed to embark.

Dr. French reminded her students that as they paddled along they should especially watch for the wood duck, a species of waterfowl found along the inland and coastal waterways of Alabama. The nearby Choctaw National Wildlife Refuge served as a breeding habitat and preservation domain for the bird. She showed them a picture of the beautiful and colorful feathered animal, and requested they alert everyone if they saw it along the route. After committing the duck's features to memory, Fawzy nervously put on a life vest, grabbed the binoculars he had obtained for the occasion, and sat down in the canoe of his professor.

The caravan drifted along uneventfully for more than an hour, with few of nature's flying wonders to behold and no sightings of a wood duck. The weather threatened to become an issue as the wind stirred, the sky darkened, and a light rain began to fall. Everyone worried that a thunderstorm was brewing. Suddenly, looking intently through her binoculars, Dr. French stood straight up in the canoe and pointed excitedly toward the shore.

"There's a wood duck!" she shouted, yelling loud enough for the others to hear.

The force of her voice and suddenness of movement startled Fawzy—already anxious from the water and weather—to such an extent that he, too, attempted to rise to his feet. The abruptness of both occupants standing up in the canoe, combined with the river's choppy currents, caused the slender vessel to rock and lurch violently, thrusting both passengers into the waterway before capsizing from the turbulence!

Dr. French swam safely to shore, pulling the canoe along with her, but Fawzy went under, gurgling water and gasping for air. Fortunately, the river wasn't very deep at this point, but Fawzy was swept along until he soon found himself hung up under a tree near the river's edge, trapped by roots and branches and debris. Completely disoriented, panicky from his phobia, having swallowed a good bit of water, and finding it difficult to breathe, Fawzy sensed he was drowning.

He had survived many close calls with death over the years in Israel, Gaza, and Jordan. Now, once again he believed his life was about to end, this time in Alabama's Tombigbee River. Images of his mother, family, and friends began to flash before him. Finally, after what seemed an eternity, Dr. French and fellow students arrived, freed him from the entanglement, and quickly brought him to shore.

Nicked and bruised and emotionally battered, but once again breathing normally, Fawzy refused to board the canoe a second time. While the rest of the group resumed their trip, Fawzy was taken to a nearby medical facility to be thoroughly checked. Badly shaken and traumatized but otherwise alright, he vowed never again to engage in aquatic activity.

Surprisingly, at the end of the semester Fawzy received an "A" in Ornithology. He later joked that the course almost killed him, that he nearly gave his life for a

wood duck. In future sermons he frequently used the
scary experience analogously to illustrate the sinner
helplessly drowning in the midst of certain spiritual death,
hopelessly ensnared by the sin of this world, before God's
amazing grace comes to the rescue.

Fawzy roomed with Gary his first year in Mobile,
a situation they enjoyed complaining about to anyone who
listened. Fawzy grumbled that his American friend was
the sloppiest roommate on campus. Gary groused about
having to live with "a crazy cheapskate Jew." In truth,
they liked and respected each other immensely.

On one occasion, however, their friendship was
sorely tested. In 1975 First Baptist Church of Fairhope, a
sizeable congregation on the eastern shore of Mobile Bay,
invited Fawzy to be their summer youth minister. Not
long after accepting their offer, Fawzy was presented with
another opportunity.

Gary wanted to spend the summer in Alaska so he
could see his fiancée Darby and participate in pioneer
mission work, a form of ministry he loved. His problem
was how to afford the ambitious trip. For several weeks
he scouted around for summer employment in the land of
the Eskimo before securing the promise of a job that paid
excellent money.

Gary promptly found his roommate to tell him the
good news.

"Fawzy," he announced in an excited manner, "I
finally got a job! It's on the oil pipeline. A friend up
there says they're looking to hire a bunch of people. You
might want to come, too, instead of staying here all
summer."

Gary went on to explain that the work would pay
$25 an hour for at least forty hours each week. The

potential wages made Fawzy's head spin, immediately capturing his interest. So far he had lived off low-paying campus jobs, along with donations from churches and the generosity of friends. The Lord had always provided for his needs, but maybe this was God's way of relieving the financial pressure and funding his final year of college.

Fawzy quickly made up his mind to accept Gary's invitation—without a lot of prayer, he later acknowledged. It would be a fun trip with his good friend, and the money was too good to pass up. He called the pastor at Fairhope, Dr. H. B. Shepherd, and expressed regret that he would not be able to serve the church after all. He was going to Alaska for the summer!

The trip was an utter disaster from the beginning. They were due at the job site a week following spring classes or risked losing the prized employment to others. In lieu of airline tickets, Gary bought a high mileage Plymouth Fury to save money. He reasoned they could use it for the long trek across the U.S. mainland and Canada, and also for transportation while in Alaska. When they returned at the end of the summer, he could sell it and recoup some of his investment.

If they took turns driving around the clock, the two roomies figured to be in Alaska in four or five days. They hadn't left Alabama, however, when their vehicle began to show its age. Between Birmingham and Nashville they watched warily as the needle on the car's temperature gauge gradually rose toward the red zone and the capital H. The engine was running hot! They pulled over, unlatched the hood, and beheld a cloud of smoky steam billowing forth. Thus began a ritual from the Tennessee border to the northern edge of the Rocky

Mountains of stopping every hundred miles or so to give their horse and buggy a much needed drink of water.

On day three of the journey they reached Canada, and it was there the old clunker died of too much thirst. The Plymouth was towed to a local garage in Valleyview, and the two preacherboys decided to camp out in Alberta's Williamson Provincial Park to await repairs. Four days and $700 later, they were on their way again. Low on funds and with no time to spare, they hurried toward their destination with a hope and a prayer—and a little more foot to the pedal.

They had almost made it out of maple leaf country when they encountered another obstacle. At the Alaska border, U. S. immigration officials refused to let Fawzy re-enter. Unknowingly, he had violated terms of his visa by leaving the United States and crossing into Canada. After a lengthy delay and much pleading, Fawzy finally obtained admittance under two restrictive conditions: he could not be employed in Alaska, and he must check in with the Immigration and Naturalization Service each day while his case was pending. Otherwise he risked immediate deportation back to Jordan.

Distressed and discouraged, the pair journeyed on to the pipeline's personnel office, but as suspected, their jobs were no longer available. Gary's fiancé's family graciously took them in while he searched for work, and in Kenai he was hired to drive a pick-up and delivery truck for a laundry service. It paid $4 an hour, far less than he had anticipated making on the pipeline. He also found a position house-sitting, providing the two homeless friends a place to reside for the summer.

Poor Fawzy dutifully reported to the INS each day, but ultimately defied their work edict. Money was

needed for the return trip to Mobile and to pay off a
considerable credit card debt—Mama Cochran's!—that
he had accumulated. Fawzy used his past skills in the
construction industry to land a job installing linoleum
floors in mobile homes, an arrangement never discovered
by the immigration authorities.

Toward the end of the summer, the two young
ministers were asked to lead revival services at Muldoon
Road Baptist Church in Anchorage. During Sunday
morning worship, Fawzy shared his testimony and it was
broadcast live around Alaska and into neighboring Russia.
Years earlier, as an atheist, Fawzy had gone to Russia
representing the Communist Youth Club of Nazareth.
Now, amazingly, he was given the grand privilege of
declaring to Russians how God had radically changed his
life through Jesus Christ!

Each preacherboy received a generous love
offering for his efforts during the revival. The money
helped purchase two plane rides back to Mobile, bringing
their summertime odyssey to a welcome conclusion.
Before leaving, Gary sold the Plymouth Fury to an
obliging future father-in-law, and kissed Miss Alaska
goodbye until their wedding. Fawzy shook the dust of her
state off his feet, solemnly vowed never to return, and
eagerly looked forward to kissing the far more hallowed
ground of Alabama.

****

In May of 1976 Fawzy and I donned caps and
gowns and proudly walked together in formal procession

to receive diplomas from Mobile College. Our
undergraduate lives were finally complete.

For me the immediate future was clear. I would
leave for Kentucky in a matter of days to pursue a Master
of Divinity degree at the Southern Baptist Theological
Seminary in Louisville. There I turned a three year
program of study into six, homesick enough midway
through to leave and take jobs teaching at Woodland
Christian School and preaching at Hatchechubbee Baptist
Church, each less than a thirty minute commute from
Beauregard. After returning to seminary to finish the
degree, I once again came home to Lee County to serve as
the single pastor of Smiths Station Baptist Church.

Fawzy's post-baccalaureate plans were much less
settled. Although the immigration violation of the
previous summer had been resolved, his student visa was
set to expire, and he feared having to return to Jordan.
Going back to the Middle East was not a pleasing
prospect; it could mean imprisonment if the Jordanian
authorities learned he was there. Fawzy felt like the
proverbial man without a country. Compounding his
angst was the necessity of leaving his college-owned
apartment and finding temporary accommodations.

Gary mentioned Fawzy's predicament to Brother
Robert, who promptly insisted he come to Beauregard
until something worked out. Fawzy packed his clothes
and few belongings for what he anticipated to be a short
visit. Meanwhile, Robert contacted the office of U.S.
congressman Bill Nichols and was told Fawzy's best hope
for obtaining residency was to apply for political asylum.
Robert escorted Fawzy to the INS offices in Atlanta,
where officials issued a temporary visa until the lengthy

application process for permanent status could take its course.

Robert and Shirley also solved Fawzy's housing dilemma. "We want you stay with us for as long as you need to," they assured him. Fawzy demurred, stating the burden was too much. They were adamant, however, and he gradually moved his things into a spare bedroom—though only a few items at a time lest they should change their minds.

While they awaited INS's decision, Robert lined up speaking engagements for Fawzy, believing his testimony for Christ should be shared. He also designed a brochure containing a short biographical sketch, the names of churches where Fawzy had spoken, and a collage of positive comments from pastors. He then mailed it to a network of ministers and churches with whom he was familiar, asking them to consider having Fawzy share his testimony and preach at future services and events.

From these initial efforts a fledgling evangelistic ministry was born. While living with Robert and Shirley, Fawzy spoke in churches almost every weekend. He found the greatest of joys in sharing the gospel, in seeing people come to know Christ and having their lives transformed—just as had happened to him. He began to sense the call to do it for the rest of his life.

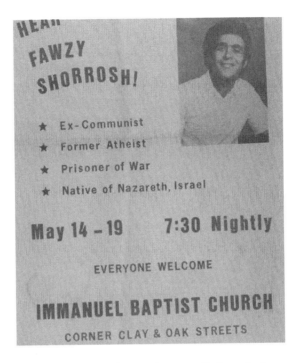

A flyer for one of Fawzy's evangelistic revivals.
This one was held at the church where I was
interim pastor in Louisville, Kentucky.

In affirmation of his call, Providence ordained
Fawzy to the ministry of evangelism on November 7,
1976, a sacred occasion highlighted by the arrival of his
mother from Nazareth. It had been nearly ten years since
Farouse Shorrosh had seen her sixth child. The happy
reunion of mother and son was made all the sweeter as
they embraced for the first time as fellow believers.

From the moment Fawzy decided to receive
ordination, he wanted his mom to be present. It was she
who first shared with him about the Lord and endured the
atheistic fury of his younger years. Farouse was the only

one who had faithfully prayed for him and loved him throughout his life. How proud she would be to see her formerly godless son undertaking the work of bringing people to Christ as his life's calling!

Fawzy's desire turned into a joyful reality when friends at Providence and other churches paid for her travel expense to this country. So excited was Fawzy to see his mom that he drove to New York to meet the plane. Both were reduced to tears in the JFK terminal, hugging tightly for several emotional moments before beginning the long, happy process of catching up. Much had happened since the spring of 1967 when Fawzy left Nazareth for Jerusalem and ended up in Gaza, Jordan, Lebanon, and now America.

Fawzy and his mother, during
their joyful reunion in 1976.

Fawzy took his mom to Robert and Shirley's, where she visited for most of a month. Communication proved a challenge since Farouse knew little English and her hosts spoke no Hebrew or Arabic. Fawzy gladly served as house interpreter.

The Dismukes were repeatedly moved by the tender affection displayed between mother and son. How they relished their brief time together! Often Fawzy simply lay on the couch, his head resting in his mom's lap, while enjoying the comforting strokes of her hand across his forehead. He listened with delight as Farouse softly hummed the Christian hymns of her home church in Nazareth. These were the familiar songs of his childhood that now resonated much more deeply within his soul.

A day or so into the visit, Fawzy decided to build a small fire in the Dismukes' back yard. He wanted his mom to cook the same boyhood dishes that had so satisfied his taste buds while growing up. Oh, how he had missed her Galilean cooking through the intervening years! Farouse gladly obliged, but gently informed Fawzy that she had modernized since he saw her last— now she cooked on appliances *inside* the house. Falafels, kafta, lebani, and Bible bread were some of her son's favorite foods that she expertly prepared once again.

An astounding coincidence occurred during her short stay. Fawzy's brother Foad decided to leave his ministry in war-torn Lebanon, arriving in America not long before Farouse. He and his family immigrated on a special visa arranged by relatives in Chicago. Learning that Fawzy was temporarily staying in Beauregard, Foad called, hoping to surprise his brother with the news he was now in the States.

Fawzy was indeed surprised, but one-upped his older brother with his own astonishing news: their mother was also in America! Foad immediately boarded a plane for Atlanta, where Fawzy and Farouse met him. Once again there was a tear-filled Shorrosh family reunion. It had been practically three decades since Foad left Nazareth for ministry in Jordan and Lebanon, and this was the first time he had seen his mother. Foad, too, spent several days with Robert and Shirley before returning to Chicago.

A thrilling moment in Farouse's life was when she sat in the congregation at Providence to hear her boy preach and see him set apart for ministry. Appropriately enough, the choir sang a rendition of "O Happy Day," and Shirley couldn't help but smile as Farouse softly sang along in Arabic. One of Fawzy's college buddies, Suhail Massad—also from Nazareth—came especially to translate Fawzy's sermon for Farouse, as well as the rest of the ordination service.

While ordination to the gospel ministry provided an emotional and spiritual high for Fawzy, saying goodbye to his mom was an exceedingly sad occasion. Once more they would be separated by thousands of miles, with no way of knowing when they could embrace again. To their immense sorrow, nineteen years would pass before another blissful reunion.

Six months following the ordination, Fawzy's spirits were boosted considerably as he experienced another ceremonial milestone—the rite of matrimony. He met Donita Martin while leading a revival in Mississippi and soon asked her hand in marriage. Exactly a year and a day after moving in with the Dismukes, Fawzy moved out to make a home of his own with Donita.

In addition to love and companionship, marriage offered an unintended solution to Fawzy's visa problems.

By marrying an American citizen, he could apply for permanent residency status through his spouse, a much preferred alternative to political asylum because of the extra rights and privileges it afforded.

Two weeks after their wedding, the newlyweds accompanied Robert to Atlanta where Fawzy conferred again with immigration officials. His change in marital status was duly noted, and the process of applying for residency restarted. Within a few months a green card was issued, a major step in his ultimately successful journey of becoming a naturalized American citizen.

Fawzy resided in Beauregard for the next five years, with two delightful children, Sonja and Meisho, arriving to bring much happiness. There he continued the itinerant ministry of evangelism while also working secular jobs to provide for his family. In 1982 he and Donita relocated to her native Mississippi, a decision that weighed heavily upon Robert's heart. He deeply missed his beloved Israeli friend and brother in Christ, and in fact, would never see Fawzy again.

****

Only a month after Fawzy came to live with Robert and Shirley, Providence voted to begin a camp and retreat ministry. Land and building committees were appointed and empowered to begin the process of purchasing property and planning for construction to accommodate the church's new undertaking.

Of course Robert's fingerprints were all over the venture. He had long seen the advantages of reaching people for Christ in attractive natural settings, far removed from the cares and enticements of the world. For fifteen years he had worked in camps for troubled boys, first volunteering with the Columbus Juvenile Rehabilitation Program while pastor of Pine Grove in Phenix City. For the past nine years he had taken church youth to Camp Ada in Florida for a week of ministry and recreation. At Providence he had also led numerous retreats geared toward specific segments of the church, spiritual outings tailored to men, women, couples, college students, and junior boys and girls.

Now Robert wanted to invest in the development and operation of a camp and retreat center that not only could accommodate the needs of Providence's membership, but other churches in Alabama and surrounding states as well. Its stated purpose would be to serve those who wished to get away and focus on the things of the Lord for a weekend or longer.

The idea had been percolating in his mind for years, a vision he shared with Shirley and close friends like George Palmer. George, his childhood pal from Dothan and now fellow Lee County pastor, often went with Robert to the camps for juvenile offenders held at Roosevelt State Park in Pine Mountain, serving as counselor, chief cook, and bottle washer. He shared Robert's passion for this kind of ministry and frequently accompanied him on trips to scout possible locations for a center.

The means of financially securing the land led to a mild disagreement between the lifelong friends. George thought it wise to purchase the acreage through individuals rather than the church, worried that Providence's future leadership might not share their

vision. But Robert insisted it should be a ministry of
Providence, believing that its initial development and
long-term success were enhanced if the tent of ownership
was broad and church-based. Robert's reasoning was
sound, but George's concern proved prescient.

Robert felt they needed at least 150 acres in a rural
setting, land adaptable for the buildings, roads, ball fields,
and lake necessary on the ideal campsite. Isolation and
development potential were keys in his quest for suitable
property. Obviously, purchase price was a major
consideration as well, but he believed that if the right spot
were found, God would provide the money.

The Land Committee suggested a desirable tract
near Uchee in Russell County. It was approximately 200
acres in size and removed from residential areas, with
terrain that could easily accommodate a sizeable lake
surrounded by a complex of cabins, pavilions, and athletic
fields. The location was less than twenty miles from
Providence, between Beauregard and Hurtsboro, a hilly
mass of ground filled with pine and walnut trees, ancient
sea shells, and Indian relics. No recorded dwelling had
ever occupied the site. On a clear day, from its highest
point, the city of Auburn might be seen in the distance.

Robert immediately fell in love with it. By happy
circumstance the owner of the property, Gus Walker, was
an old acquaintance of Robert's from Hurtsboro and
willing to make the land available for the purpose the
church intended. A deal was tentatively struck.

With facts and figures in hand, the committee
made its recommendation, and the church authorized
acquisition of the property. The transaction hit a few
snags, delaying consummation, but in February of 1979
Providence voted to purchase 188 acres of Walker's land,

paying $6,678 in cash and financing the remaining $46,000 over five years. Robert finally had his campground.

He immediately thrust himself into the improvement of the site, holding a camp workday in March and overseeing the clearing of trees and the building of fences through the summer. The blueprint he had in mind included excavation of a lake and construction of sleeping facilities along its shore, as well as a separate pavilion for cooking, dining, worship, and Bible study. Fields designed for recreational purposes were also part of the master plan.

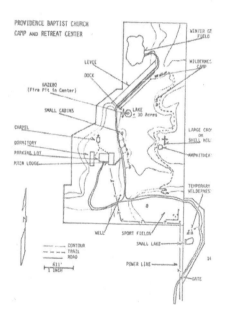

A diagram of Robert's vision for the campground he led Providence to purchase. Sadly, most of his plans were never realized.

The development process moved at a much slower pace than Robert desired or anticipated. Pastoral duties, health issues, financial challenges, and an unrelated building project all interfered with its progress. Nevertheless, Robert retained his enthusiasm. Commenting on a trip to the campsite during the summer of 1982, he wrote:

> *This past Monday Gary Dennis, George Palmer, and your pastor rode down to the Camp and Retreat Center. What a thrill it was to turn off the highway and down the road to the Center. It was exciting to see the power poles leading back to the Center. It was also exciting to see that the third cabin is almost completed. After sitting in the shade, surrounded by a cool breeze and eating some delicious watermelon, I visualized a hillside covered with youth and adults learning about Jesus and growing as Christians. I also visualized near where I sat a campfire surrounded by young people and adults sharing testimonies and singing the beautiful hymns and choruses in honor of our wonderful Lord. Someday this facility will not only be a blessing to this church, but to many other churches and people* (Providence Bulletin, August 22, 1982).

By the following summer the church was able to pay off the campground debt several months ahead of schedule. After announcing the good news to the congregation, Robert urged them to contribute toward the next phase of their outdoor sanctuary.

We are now looking forward to the day when we can complete the initial stage of the camp which will be completion of the wilderness camp. This camp will consist of six cabins, dining facilities, rest rooms, and an athletic field. Three of the six cabins are in the process of completion. The dining pavilion is under construction. The dining pavilion is a building 40 ft. by 60 ft. which will serve as the cooking area, dining area, study area, and worship center. The next step in the completion of this building is covering it with shingles. The only way we have to get these shingles is for our people to provide them. We need 30 squares of shingles to cover this building. We need 30 people that would give the money to purchase 1 square of shingles. The shingles will cost about $25.00 per square (Providence Bulletin, June 12, 1983).*

Though the land was now owned free and clear, much more in the way of hard labor and monetary donations were needed to make the camp and retreat center ready for use.

The day after asking for shingles, Robert left for the Florida panhandle to direct the church's fifteenth annual edition of Camp Ada. The 1983 version, with its theme "Growing in Christ," was conducted differently than the others. Robert invited the preacherboys to bring the youth of their churches to join with Providence. As a result, camp attendance was the highest ever, with 133 overcrowding the cabins, restrooms, and dining hall. Fifteen youth made professions of faith, and one, Michael Flowers—later a long-time state missionary and camp director for the Georgia Baptist Convention—committed his life to the gospel ministry.

Jimmy came down with his group from Georgetown, Billy did the same from Waynesboro, and I brought my young people from Smiths Station. Once again we delighted in studying the Bible, creating funny skits, laughing at King Bobo, and singing around the campfire. Most of all, we enjoyed being with Robert. No one knew it would be his last trip to Camp Ada.

Billy with Robert, at his final Camp Ada.

****

As a Type 1 diabetic, Robert's health had never been good. He constantly battled fatigue and circulation problems. Kidney stones repeatedly attacked his body, twice requiring surgery and putting him in the hospital for eleven days in 1974.

The disorder's potentially harmful impact upon his heart, eyes, kidneys, and feet required close monitoring.

The daily regimen of insulin injections, blood sugar tests, and dietary management tended to wear him down. Remarkably, Robert largely masked the effects of the illness from church members and friends with his ready smile and upbeat attitude.

He was keenly aware of the severe physical complications that often awaited those with chronic diabetes, as well as their relatively shorter life span. As Robert moved steadily through his forties, the future security of Shirley and the children weighed heavily upon his mind.

Should the disease incapacitate him or prematurely take his life, where would his family live? The home where they resided belonged to the church, and if he were no longer pastor, they would be obligated to move elsewhere. The prospect troubled Robert and Shirley, and they began to pray in earnest that the Lord would bless them with a home of their own.

Through the years of their ministry, first in Louisville, then in Troy, Phenix City, Hurtsboro, and now Beauregard, they had always rented a residence or lived in church-owned housing. They often dreamed of buying a home—nothing elaborate, just something elegantly simple—that would be theirs alone to fashion and enjoy. Shortly after moving to Providence, they decided that their next church stop must allow their dream to come true.

But on Sunday, August 6, 1978 as Robert officially completed a decade as pastor, and as he and Shirley simultaneously celebrated their twenty-fourth wedding anniversary, they felt they would be happy to remain in Beauregard for the rest of Robert's ministry. They were not content, however, to reside that long in

Providence's parsonage. At a lay renewal conference the same year, Shirley mentioned their desire to build a home to a few friends, who made it a matter of prayer.

Two church members she took into confidence were Billy's parents, Frank and Frances Duncan. The Duncans were in the process of building their own home when Robert and Shirley first arrived in the community. Robert came to know Frank by occasionally stopping by the house as it was under construction, and that friendly episode helped motivate the whole family to become more involved at Providence.

In subsequent years the Duncans purchased an adjoining acre of property that fronted the main highway through Beauregard. After much thought and prayer, Frank and Frances believed the Lord was leading them to donate the land to the Dismukes. They had no immediate use for the extra parcel, and Robert and Shirley had meant so much to their family. It struck them that this was probably the very reason they had bought the lot in the first place, the reason the Lord had enabled them to pay off its loan quickly, so they could give it away to their pastor.

With land to build on, Robert and Shirley began seeking the Lord's guidance about the actual construction of a home. Neither wanted to take out a loan; interest rates were exorbitantly high at the time, approaching 20%, making a mortgage unaffordable. They believed that moving from their rent-free pastorium only made financial sense if the new house were substantially debt free. They decided it must be built incrementally, as the Lord provided the means.

In the spring of 1980, Robert heard that the military base at Fort Benning was selling many of its older army barracks. After doing some investigation, he found that the lumber constituting the framework of the former soldiers' quarters was in excellent condition and could easily be reused in the framing and flooring of a house. He and Shirley decided to step out on faith and purchase one of the barracks for approximately $300.

New owners were given ten weeks to completely remove the building from the army base. For ten Saturdays the Dismukes and a few church members traveled the forty miles to Fort Benning. They disassembled "Goliath," as the wooden behemoth was affectionately dubbed, hauled off tons of debris, loaded the useful lumber onto various trucks, and brought it back to the acre of ground in Beauregard. There others gathered through the week to remove hundreds of nails embedded in the wood. The construction of their dream house was at hand!

Next Robert and Shirley worked with an architect in the church, Paul Weatherly, to draw up house plans. The blueprint called for approximately two thousand square feet of living space and a two car garage. Three bedrooms, two baths, a combination living and dining room, and a kitchen and breakfast area comprised the main sections of the layout.

On August 3, the occasion of Robert's twelfth anniversary as pastor, the church took up a love offering expressly for the purpose of raising the house. By the time autumn rolled around, construction was well underway. Robert talked about its beginnings in his pastor's column, one of the few times he mentioned the house in the Sunday bulletins.

Please allow me the privilege of sharing with you something on my heart. When young couples fall in love, begin to think of marriage and spending the rest of their lives together not only on this earth, but in heaven also, they begin to make many plans. Shirley and I were no different from any other young couple in planning and looking forward to the years ahead. We talked much about the family we wanted. We wasted lots of paper drawing the home we dreamed of building. One week after marriage, when I surrendered my life to the Gospel ministry, these plans were changed. Not the plans for our family, but the plans for a home. After some eight years of marriage God gave us a son and some three years later God gave us our daughter and we were happy. Now after twenty-six years of marriage and ministry the Lord is completing the dream Shirley and I have carried in our hearts these past twenty-six years. The dream started to form into reality last May 15th, when some of the men, women, and young people went to Fort Benning, Georgia, to tear down an army barrack to be used in building this home. Many Saturdays were given up and many hours spent and finally the last board was off and the dream was closer to reality. God continues to provide workers to dig a foundation, pour concrete, lay blocks and the dream was taking form. Day by day the dream comes closer to reality and I am confident that soon the dream will be a completed reality. These have been happy days as we have thought of doors, windows, bathrooms, walls, floors, and all that goes into the completion of a house. As I reflect back over these past twenty-six years, and the places we have lived, I am so thankful that God allowed our dream to become a reality at this very place. I am so thankful that God knew it would be this way and at this very place twenty-six years ago. We will call this the house that "Faith, Hope, and Love" built because this has been so very evident during these past few months. Thanks be unto God who gives us the desires of our heart (Providence Bulletin, October 26, 1980).

The church responded with extraordinary support. Sunday School classes raised money through yard and bake sales to buy building materials and supplies, and then set dates to meet at the house to use them. The brotherhood, women's missionary group, adult choir, youth, and other organizations spearheaded similar fundraising campaigns and workday events.

The combined generosity of three non-church members especially provided the financial wherewithal to quicken the pace of construction. Neil Koon, Herbert Herring, and Bill Ashcraft were business partners at a real estate firm in Phenix City. Robert came to know them in 1973 during a trip to the Holy Land led by his good friend and their pastor, John Rigby. Reverend Rigby had enlisted their aid to sponsor Robert's participation on the trip.

These Christian businessmen were impressed with Robert and kept up with his ministry in subsequent years. Learning of the house project, they soon became key financial backers. Early on they contributed bricks for the foundation, paid for the framing of the house, and donated the exterior wood siding, windows, and doors. Without their support it's hard to see how the dream could have been realized.

People met on Saturdays and often during the week to work on the house. With the notable exceptions of framing and bricklaying, most of the work was performed by church members and friends. Few, if any, were professional builders, and many did labor entirely new to them. Most had other jobs to think about, but gave willingly of their time, toil, and talents. They relinquished hunting trips, football games, shopping expeditions, and family times to help build Robert and Shirley's house.

By late 1981 the exterior construction was almost complete. The walls were up and the roof was attached. Shirley decided to write an open letter to the membership of Providence, thanking them for what had been done on their behalf. The letter was printed by columnist Betty Baggott of the local Opelika-Auburn News. Shirley recounted the genesis and history of the house project, and then shared her emotions.

> *I am writing out of a heart full of love, from both Robert and myself, for the kindness and deep love shown to our family from our beloved church membership...Our house is really beginning to look like a house now. We were hoping to complete it soon, but our dream began to fade when Robert became very sick again. We felt discouraged, but learned that the work was being continued by the men of the church. How do we ever repay these dedicated men? There is no way to show our deep appreciation. Each day we*

pray, "God, please bless them in a special way."
Each of them labor in love. We feel it is for God
and for us. Betty, you, with the heart of a pastor's
wife can understand how we feel and how this
whole venture of love moves us to tears. Just
maybe this letter can be used to show those in
strife torn churches that there are churches where
pastor and people love and work together! There
are churches where people go beyond giving of
their money and prayers, to give of themselves in a
sacrificial way (Opelika-Auburn News, January 8,
1982).

The column was later picked up and published by the
Alabama Baptist denominational newspaper. Soon
Robert and Shirley heard from folks all around the state.

Following publication of Shirley's letter, the
church bulletin for January 17 announced that $5946 was
needed to finish the interior of the house. It also listed
individual amounts required to complete various
sections—master bedroom: $542; master closet: $275;
master bath: $153; great room: $1388; Susan's bedroom:
$570; hall bathroom: $262; bedroom closet: $214;
David's bedroom: $570; kitchen (less cabinets): $794;
cabinets: $500; utility room: $263; insulation: $615.
(Inexplicably, the figures actually total $6146.)

Little by little, contributions came in and
construction continued accordingly. Someone called
Robert to say they would buy the house's heating system;
another committed to purchase the garage door;
somebody else pledged to pay for the dishwasher.
Families and individuals donated everything from carpet
to commodes to cabinets.

By the end of the summer, about half the money had been raised. After more than two years of building bit by bit, Robert and Shirley were anxious to move in, their impatience especially prompted by Robert's deteriorating physical condition and mounting health concerns. Only $3000 was needed to finish the job, but that could take several more months. They decided to borrow the money to bring the project to a conclusion. It would be their only debt on the house, a liability erased within a year.

In December the pristine home was ready for occupancy. With great fanfare and satisfaction, members and friends helped the family transport their belongings from the parsonage three miles away. Someone brought a load of chopped wood and piled it high in the backyard for use in the new wood-burning stove. Others planted trees in the yard to commemorate the occasion.

Cherished furnishings quickly enabled the house to feel like a home. Shirley found curtains that she and Robert had used in their first apartment in Dothan twenty-eight years earlier. After cleaning and mending, she proudly hung them in their modern new kitchen. Robert repaired and refinished several pieces of old furniture in anticipation of the move, and took great pleasure in their placement throughout the house.

Three days before Christmas, the family spent their first night in the new residence. Robert and Shirley's dream had come true, made all the more special because it was built from the "faith, hope, and love" of a pastor and his people.

The house that "Faith, Hope, and Love built."

On January 30, 1983 Providence's bulletin carried the following announcement:

> *The Deacons and their Wives*
> *of Providence Baptist Church*
> *Cordially invite you to an Open House at the*
> *New Home of their Pastor*
> *Rev. Robert and Shirley Dismukes*
> *Sunday the sixth day of February*
> *at two o'clock through four o'clock PM*

As the couple welcomed scores of well-wishers into their new home on a cold and rainy winter's afternoon, Robert sat in a wheelchair, the effects of diabetes obvious to all. His countenance was full of great joy, however, as he greeted each individual by name—his eyes sparkling, his smile wide, his handshake strong.

Robert's immense delight on that magnificent occasion would have been scarcely diminished had he known he would live in the house for less than a year.

****

Robert's reliance upon a wheelchair had begun more than a year earlier when he suffered a heart attack on November 11, 1981. The day had been a bit more stressful than usual as he moderated a church business meeting where budget issues for the coming year were debated. After going to bed that Wednesday night, he awakened complaining of chest pains. Shirley rushed him to the hospital in Opelika where he stayed for more than a week.

Complications stemming from the coronary ailment were debilitating. For three months Robert was largely incapacitated, checking in and out of hospitals on five occasions. When not in the infirmary, he rested at home, quietly suffering the worst physical ordeal of his life. Little in the way of pastoral ministry could be done.

Though absent from pulpit and church, Robert continued to pen his pastor's columns, as in a bulletin entry written little more than a week following the traumatic event.

> *Even though I could not be present with you last Sunday for a glorious worship experience on Sunday morning, I joined with you from my hospital room in the ICU unit of the East Alabama Medical Center by radio. I was so pleased to hear the choir sing the call to worship and to hear Dr. Smith announce the beautiful hymns of worship. I am also deeply grateful for men like Fred Woodall and Gary Kenney who will stand in the pulpit in my absence to present the Gospel of Christ.*

*Please continue to pray that God will give a
speedy recovery that I might soon be able to greet
you from the pulpit each Sunday morning and
night* (Providence Bulletin, November 22, 1981).

Robert was not granted the rapid recovery he
desired. While in the hospital he began to notice
something amiss with his left foot. When standing or
walking, he experienced intense pain in the lower
extremity, discomfort that did not quickly subside. After
returning home to convalesce, the foot started to swell and
darken in color, and the pain grew more severe. It hurt so
bad that a good night's sleep was impossible, and getting
through the day unbearable, without the aid of morphine.
Robert spent the Christmas holidays in agony.

The doctors were at a loss to help him, and one
physician, Dr. Richard Dempsey, offered a frank
assessment: "Robert, you're going to lose that foot."
Though Robert and Shirley knew of the danger, they had
not mentioned it or allowed its consideration. The
surgeon's haunting words jolted them with grave alarm.
As the calendar turned from one year to the next, their
chief concern switched from strengthening Robert's heart
to saving his leg.

By the middle of January the foot was no better,
and when Robert went to the hospital seeking relief, other
tests revealed a coronary blockage requiring immediate
attention. Shirley's niece, Sally Deneen, worked in
Atlanta as a nurse in the coronary care unit at Emory
University Hospital, and she arranged for an angioplasty
procedure to be performed. Emory's medical staff would
also take a look at Robert's foot.

The angioplasty was successful, but Emory's doctors recommended that Robert's foot undergo amputation in the interest of his overall health. While lying in intensive care, Robert pondered and prayed about the decision he alone must make. Over the past two months the pain had worsened, and the only way he functioned at all was through the aid of powerful pain killers, a dependence his body could not long sustain.

Life was miserable and ministry impossible in his current physical condition, and there was no prospect of relief in sight. Yet life would be difficult and ministry complicated by the loss of his lower limb. How would he preach? Visit prospects? Kneel to pray? How could he baptize with only one leg? These and other concerns Robert brought to the Lord in the quietness of his hospital room, while watching an over-sized clock on the wall tick off the seconds, minutes, and hours of his forty-ninth year.

It was when Robert prayed, "Lord, I'll give up this leg if you can still use me without it," that he found inner peace and strength amid the intermittent pain pervading his chest and foot. The excruciating decision to have such a vital body part forever removed was made easier by the response he felt he received to his prayer. The Lord told him, "Robert, you just win people to Me, and I'll take care of the rest."

He wanted the surgery done in Opelika, and on January 22 Dr. Dempsey performed the amputation just above the knee. For the next six months Robert waited for the wound to heal sufficiently—a slow process for diabetics—before being fitted with a prosthetic device. He healed nicely and experienced no significant complications from the operation or medicines.

Robert's left leg was amputated in early 1982.

Amazingly, on the first Lord's Day of February, two weeks and two days following surgery, Robert returned to the pulpit after an absence of nearly three months. That same Sunday he wrote about how much he regretted functioning in only a part-time capacity, and how appreciative he was for the church's understanding and support.

> *Words are totally inadequate to express what I feel in my heart toward this congregation. Since my initial sickness this past November, I have experienced the power and presence of your love and prayers. You are the greatest congregation on earth. I feel like the apostle Paul when he said to the Christians of Philippi, "I thank my God in all my remembrance of you, always offering prayer with joy in my heart for you all." I want you to continue to pray for me during these days of recovery. I am looking forward to the time real*

soon when I can be back in full service for our blessed Lord and His church. God bless you. I love you, every one of you (Providence Bulletin, February 7, 1982).

Opelika's First Baptist Church loaned a wheelchair for Robert's use, and as the worship service began, Providence's deacons lifted the chair and its occupant onto the sanctuary's stage. This was the first time most in the congregation had seen their pastor since early November, and as he appeared before them in a noticeably weakened state, with more than half his left leg missing, anxious looks registered on the faces of those in attendance. True to form, Robert eased the tension by declaring that now he must especially trust his deacons, since they were going to carry him up to the pulpit every Sunday! As Robert sat in the wheelchair and preached his morning message, the love of pastor and people was never more evident.

The ensuing weeks saw Robert grow physically stronger and commence using a walker and then crutches to get around. He still needed support when ascending the auditorium's platform, but soon was able to sit on a stool behind the pulpit to deliver his sermons. When Robert received an artificial limb later that year, the church built a rail alongside the pulpit area which he deftly used to climb the steps unaided, grabbing the rail with one hand while hoisting his new leg with the other.

Because his heart was so weak, he was unable to be fitted with the kind of prosthesis he wanted—a hydraulic leg, relatively easy to maneuver. Instead, his prosthetic device consisted of a leg-shaped rod encased in foam and covered with a stocking, then surrounded by a thick, heavy belt at the top. It was uncomfortable and depressing, and he never gained confidence in the apparatus. Robert soon dispensed with it altogether except on public occasions. Crutches became his constant companion, a guard against falling and hurting or embarrassing himself. At home he also used the wheelchair and walker to navigate his way.

A month or two before Robert received the new limb I arrived back in Beauregard fresh from earning a seminary degree. Prior to beginning full-time pastoral and professorial careers, I took the job of summer youth director at Providence, delighted by the opportunity to spend time with Robert. I observed first-hand the struggles he endured in order to function each day. I also witnessed his unwavering devotion to the Lord and gritty determination to carry on with ministry—twin commitments not compromised in the least by the tumultuous events of recent months.

Despite personal adversity, Robert's
ministerial focus never wavered.

Robert came into the office on his crutches almost every day. He sat at his desk and planned the church's programs, prepared Sunday sermons, met with individuals, and spent time in prayer. He visited hospital patients, skillfully maneuvering from room to room in a wheelchair especially provided for his use. Though obviously weak and sick himself, he often appeared at my youth events and in the homes and businesses of the community, carrying out pastoral duties as best he could.

Upon returning home thoroughly exhausted after each day's work, he voiced pangs of guilt because of so much in the way of ministry left undone. There were prospects to see, church meetings to lead, community events to attend. "My heart's willing," he would frequently say, "but my body just won't cooperate." Sitting on the couch or reclining in bed, he hoped to rest enough to go again the following day.

Robert's illness might have spelled the end of work on the new house, since he was no longer able to carefully supervise the project. But as Shirley's letter— published two weeks prior to the amputation—attests, his sickness produced the opposite effect. Enthusiasm for the house renewed and contributions increased. The church became even more involved, with members redoubling their efforts during their pastor's time of crisis. If they were not able to give Robert his health, the congregation reasoned, they could at least give him a home.

The dwelling was finished less than a year following the loss of his leg, and Robert sat proudly in a wheelchair at the Open House celebration welcoming church members and friends to the family's new residence. In ten months time he would trade his earthly home for one far more glorious.

****

Immediately upon returning to the pulpit following his heart attack and amputation, Robert led Providence to begin a capital campaign entitled "Debt Free in '83," an effort to pay off all outstanding loans on church properties before the congregation's centennial celebration, an anniversary upcoming in 1984. Robert not only had the vision of financial freedom for his personal residence, but desired that status for God's house as well. He requested an initial commitment from seventy families to donate an extra $250 on top of their yearly church tithes and offerings.

Providence responded in a fabulous way. Only sixteen months later, on June 9, 1983, all mortgages were erased and the entire church plant, including the Camp and Retreat Center, was free of debt. A grand gala was planned for August 7, a date coinciding with Providence's ninety-ninth birthday and Robert's fifteenth anniversary as pastor. The Homecoming and Note Burning Celebration, as it was dubbed, featured Sunday School, morning worship, dinner on the grounds, and a special afternoon service of ceremony and praise. Highlighting the observance was a symbolic burning of the loan notes held on the sanctuary, children's building, and camp land.

In his pastor's column, Robert could well have called attention to his own accomplishments in leading the church to an impressive milestone. From a membership of 336 when he arrived, it had grown to over 1100, with 632 baptisms recorded during the course of his stay, and more than twenty men called to the gospel ministry. A budget of $25,000 had expanded to $225,000. The initial monetary debt of $93,000 had been completely eliminated, so that currently the church didn't owe a dime, even though it had built new facilities and bought additional property during his tenure.

Instead, Robert focused upon the church's real reason for meeting together that Sunday, while also issuing a challenge for the future.

Today is a very special day in the life of Providence Baptist Church. The purpose of our assembling together today is the same as every other Lord's Day....to worship God. Today the very theme of our worship is built around praise and thanksgiving. While the names of many people will be heard and recognized today it is the name of Jesus that stands above every other name. For the past 99 years the Providence Baptist Church has been a lighthouse in this community sharing the message of Christ to all who would hear. Through these years this church has cast its shadow of influence and witness around this community and its arms of compassion and love have reached even unto the uttermost parts of the earth. In God's span of time, I praise Him for permitting me to come as Pastor of this great church in August of 1968. These past fifteen years have been wonderfully exciting. As I think back over these years and read the history of the past 99 years I praise God for the great team of pastors I have had the privilege of serving in the same local fellowship of believers with. This is not a

time to stop and simply reflect upon the glorious
years of the past but the God given future before
us. I joyfully and eagerly anticipate what God will
do with an obedient and submissive church in the
days and years ahead (Providence Bulletin,
August 7, 1983).

Among former pastors in the congregation was
Robert's immediate predecessor, Thomas Preston. It was
Reverend Preston who oversaw construction of the
church's current sanctuary two decades earlier. Asked to
resign five years into his term, Preston's acrimonious
departure opened the door for Robert's arrival and
everything the Lord accomplished through his ministry, a
ministry now crowned by the joyous celebration in which
both men participated. Fifteen years were long enough to
heal old hurts and make peace with Providence.

Included in the festivities was a small but heartfelt
gift. Though Robert steadfastly refused to accept
accolades of any kind, preferring to give credit to God
alone, the preacherboys felt their pastor's labor for the
Lord should not go publicly unrecognized. Knowing the
fragility of his health, we chose the occasion to surprise
him with a token expression of our enormous appreciation
for his dedicated ministry.

I suppose we should have presented him
something more useful or lavish—maybe a set of biblical
commentaries or new wood-working machinery, perhaps
the latest technical gadget or keys to a new car. We opted
instead to give him words and names engraved upon a
simple plaque, a keepsake to convey our eternal affection.
It read:

Presented to Robert Dismukes
Pastor, Providence Baptist Church
August 7, 1983
In loving gratitude
For your faithful service and commitment
To our Lord Jesus Christ
The Preacherboys
Jimmy Blanton
Rick Cochran
William Cox
Harold Cummings
Max Cummings
Gary Dennis
Billy Duncan
Steve Golden
Tommy Hilyer
Mike Hutchinson
Gary Kenney
Andy Patillo
Jerry Ray
Cliff Roberts
Fawzy Shorrosh
Freddie Simpkins
Roger Smith
Fred Woodall

The plaque still hangs prominently in the house
that "Faith, Hope, and Love built."

****

As 1983 closed its doors, Robert's thoughts as pastor focused upon the two aspects of ministry he loved best: young people and missions. Moving the church forward in these areas consumed much of his thoughts and prayers.

One of his goals over the years was to lead Providence to the point where it could hire a full-time Youth Director. Recent health issues had limited his own involvement with young people, and summer or part-time youth workers were unable to render the degree of care needed by this age group. Nor could they effectively reach the large number of unchurched teenagers and children living in the Beauregard community.

Robert believed that as Providence approached its centennial year, the time had come to add such a staff member. He successfully lobbied the church's Budget Committee to allow salary for the new position, and published his view of the matter to the congregation on the Sunday after Thanksgiving.

> *For the past 20 years a large portion of our budget has gone to debt retirement. We praise God that this past August this debt was completely retired. Part of the money that was used for debt retirement will be used for much needed renovation on our present buildings. One of the new items in the Church budget is money for a Youth Director. Many of our people have expressed their desire for a person to work in this area. God has blessed this Church through our work with the Youth. We have a great army of children and youth that need our constant attention and guidance as a church. I cannot*

think of another area in our church where God's money could be better invested than in the area of our youth (Providence Bulletin, November 27, 1983).

The other leading issue on his mind was the church's yearly promotion of international missions, known as the Lottie Moon Christmas offering. The offering, named in honor of an esteemed former Baptist missionary to China, is a collaborative effort among Southern Baptist churches that singlehandedly supports thousands of missionaries serving in foreign lands. The project was especially dear to Robert's heart and enjoyed his enthusiastic support. According to church records, he annually led Providence to contribute as much as 175 times the amount collected for Lottie Moon in the year prior to his arrival.

Now, with another December rolling around, Robert concentrated upon missions on the first Sunday of the month, as was his custom. The sermon would have an evangelistic thrust, the music a missionary flavor, and the bulletin a prominent amount of advertising for the offering. Robert devoted his entire pastor's column of approximately three hundred words to publicize the Christmastime collection. The final paragraph expressed his personal reasons for giving to Lottie Moon, while encouraging others to do the same.

At this season of the year when we are thinking about Christmas gifts it is well for us to turn our attention to the greatest of all gifts, GOD'S CHRISTMAS GIFT TO MAN. What greater way could we as believers show our love and

appreciation to God for "His Unspeakable Gift"
than giving through the Lottie Moon Christmas
Offerings so those around the world may know
HIM? (Providence Bulletin, December 4, 1983).

As if divinely ordained, a challenge to support missions comprised Robert's last written words to the congregation.

Several hours before Providence's members perused his column in their Sunday bulletins, Robert was awake suffering from coughing spells and insomnia. Compounding these problems were a recent loss of appetite and little or no urination. A general feeling of bodily fatigue besieged him. He was in no shape to preach, so Shirley insisted on calling one of the older preacherboys, Gary Kenney, to fill the pulpit.

Shirley drove Susan to church but skipped Sunday School to care for Robert. At her husband's urging, however, she reluctantly left again to attend worship, though he was all she could think about. Her worst fear was that his body was shutting down. When she returned home to find that he still had not eaten or been to the bathroom, she called their physician, who happened to be on hospital duty. She was advised to bring Robert in right away.

During his examination at the hospital, Robert suddenly started coughing and turning blue. They ushered Shirley out of the room as additional medical personnel rushed in and promptly carted him away to the intensive care unit. She then heard the hospital CODE alert sound; they were losing him. Shirley sat anxiously all alone in the waiting area, praying and attempting to reach David and Susan.

After a multitude of excruciating moments, she learned that Robert had revived but would remain in intensive care. Twenty-one year old David, now married and living on his own, arrived to sit with his mother. Susan, eighteen, chose to cope with her dad's crisis by staying with friends.

Late in the afternoon Robert was finally stable enough to receive visitors. Shirley and David entered his room, and as much as he was able, Robert said his goodbyes to each of them; he correctly surmised that his life was not long for this world. In a particularly poignant moment, he asked David to take good care of his mother.

Shirley waited at the hospital with church members throughout the night and past lunch the next day, going in to see Robert at every opportunity. On one of her visitations, Robert grew agitated with excitement and sat straight up in bed. He proceeded to relate, in mostly broken sentences, how he had seen a vision of heaven. He told how much he wanted to describe it, but was commanded not to share the scene because people would not believe it. In a loud voice he shouted, "Praise Jesus!" and began to speak clumsily in a way that Shirley could not comprehend. Finally, he fell backward, exhausted and unable to continue.

After being at the hospital for more than twenty-four hours, Shirley went home Monday afternoon for a brief respite, asking Associate Pastor Carlos Golden to monitor things in her absence. She had only been gone a short time when Carlos called to summon her back. Upon her return, Billy and Fawzy, who had arrived together from Mississippi, met her with the news that Robert had died. Though grief stricken, Shirley was secretly thankful she had not been there. God had planned it that way, she believed, to save her from having to watch her beloved husband's final breath.

Robert's funeral was held on Wednesday, December 7, a sunny, cool, breezy day, with temperatures settling into the low fifties. Providence was packed, every seat taken, with many unable to enter the auditorium. Shirley and the family walked into the sanctuary to the tune of one of Robert's favorite songs, "Alleluia!" Appropriately, Dr. Tom Smith and the choir substituted for "Alleluia!" the words recently written in Robert's Bible, "I am Ready!" As the gathering spontaneously sang along, all were quite convinced that no one was more ready to meet the Lord than Brother Robert.

The service was truly the celebration of an extraordinary Christian life, its atmosphere more like a festival than a funeral. Shirley asked the preacherboys to speak, and I and others shared about the impact Robert had made upon our lives. In what was undoubtedly the memorial's most touching moment, Billy took from Robert's Bible the sermon he would have preached the previous Sunday morning and delivered it word for word from the manuscript. Robert's last message on evangelism and missions did not go unheard.

Later that day the funeral party moved from Beauregard to Dothan, Robert's hometown. In City Cemetery, not far from the church where he accepted Christ thirty-one years earlier, his earthly body was laid to rest under an unadorned marker with three words etched in stone: "Reverend Robert Dismukes."

As mourners gathered around the grave, a final song was sung. It's a song that affirms the testimony of this simple, humble man who walked with Christ, a man

God used to bring the power of the messianic age to so many, and whose spiritual legacy is yet unfinished.

> *"God is so good.*
> *God is so good.*
> *God is so good.*
> *He's so good to me."*

Epilogue
"Pass It On"

There is another song that encapsulates the spirit of our messianic age, a tune we loved to sing during our Seekers meetings and revivals. It's a musical echo I often hear at Memory Rock.

It only takes a spark
To get a fire going.
And soon all those around
Can warm up in its glowing.
That's how it is with God's love,
Once you've experienced it.
You spread His love to everyone,
You want to pass it on.
I'll shout it from the mountaintop!
I want my world to know!
The Lord of love has come to me,
I want to pass it on.

In our own religious journey, it was Brother Robert who provided the spark of God's love, lighting the spiritual fire that burned so brightly in Beauregard. The flames soon spread to other churches and communities, who likewise basked in the warm glow of the love of God found in Jesus Christ.

Looking back upon that marvelous era, it's also a song that captures well Robert's "purpose driven life." It's evident to me now that he understood and put into practice the most vital thing about the Christian faith—he passed it on.

Every Gospel and the book of Acts conclude the story of Jesus with a form of what Christendom calls the Great Commission. The Lord explicitly instructed His disciples to go and share the good news of what He had done for them—and what He wants to do for others. He commanded His followers to pass it on.

It was Christ's mandate to evangelize the world, to be on mission for the gospel that Robert so personalized and perpetuated. More than anything else, this characterized him as a minister and as a mentor.

In the years since his death, his protégés have striven—by various and sundry means—to make his spiritual purpose our own. We, too, have sought to pass it on.

Jimmy Blanton—aka Jerry Lewis!—has remained in the state of Georgia to fulfill the Lord's calling upon his life. Following a decade as pastor of Georgetown Baptist Church, Jimmy served in the same role at First Baptist of Warner Robins. He moved on to become the Director of Missions for the Columbus Baptist Association of churches, where since 1994 he has led nearly fifty congregations in sharing the good news while also expanding the organization's extensive collection of social ministries. The CBA provides a medical clinic, clothes closet, food bank, home repair assistance, and numerous life enhancement skills, each offered in the name of Jesus from a needs-based approach.

Jimmy, unfortunately, still sings like a prisoner.

Gary Dennis—Marshall Dillon!—has spent most of his life in Louisiana as pastor of several Baptist churches, including Old Mount Zion in Albany, and

Creekside, Ebenezer, and Celebration Fellowship in the Hammond area, where he resides. Gary's passion, however, is an organization he founded in 1994 called In His Steps. Its ministry specializes in sending mission teams to gospel-deprived areas—yes, even to darkest Africa. In particular, however, it focuses upon the indigent in Mexico, supplying food, medicine, clothing, and housing while also building churches and sharing Christ through worship, pamphlet, film, and personal witness. IHS has helped establish Casa Mami, a Christian orphanage in Renosa that cares for approximately one hundred young women, and Living Waters Mexico, which drills fresh water wells in disadvantaged areas of the country.

Thankfully, Gary finally stopped asking the ladies for a holy kiss.

Billy Duncan—the Sundance Kid!—has made a career of the pastorate, perhaps emulating Robert's ministry path most closely. After serving in Mississippi during seminary years, he returned to his native state to lead three Baptist congregations. A two year stint at Westmont in Birmingham was followed by thirteen at Highland Avenue in Montgomery, and then a brief stay at Heritage in Dothan—Robert and Shirley's home church. Family health issues forced Billy to resign the latter and take a year's sabbatical before moving to Georgia to shepherd Beallwood Baptist in Columbus, where he has been pastor since 2001.

Billy's sermons, they say, have yet to be shortened.

Tommy Hilyer—our Harpo Marx!—served in Spain for almost a decade as missionary to the University of Seville, while also working among the city's indigenous Baptist churches. After helping coordinate evangelical efforts at the 1992 World's Fair in Seville, he came home to study and teach at Auburn University before heading back to Western Europe under a second missionary appointment. Based again in Spain, he joined efforts to evangelize the Saharawi people—approximately 100,000 Spanish Islamic refugees displaced from their Moroccan homeland in the northern African nation of Algeria. Since 2001 he has been back in the States and presiding once more over a classroom, this time at a high school near Nashville, Tennessee.

Tommy long ago abandoned his afro-style hairdo.

Fawzy Shorrosh—the Fonz!—has lived in Mississippi since leaving Beauregard in 1982. Hundreds of churches through the years have heard his dynamic testimony for Christ in their worship services, revivals, crusades, and conferences. In addition to carrying on the ministry of evangelism, he has also served as pastor of West Shady Grove Baptist Church in Waynesboro, where he makes his home.

Fawzy continues to avoid hot dogs, catfish, canoes, and the state of Alaska.

As for me, after seminary and a brief period of ministry in Alabama, I became pastor of two sweet churches, Beaver Dam Baptist in Troy, Virginia and First Baptist in Shellman, Georgia, while also earning a doctorate along the way at the University of Virginia. The less stressful life of a professor followed, and since 1993 I've taught the New Testament at Brewton-Parker College in Mount Vernon, Georgia. There I've delighted in passing on to students the Christian faith passed on to me—the same faith now passed on to you, dear reader.

Unlike the friends of my youth, I'm not sure what memorable character I tend to resemble. It would suit me just fine, however, to look a little more like Robert Dismukes, for then I would look a lot more like Jesus. Indeed, Robert's sterling example of a Christ-like life was the spiritual inspiration—and is the enduring legacy—of our messianic age.

Acknowledgments

The genesis of this book may be traced to a late night snack I shared a few years ago with lifelong pal Gary Dennis. It was Christmastime, and we decided to get together at the Auburn IHOP to catch up and reminisce, as we often did when home for the holidays. In the midst of friendly banter, Gary suggested that someone should write the story of the Seekers and everything the Lord had accomplished through the ministry of Brother Robert.

I was enthused by the idea and proposed we collaborate on the effort. Gary demurred; he was just beginning Ph.D. work and didn't think he had the time or energy to commit to it. The project fell to me and the end result is this volume. It has been a labor of love, a spiritual journey down memory lane that I have thoroughly enjoyed.

The book would not have been possible apart from the kind assistance of numerous individuals who shared their past memories, historical documents, dated photographs, and helpful expertise.

Foremost in her generosity was Shirley Dismukes, who patiently answered endless questions and carefully searched long-hidden files for relevant information.

Colleagues Jimmy Blanton, Gary Dennis, Billy Duncan, Tommy Hilyer, and Fawzy Shorrosh served as key resources, making time in their busy schedules for multiple interviews.

Fellow Seekers Dianne Kennedy, Judy Patterson, Marcy Underwood (their maiden names), and Andy Patillo offered invaluable eyewitness input.

Family members, especially Shirley Myrick, Ernest Ray, Jr., and Jimmie Clyde Kasulka, recounted significant events, facts, and anecdotes.

Also rendering valuable insight and materials were Valeria Brown, Gertrude Dennis, Wilmer and Sylvia Dismukes, Frank and Frances Duncan, Blanche Hilyer, Gerald and Jane Long, Mike and Reba McCutcheon, George and Sarah Palmer, Susan Patrick, and Nathan and Jenny Smith.

Dr. Rusty Sowell and the staff of Providence Baptist Church graciously opened their records and provided work space from time to time.

Editor Andy Overett and Lighthouse Christian Publishing were kind enough to extend an invitation to publish the manuscript and oversee its production.

Of course, without the Lord's daily supply of grace and strength I would not have gotten past page one.

I wish to thank all of these and unnamed others for their myriad contributions to this volume.

Finally, I wish to express gratitude to the readers of the book. I sincerely hope it has been a blessing, serving to strengthen Christian faith. I would love to hear from you, and may be contacted through Brewton-Parker College at jray@bpc.edu and on Facebook at facebook.com.

Jerry Ray
July, 2012

Book Ordering Information

Our Messianic Age may be purchased from select bookstores and the following book retailers:

Lighthouse Christian Publishing
www.lighthousechristianpublishing.com
(View their catalogue online)

Amazon
www.amazon.com
(Paperback and Kindle versions available)

And most retailers supplied by
Ingram/Spring Arbor distributors